GOVERNING AMERICA'S ECONOMY

James W. Lindeen, Ph.D.

The University of Toledo

PRENTICE HALL, Englewood Cliffs, New Jersey 07632

Library of Congress Cataloging-in-Publication Data
Lindeen, James W.
   Governing America's economy/ James W. Lindeen
     p. cm.
   Includes bibliographical references and index.
   ISBN 0-13-097031-X
    1. United States–Economic policy. 2. Fiscal policy–United States. 3. Labor policy–United
States. 4. Business and politics–United States. 5. United States–Politics and government.
I. Title
HC103.L44 1994
338.973–dc20   93-17155
                                               CIP

Editorial/production supervision, electronic page make up,
       and interior design: Mary Kathryn Bsales
Acquisitions editor: Julie Berrisford
Editorial assistant: Nicole Signoretti
Prepress buyer: Kelly Behr
Manufacturing buyer: Mary Ann Gloriande
Cover design: Maureen Eide
Editor-in-chief: Charlyce Jones Owen
Marketing manager: Maria DiVencenzo
Copy editor: Barbara Conner

 © 1994 by Prentice-Hall, Inc.
A Paramount Communications Company
Englewood Cliffs, New Jersey 07632

Printed in the United States of America
10 9 8 7 6 5 4 3 2 1

ISBN 0-13-097031-X

Prentice-Hall International (UK) Limited, London
Prentice-Hall of Australia Pty. Limited, Sydney
Prentice-Hall Canada Inc., Toronto
Prentice-Hall Hispanoamericana, S.A., Mexico
Prentice-Hall of India Private Limited, New Delhi
Prentice-Hall of Japan, Inc., Tokyo
Simon & Schuster Asia Pte. Ltd., Singapore
Editora Prentice-Hall do Brasil, Ltda., Rio de Janeiro

CONTENTS

PART THREE
GOVERNMENTAL INSTITUTIONS
AND PROCESSES   89

Chapter Six
Popular Politics   91

Chapter Seven
The Three Great Branches   106

Chapter Eight
Governmental Functions: Supportive, Regulatory,
Managerial, and Entrepreneurial   124

PART FOUR
MANAGING THE ECONOMY   141

Chapter Nine
Managing the Economy: Fiscal Policy   143

Chapter Ten
Managing the Economy: Monetary Policy   165

PART FIVE
SUBSTANTIVE ECONOMIC POLICIES   187

Chapter Eleven
Structure and Performance in the Marketplace: Monopoly and Antitrust   189

PREFACE

Politics and economics are inextricably linked. Sometimes the connection is obvious: Everyone understands that taxing, spending, and budgeting, as well as deficits and debt, are economic matters through which the winds of politics blow freely and often. The linkage is obvious, too, in business and government relations, factors like antitrust, economic regulation, fairness in advertising, and the treatment of capital gains. But often the nexus between economic and political life is not so clear, and the public fails to perceive how *politics* legitimately fits into the savings and loan debacle, education reform, or health-care policy. Many are slow to perceive an *economic* component to civil rights, national defense, or reproductive rights. But scratch away at the surface rhetoric and two truths emerge. One is the homily that it's not the money, it's the amount. Economics is always important grappling with public issues. The other is that democratic politics is an appropriate alternative to the marketplace for allocating the values that people hold dear in a democracy.

Political and economic forces often coexist, but which way does the causal arrow point? It may be easiest to recognize politics as the determining agent. Certainly the New Dealers of the 1930s sought to apply governmental remedies to the problems of the economy, and so, too, have many of those who came to Washington with President Clinton in 1993. Politics is seen as a causal force by the advocates of Reaganomics as well, but usually it carries a negative sign rather than a positive one. Their goal was to insulate market-based decision making from what they perceive as the meddling of regulators and planners.

The arrow of causality also flows from the economic realm to the world of politics. Students of public opinion know that the socialization process and prolonged exposure to the rhetoric of market superiority can foreclose consideration of policy alternatives very early in the policy life cycle. Corporations, trade associations, and labor unions also use their considerable resources to influence the action of government through campaign activity, PAC donations, and lobbying, as well as through the litigation that is so much a part of the policy process.

For a number of years my students and I have been trying to untangle the causal flows, comprehend the historical forces, explain the institutional processes, and understand the leading substantive areas of economic policy-making in America. One of our problems, however, has been the lack of a suitable core textbook. Thus, *Governing America's Economy* has been developed to fill that void.

One of the first keys in unlocking the relationship between politics and economics is recognizing a certain dissensus in the field of economics itself. Although we often hear the phrase "Economists all agree...,"one certainty is that there are a number of economic perspectives. The axioms of the neoclassical school were rebuffed by Keynesian prescriptions during the Great Depression, only to be synthesized after World War II in the neoclassical post-Keynesianism of Paul Samuelson. Institutional or labor economists developed their own insights about the importance of institutional power. By the early 1980s the supply-side remedies of Arthur Laffer briefly held center stage, to be followed swiftly by the monetarism that has such a strong appeal to those who prefer a smaller government.

War is too important to leave to generals, and economic issues need to be examined from the perspective of political science. Economists, a wholly admirable group of colleagues, conduct their analyses with elegant, parsimonious models that often exclude the hopes and dreams of individual citizens in a democratic society. Measures of non-market-based power are rare, and there may be little appreciation for the legitimacy of political discourse. Similarly, the approach to public issues that typifies the work of professional students of business tends to focus more on specific applications and to reflect the concerns of corporate America.

It is imperative to approach the issues of economic policy from a historical perspective for at least two reasons. First, little that occurs in politics or economic policy is truly new. Often we hear someone assert that this or that problem is "unprecedented," and the lack of historical insight that this terms connotes means that we fight the same battles over and over again. History helps us to understand our heritage, which is especially important for marginalized interests and people, such as organized labor today.

Another major task of this book is to explain the behavior of the governmental institutions and policy-making processes that are important for economic policy. Governmental institutions exert their own influence over policy. Just as economic activity occurs in a marketplace that must be carefully specified, so too politics takes place in institutional settings that have their own characteristics. The legislative role in policy-making, for example, occurs in a post-Reform Congress that differs from Congress of the early 1980s. The administrative process must also be addressed in the context of behavioral realities. Organizations have lives of their own that determine what they can and cannot accomplish.

Since the Employment Act of 1946, one of government's most important roles has been to react to fluctuations in the business cycle. In Part IV we examine the politics of fiscal and monetary policy in the context of managing the economy rather than as particular aspects of public finance. Three additional policy areas are also singled out: antitrust, organized labor, and international trade.

Finally, a concluding chapter examines the American economic and political systems in comparative perspectives. The American mixed economy and pluralist democracy are the joint product of a unique sociopolitical culture. Capitalism comes in many varieties. The American version is the product of decades of evolution, involves complex interrelationships with government, and has been called mixed capitalism by many scholars. Democracy also takes many forms, and the notion of pluralism has emerged since 1960 as the dominant conceptualization of it. Both features, mixed capitalism and pluralist democracy, are the result of a sociopolitical culture that itself is the product of the Enlightenment and classical liberalism. This suggests that American economic and political institutions do not travel well and are not easily transplanted to systems that lack our cultural values—which means that the emerging free regimes of Eastern Europe, for example, should be wary of attempting to clone American institutions. Each system must find its own way, as painful as that may be.

The book's length is appropriate for a college-level academic term. The fourteen chapters, if read at a rate of one each week, are the right length for a semester system. At the same time, my own experience with the quarter system shows that it is highly serviceable there as well.

Any writer is indebted to a great number of people. In this case, special thanks are owed to Sakari T. Jutila, Ronald Randall, Carter Wilson, and Mark Denham for their contributions in reading and critiquing this manuscript at its various stages of development, and to Shirley Lindeen for her many insights and unfailing enthusiasm and good cheer. The skill and patience of Linda Neuhausel were invaluable in producing the various drafts of each chapter. And thanks are owed especially to the insights of the hundreds of students who have offered their views on earlier incarnations of this manuscript and whose comments have been particularly important. Thanks, too, to Margaret Kahn, University of Michigan; and Ron King, Tulane University; for reviewing the manuscript. Despite their efforts, and the help of others as well, the errors of fact and interpretation that are sure to surface remain mine alone.

I hope you find the book to be useful in unraveling the secrets of the American political economy.

PART ONE

AN INTERDISCIPLINARY PERSPECTIVE

Governing America's economy is a daunting undertaking. With a population in excess of 255 million, the extent of economic activity is great and the number of job descriptions seems even more so. It is easy to develop a list of economic concerns that trouble those in the United States. The specter of inflation is a perennial topic, especially among the more well-to-do. The threat of unemployment, particularly among those who already enjoy less in the way of material goods, becomes greater as the monthly unemployment figures rise. The ups and downs of the business cycle, and the role of government in stabilizing it, interests many, as does the issue of whether the nation's level of saving and investment is sufficient to carry it into the world competition of the next millennium. When important new initiatives, such as the North American Free Trade Agreement (NAFTA) enter the public debate, they too become causes for public concern. Should the fate of these issues be left to the mechanisms of the marketplace or should government take a hand in solving them?

The troubles of effective governance are hardly less troubling when one examines economic policy. Many public concerns, while seemingly important in their own right, can be seen to harbor a considerable economic component upon closer inspection—race, women's rights, drugs, foreign trade, and foreign aid. Other concerns are voiced about how governmental institutions themselves can be expected to operate. Can bureaucracy ever be made efficient and effective or is overregulation inevitable? Can Congress ever avoid the snares of the special pleaders and lobbyists? Does everything eventually make its way into the expensive judicial system before it can be settled? With national, state, and local levels of government that have their own agendas and rivalries, the opportunity for dissensus is always present. Overall, what sorts of people really govern the United States, and with what effect?

This is a book that approaches the inter-relationship of government and of economics in three major ways. One is by developing a historical overview of this relationship as it has unfolded across more than two centuries of experience. A second is by examining those governmental structures that both determine and react to the economic forces that populate their environment. The third is by exploring public policy in six policy arenas—fiscal policy, monetary policy, public finance, antitrust, organized labor, and international economic issues.

Before we advance into these realms, however, it is important to plot our initial position, to get our bearings, and to cut away a certain amount of analytical underbrush. First, it is a good idea to consider the nature of politics and of economics. Chapter One takes us into the differences between governments and markets, or between centralized command-based decision-making and decisions that emanate from decentralized market-based processes. We may find that the neat lines that separate that which is economics from that which is politics sometimes are blurred.

Another preconsideration involves the differences that distinguish among differing viewpoints within the disciplines of economics and political science. Chapter Two attempts to sort out the so-called schools that are found within each. In the end, you may become more wary whenever you hear someone say that economists all agree that this or that is so. Similarly, there are many important ways in which students of politics are far from consensual in their views of just who governs and how they do it.

CHAPTER ONE

ECONOMICS AND POLITICS IN AMERICA

Politics involves both conflict and accommodation. The conflictual component emanates from many sources. Some of it is embedded in differing moral and religious judgments, such as the deep division over abortion—right to life versus freedom of choice. Other conflicts arise from ethnic or racial differences that are traceable to European rivalries or to the hardships that black Americans have experienced throughout their history. Some of it begins with differing notions of how much freedom a free people can tolerate versus how much order is necessary to ensure that liberty does not become license. This conflict surfaces in issues of rights of the accused and freedom of speech. But the greatest basis of political conflict has economic roots.

POLITICS AND ECONOMIC ISSUES: CONFLICT OR ACCOMMODATION?

Consider some of the economic issues that concern Americans today. Arguably, those who are in their teens and twenties today are the first generation whose prospects are less bright than those of their parents. This fact is striking, given the importance of upward mobility as a part of the American dream. The failure of the economy to create new jobs apace with the growth in population—jobs that are financially and professionally rewarding—is cause for further concern. Many fear that this failure is due to structural changes in the economy as it has moved away from a manufacturing base and into a service mode. The extent to which job loss is the result of mergers and takeovers, and those who are laid off are white-collar employees, has given rise to the term *dumpies*—downwardly mobile professionals, who trained to be accountants, computer programmers, and engineers. Some people continue to worry about inflation, although the more important problem of the 1990s seems to be inflation's trade-off, unemployment. There is also that perennial favorite, taxes. This is a bifurcated issue: Some people are distressed about the magnitude of taxes, others about the fairness of the taxing system itself. Foreign threats also loom as a source of concern, as does the disintegration of the infrastructure of highways, bridges, and transportation facilities. The freer trade that was heralded in the 1930s by Democrats as a boon for U.S. exports now elicits the fear that America's leading export will be its jobs, as deindustrialization shifts manufacturing to low-cost "offshore" countries of the Third World. Simultaneously, the importation of cheaper products from overseas may undercut American products. These concerns and others flow easily from mainstream Americans who accept the tenets of what might be called the American system.

Additional concerns are more likely to be voiced by those who question many of the fundamentals of the dominant political–economic paradigm. Among them are the seeming intractability of the problem of poverty thirty years after war was declared on it during Lyndon Johnson's Great Society. Added to this is the homelessness that is not limited to the streets of major cities. And why is it, these dissenters ask, that the problems of the well–to–do are addressed quickly and with little thought of total cost, whereas those of the underclass are elbowed aside by the lobbyists for special interests who clog the corridors of Congress. The bailout of failed savings and loans is exemplary here. Then there is the lack of certain items that are commonly supplied as public goods in almost every other Western industrialized country. Thirty percent of Americans do not have access to affordable health care. Those without access to automobiles or airline transportation have little in the way of public transportation to fall back on.

To what extent can the government respond to these concerns? In general, advocates of activist government (modern–day liberals, Democratic party activists, and those in the "reform" tradition) are optimistic about what the public sector can do. They espouse policies that they hope will raise the level of those at the bottom (generally at the expense of those above the median) while simultaneously raising the lot of everyone through economic expansion. Meanwhile, those who are suspicious of government (contemporary conservatives, Republican activists, and market–oriented theorists) contend that reliance on market mechanisms should be paramount because governmental intervention inevitably does more harm than good.

A wholly different view of politics, one often unnoticed, is that it is concerned also with accommodation—with reaching solutions to the problems that confront the diverse population of the modern, industrialized nation that is the United States. Politicians respond well to situations in which contending parties, labor and management, for example, come forward after arranging an agreement between themselves.

There is considerable evidence of the government acting in accommodative ways. In roll–call voting in Congress and most state legislatures, the majority of outcomes are one–sided affairs, with Republicans and Democrats on the same side. Accommodation is also seen in the two–party system. Unlike the ideologically based conflict among the multiparty systems of most other industrialized nations, both American parties accept the fundamental tenets about the underlying political–economic system. And accommodation can be seen electorally, where contests for office are won or lost on the decisions of those 10 to 20 percent of the electorate who constitute the middle of public opinion.

Because of the accommodative nature of American politics, disagreements over economic issues seldom involve the question of whether or not to address the mainstream problems of job creation, mergers, unemployment, poverty, or foreign trade. Instead, the concern is when to put these issues on the agenda; how best to address them; how much governmental intervention will occur; and especially, how much money to spend on them. Indeed, it may be that the problem with the American political economy is not that there is too much conflict but that instead there is too little.

THE ECONOMIC FACTOR IN POLICY ISSUES

Although economics and politics are closely related in the United States, there are contrasting perspectives about the importance of the former to the latter. Economic determinists see the hand of economic forces nearly everywhere. Indeed, there are policies and programs in which the economic factor is paramount. Public finance (taxing, spending, the national debt, and the value of money) is one of them, and the behavior of economic institutions—savings and loans (S & Ls), securities firms, and the markets in which they operate—is another. Many people also insist that policies dealing with the structure and behavior of the marketplace are uniquely economic as well. False advertising, mergers and monopolies, and coping with the problems of the business cycle and unemployment could be cited here, too. In other policy areas the economic component might be perceived as predominant, even though it is accompanied by lesser, noneconomic forces. In transportation deregulation, for example, the major theme of economic reform that appears in restructuring the nation's airlines is joined with minor concerns about public safety and convenience. But even with issues like education, drugs, reproductive rights, or product safety, the economic determinist would brush away surface concerns in order to get to a "bottom line" that is fundamentally economic.

The alternative view is to discount the importance of economics altogether and to stress instead the significance of other factors. Budgets and public finance, in this view, are only monetary representations of deeper substantive concerns over medical care, weapons systems, or moral values. As for banks and the S & L industry, they are only institutional vessels for ensuring the good things of life—obtaining better housing or anticipating a more comfortable retirement. Those who diminish the importance of economic factors turn instead to other causal forces, among them the centrality of individual leadership by people who act directly in the political sphere, as did Franklin D. Roosevelt, or who operate from behind the facade of the marketplace only because they find it more convenient to do so. Or, they might say, economics easily gives way before such urgent concerns as protecting passenger safety by requiring safer automobiles regardless of cost. Certainly economics took a back seat to the defense of liberty during World War II. The costs of defeating the Axis powers drove the national debt from 51 percent of gross national product (GNP) in 1941 to 128 percent by war's end. When it came to winning, money was no object.

Table 1–1 suggests the relative importance of economic and other factors in the political process. Whereas national security, gender, race and ethnicity, crime, and morality are underlying themes in two or three areas; family life is important in four; and health and safety emerge in nearly half, an underlying economic concern is present in nearly two–thirds of these programs. What does this say about the role of economics? Not that it is the sole determinant of most programs but rather that it shares a causal role with a changing collection of other forces—sometimes with family life or ethnicity and then again with national security, morality, or criminal justice. It also says that the economic factor does not stand alone but rather is nearly always one instrument in a changing matrix. And if we change our own perspective by glancing down the columns of the table, we see also that the economic hand is present in a greater number of programs than is any other factor. It affects more policy programs than does health or safety, for example, and appears more frequently than morality or gender or ethnic conflict. If economics combines with other factors to form a kaleidoscope of explanatory ensembles, it also shows greater virtuosity across a wider range of programs.

The importance of economic factors in politics is well known. In the literature on comparative state politics, for example, Thomas Dye (1966) found economic development to be the most important explanation of variation in state public policy outcomes across a wide range of issues. An analysis of congressional voting has shown that economic measures are usually present in determining the results of roll–call voting (Clausen, 1973).

Table 1-1. Underlying Factors in Governmental Programs

	Economic	Health/Safety	Family life	Morals	Crime	Ethnicity/Race	Gender	National Security
Antitrust: takeovers and job loss	X		X					
S & L insolvencies	X			x	X			
Aid to Israel	X							X
Education: elementary and secondary	X		X			x		
B-2 Bomber program	X							X
Homelessness	X	X	X	x				
Environment: Clean Air Act of 1990	X	X						
Drug use: cocaine	X	X	x	X	X	x		
Compensation: equal pay for equal work	X		x	x		x	X	
AIDS: treatment and research	x	X	x	x				
Consumer product safety	x	X	x					
Hiring: racial discrimination	x			X	x	X	x	
Reproductive rights: choice		X	X	X			X	

DECISION-MAKING ALTERNATIVES

It would be nice if, as an old song once said, "the best things in life are free." Instead, many of the things that people need are in short supply, and humankind has developed a number of ways of reallocating them. In addition, some things cannot be divided among people at all, like moral issues. For example, the most zealous of the antiabortion "right–to–life" advocates would make abortion illegal under virtually all circumstances—an all–or–nothing approach.

People have developed a number of ways of making societal decisions. The most primitive of them must be brute force, whether at the individual level in prehistoric cultures or on the international level through war. Religion and social hierarchy, both of which emphasize the manipulation of important social-psychological symbols, have also been pathways to the acquisition of goods and services in settings that range from medieval Europe to aboriginal tribes still existing today. In most of the Western, industrialized world, however, there are two important alternatives for determining who gets scarce resources and under what conditions: through market–based decision making and through the political process.

Economic systems can take many forms, but in the United States particular importance has been given to the role of market–based deci-

ing. From the publication of Adam Smith's *Wealth of Nations* in 1776 (a book called the first theoretical discussion of markets) through the development of neoclassical economics after the 1880s to the policies of Reaganomics, market–based decision making has been prominent in America.

Political systems also take many forms, as we shall suggest in the following chapter. In the United States of the 1990s, however, a variety of politics called the pluralist model is believed to be the best explanation of how public choice occurs.

One of the features of American politics is that two general tendencies of resource allocation—of decision making—are locked in competition. The judgment of which is preferable, under which sets of conditions and regarding which policy areas, is subjective and changing. It does seem, however, that two distinct outlooks can be discerned among thoughtful Americans: public sector and private sector outlooks.

COMPARING PUBLIC AND PRIVATE SECTOR OUTLOOKS

A curious feature of American politics is the differing outlooks of two groups of people: those who prefer to allocate values through a private enterprise, market–oriented system and those who favor public sector, governmental activity. Whether one focuses on the policy disputes of the Reagan era, the Great Depression, or the Gilded Age of the last century, there is often a distinct line that separates those who prefer governmental intervention from those who would marketize as much as possible. Usually those who favor markets outnumber the proponents of public service. But just what is it that distinguishes the United Parcel Service (a private company) from the U.S. Postal Service? During the decade that it was a federally owned railroad, how did ConRail differ from Norfolk Western? Or how does a state agency like the Ohio Bureau of Employment Services differ from a private employment agency?

The clearest distinction between the public and private sectors is in *ownership and control.* It is the public who "owns" the streets and roads, the parks, the military installations, and the schools and universities. And it is the proprietor, shareholders, or lenders—private parties all—who own private businesses. Control, however, although it is different from ownership, might be the more meaningful. Members of boards of public institutions as diverse as universities and zoological parks may bring a perspective of private ownership to their positions—a feeling that this is "ours" and the public be damned. That public utilities are controlled to varying degrees by public regulation and that major blocks of corporate stock are owned by governmental pension plans suggest that corporate America is not altogether "private." At the same time, the regulation of privately held public utilities is often half-hearted, and there are few surprises at the annual stockholders meeting that cannot be finessed by an astute chairman of the board or chief executive officer (CEO).

That private enterprise exists for *profit maximization* and that government seeks to provide a range of fundamental services without thought of profit is another basic distinction between the public and private sectors. Firms are not always profit maximizers, however. The values of corporate citizenship often lead them to support charitable causes, and country club memberships and a host of other perquisites for executives can detract from profits that might have gone to shareholders. Similarly, the government occasionally provides services above cost, realizing that such income can reduce the burden on taxpayers. North Dakota has operated grain elevators, and the state of New York has bottled mineral water, in attempting to turn a profit. And one of the oldest names in sport, the Toledo Mud Hens baseball club not only is owned by Lucas County but also returns a tidy profit annually.

An ostensibly clear distinction between private and public exists in the area of *finance*. The private sector must rely on borrowing or selling shares of stock, whereas the public sector can call on tax revenues of the general treasury for support. However, increasing privatization has put pressure on governments to implement user fees for their services. The availability of public grants and tax abatements, moreover, shows that the public sector occasionally supports the private one as well. It is also clear that government at all levels is the sole customer of a wide range of private firms that rely on the public for support.

The popular perception is that business can make *decisions more rapidly* than can government. Private enterprise, from the proprietor of a small business to the CEO of a great corporation, has great freedom to act. Its only constraints are the decisions of the marketplace or, perhaps, the questions of a board of directors. The government, in contrast, must reach new decisions only after the time–consuming construction of coalitions of political leaders with varying degrees of interest in the outcome. Often policy can be modified only with the consent of veto groups that are in a position to block new directions. Nevertheless, the government can move swiftly in the face of a crisis like war or a natural disaster or after a critical, realigning election. And the history of business is replete with cases in which major firms have bogged down from outmoded practices, constraints imposed by labor rules, or financial woes that limit flexibility.

Efficiency, measured as the ratio of inputs to outputs, is commonly believed to be higher in the private sector because of the discipline of the marketplace, competition (e.g., refuse collection is the responsibility of the city government alone), and the belief that public employees are lazy or wasteful. Not all markets are highly competitive, however, and more than a few companies have problems with employees' productivity.

Differences in *employment practices* can be significant. Most public employees are hired on some basis of merit, either through competitive examination or educational attainment or because they "know someone" — a system known as patronage. During good economic times they may be paid less than they might be in the private sector, but the trade–off is job security. Indeed, it is very difficult to fire someone in the federal civil service. At the same time, the notion that personnel decisions in the private sector are wholly at the employer's discretion may not correspond with reality. First, union contracts can make dismissal very difficult, and second, dismissal of some employees can result in discrimination charges. Finally, personal friendships sometimes interfere with hard decisions in the private sector also.

What about *competition* as a distinguishing feature? Although we celebrate the competition of the marketplace in the free–enterprise system, Adam Smith understood that competitors would inevitably seek some accommodation to reduce its rigors. The American economy once was plagued by the monopoly problem, but the difficulty now seems to be one of oligopoly. Still, the structure of an industry is less important than whether there is workable competition within it. It is in this area of the degree of competition that government is seen as a monopolist. Nevertheless, people do vote with their feet and move from one locality to another. That this competition is real is seen in the rivalry among cities to entice new jobs from another location to their own.

Size of organization is another possible distinction. *Public* and *private* are terms that conceal as much as they reveal. Private includes a one–man proprietorship and a Fortune 500 corporate giant like General Motors. The term *public sector* refers to the 3.1 million civilian employees of the federal government; the government of the city of New York (with 395,000 employees); or a township with a payroll of 35.

The *proprietary outlook* can be summed up in the assertion "It's all mine." And justifiably so, for the entrepreneur who builds up a business is a valuable part of the free–enterprise system. This is an outlook that sometimes bleeds into the public sector when elected or appointed officials mistakenly feel that habits of a lifetime can be transported into the arena where the public's business is transacted. The consequences can be efforts to reach decisions away from scrutiny or expectations of the sorts of personal services that were forthcoming in the profit–making sector.

This exploration of the similarities between public and private is not to say that there are no differences but only to point out that the distinctions are often blurry.

POLITICAL ECONOMY

All of the topics addressed to this point—politics as both conflict and accommodation, the importance of economic values in public programs, the differences between economics and politics in decisionmaking, and the contrast between those who prefer the public or the private sector way of reaching decisions—are different facets of a larger whole: political economy.

One definition of political economy sees it as *the use of governmental power to obtain economic goals.* This is an ancient notion, for it was a principle of mercantilism during the age of exploration that the government would intervene extensively in what we now recognize as economic life. Early in our national history the state governments, and Congress as well, embarked on many efforts to support and develop the economic infrastructure—canals, railroads, and even manufacturing operations. In our own time, governmental intervention is readily seen in regulatory institutions. Many are of a protective nature, with responsibilities in the areas of consumer safety, safety in the workplace, or protection of the environment. Others, like the Federal Trade Commission, regulate economic and marketplace actions. However, despite the deregulation movement that began during the 1970s and became a central principle of conservative thought during the Reagan–Bush era, government remains a major force in economic life.

A companion definition of political economy reverses the direction of causality and sees it as *the impact of economic power on political processes.* Marxists are not alone in discerning that the private sector can have a profound effect on the workings of government. Almost at the time of our national beginning, the private sector exerted influence on the federal government to protect our commerce in the Mediterranean during the Jefferson administration. The owners of businesses were able to limit the ability of labor to organize until well into this century and to impede the flow of free trade. For a time, organized labor was able to make telling use of the muscle that came from its great size. When one–third of American workers were unionized and when union solidarity was greater than today, considerable influence could be brought to bear politically. In the last two decades the effect of corporate political action committees (PACs) and the impact of slick, expensive lobbying may have significantly increased the political power of businesses and the wealthier individuals for whom they speak.

There is a third meaning to political economy as well: analyzing and representing political processes through economic graphic notation. Among the first to use this approach was Anthony Downs (1957), who accounted for the two–party system by referring to the bell–shaped distribution of public opinion. Other notable examples include a price–theoretic depiction of the process of constitutional formation by James Buchanan and Gordon Tullock (1965) and an extensive analysis of the political process by Curry and Wade (1968). The journal *Public Choice* is a particular repository of this mode of inquiry.

PLAN OF THE BOOK

The chapters of this book explore the American political economy in three different ways. Part One seeks to introduce some of the fundamental notions of political economy. It includes this introductory chapter as well as the following one on the schools of economics and the differing perspectives about who governs in the United States.

Part Two develops the historical context within which the American political economy has developed. Chapter Three adopts the longest focus. It is concerned with the sweeping themes of three centuries of experience, from the mercantilist beginnings of colonial America through the industrialization of the Gilded Age to the Great Crash of 1929 that brought it all to an end. Chapter Four examines the half century between 1929 and 1980 and highlights the new governmental agencies and activities that arose. These years of economic cataclysm engendered an interventionist government and an alphabet soup of regulatory agencies that have persisted, to a considerable degree, to our own time. The historical focus becomes narrowest in Chapter Five, which treats the dozen years of Reaganomics and the Bush sequel.

Part Three examines the institutions and functions of government that are important to the economy. Chapter Six discusses the three great branches of government, the executive, legislative, and judicial powers. Chapter Seven addresses practical politics as seen in elections, political parties, and pressure groups. Chapter Eight examines the functions that government performs, with special reference to regulation and to the deregulation movement that began in the 1970s.

Part Four draws our attention to several selected topics in public policy. The government has sought to manage the economy in two distinctive ways. Fiscal policy, or attempts to smooth out the business cycle by varying expenditures and the taxing process, is the subject of Chapter Nine. Chapter Ten examines a management technique that has become fashionable among conservatives during the last two decades—monetary policy. Chapter Eleven addresses two important assumptions about the marketplace that are central to capitalism: antimonopoly or "antitrust" policy and anticompetitive business behavior. Organized labor is the subject of Chapter Twelve, and Chapter Thirteen examines the rapidly changing area of international political economy.

The final chapter draws from the historical, institutional, and policy chapters in an attempt to examine the relationship among politics, economics, and governance. Are democracy and capitalism inseparable, as some claim, or are they threats to each other, as Joseph Schumpeter once argued? Or is the peculiarly American style of political pluralism and mixed capitalism the result of some other set of forces?

DISCUSSION QUESTIONS

1. What are the most important issues that confront the United States today? That confront the locality you call home? How would you rate the importance of economics in each of these issues?

2. What do you think about the charge that American politics simply is not conflictual enough in addressing the problems that confront us?

3. In what ways are politics and economics different from each other and in what ways are they similar? Which is the more usual view, that they are different or that they are alike? In what ways are the academic disciplines of economics and political science different from each other? How are they similar?

4. If we view politics as concerned with compromise, or "the art of the possible," is there any relationship between the size of the economic component in an issue and the ease with which compromise can be reached?

5. What is an *economic determinist*? What problems result from adopting this point of view? Is there such a thing as a political determinist?

6. Where are the differences between public sector operations and those in the private sector most distinct? Are some of these distinctions more apparent than real?

7. How does political economy regard the relationship between economics and politics? Which is causal, and which is the result?

REFERENCES

Buchanan, James M., and Gordon Tullock. 1965. *The Calculus of Consent: Logical Foundations of Constitutional Democracy.* Ann Arbor: University of Michigan Press.

Clausen, Aage R. 1973. *How Congressmen Decide: A Policy Focus.* New York: St. Martin's Press.

Curry, Robert L., and Larry L. Wade. 1968. *A Theory of Political Exchange: Economic Reasoning in Political Analysis.* Englewood Cliffs, NJ: Prentice Hall.

Downs, Anthony. 1957. *An Economic Theory of Democracy.* New York: Harper.

Dye, Thomas R. 1966. *Politics, Economics, and the Public: Policy Outcomes in the American States.* Chicago: Rand McNally.

CHAPTER TWO

ECONOMIC SCHOOLS AND POLITICAL PARADIGMS

Schools of inquiry, common to all academic disciplines, consist of like-minded analysts who adhere, more or less, to the teachings of a particular great writer. Although some may have been founded consciously, more usually they have been labeled, and their members identified, only in later years. It is not unusual for certain individuals to fit into more than one school, to shift from one to another over time, or to disavow an apparent association with any of them. After all, it may be wiser to identify oneself as a pragmatist than to invite controversy because of some particular discipleship. Some observers contend that the persistence of schools attests to the immaturity of a discipline.

Although many economic schools can be identified, much of the conflict in political economy today can be traced to disagreements between adherents of two broad intellectual clans. One of them centers on the neo-classical tradition that espouses market-based decision making and minimal government. The other consists of those who see a need for governmental intervention in economic life and who style themselves Keynesians, post-Keynesians, neo-Keynesians, or similar kindred spirits. The first half of this chapter examines several economic schools and their seminal writers.

Political science became divided between "traditionalists " and "behav-ioralists " during the 1950s and 1960s, although the conflict was largely healed by their synthesis into "postbehavioralists" or "new institutionalists" during the 1970s. Although the schism had centered on the proper methods for studying politics, it did seem that those who insisted on empirical theory and quantification had a conservative outlook on the world. Perhaps strangely, the term *school* was seldom applied to either approach; instead, terms like *approach, outlook,* or *persuasion* were used. Thus, the analogy for economic schools in political science lies not in methodological persuasions but is found instead in the dispute over who governs. The second half of this chapter examines three prominent interpretations of how government is run—the majoritarian, elitist, and pluralist paradigms.

SCHOOLS OF ECONOMICS

The classical tradition

A seminal event in the history of economics was the publication in 1776 of *The Wealth of Nations.* The book, which elaborated on the work of earlier writers like Anders Chydenius (1765), was the product of the Scottish academician Adam Smith (1723–1790), and it heralded a *classical* period that persisted through the mid–nineteenth century. Just as Isaak Newton had reshaped thinking about the physical world three generations earlier, Smith contributed to a new social physics. Competition among individuals in a private marketplace free from governmental interference is the primary cause of national wealth, he argued. But although capital accumulation, market expansion, and division of labor were foremost in Smith's thinking, he nevertheless offered recommendations for governmental policy both in normal times and when markets might fail. Smith's massive contribution was joined by that of the Reverend Thomas Malthus (1766–1834), who added a dynamic view that population increases would outstrip the growth of nation-al economies. It was this gloomy view that branded economics "the dismal science." Most of the classical economists postulated that prices are deter-mined by the costs of production and the value of the labor that went to cre-ate them; but a Frenchman, Jean-Baptiste Say (1767–1832), recognized that value depends on the usefulness of a good rather than on the costs of the labor that produced it—an insight that was to bear fruit in neoclassical hands a century later. David Ricardo (1772–1823) did more to isolate labor as a basis for value, and John Stuart Mill (1806–1873) synthesized this corpus of knowledge by midcentury. Methodologically, Smith pioneered in inductive analysis by formulating premises and testing them against empirical data. Ricardo, however, proceeded deductively by stating hypotheses and deducing empirical laws but making little attempt to verify his results—a failure called "the Ricardian vice " by Joseph Schumpeter (1954) a century later.

As great as it was, classical economics suffered from several weaknesses. One was Say's law, which by contending that "supply creates its own demand " had omitted as much as it included and typified an inadequate treatment of aggregate demand in the marketplace. Other shortcomings were a fuzziness about the determinants of the supply of capital and the nature of physical investment. Although the classical economists were concerned primarily with macro-level analysis and the determinants of national growth and development, there was a need to descend to a more desegregated level of analysis. By the last quarter of the nineteenth century a new school had emerged, driven not only by a desire to extend the lines of classical inquiry but also by even greater concerns with micro-level economic behavior and with the locus of its activity—the marketplace.

The neoclassical school

Neoclassical economics is the name given to a view that had captured center stage by the late nineteenth century and called for minimal governmental involvement in the economy. Grounded on the teachings of the classical economists; revised by Alfred Marshall, Irving Fisher, William Graham Sumner, A. C. Pigou, and others; linked with the sociological teachings of Herbert Spencer and the theology of Henry Ward Beecher; and in conformity with the interests of the great fortunes of the day, this was the *neoclassical* economic model. By the early twentieth century it had developed a sophisticated view of how capitalist economies worked. Many of its concepts flowed directly from Adam Smith and others of the earlier classical period: (1) a reliance on individual and personal initiative, (2) private ownership of production and distribution, (3) a plurality of buyers and sellers in the marketplace, (4) active competition among sellers, (5) easy entry into the marketplace by new producers (as well as easy exit from it for the unsuccessful), and (6) prices established by a marketplace.

At least three important innovations distinguished neoclassical economics. The first was Alfred Marshall's refinement of the interaction of supply and demand through his development of two laws that governed the action of each. The second was the concept of *marginality*, the insight that each additional increment of any commodity decreases in its unit value to the holder. All things being equal, the second automobile that a person acquires adds less additional utility (is "less additionally useful") than the first; the third car adds less than did the second; and so on. This notion of diminishing marginal value is the reason that the familiar downward– sloping demand function is a curve rather than a straight line. It is also the justification for progressive rates of taxation, although the wealthy prefer to skip over the idea of marginality whenever the subject of taxes enters the conversation.

The third neoclassical innovation was the most important from the standpoint of political controversy, for sophisticated notions of *market equilibrium* were central to neoclassical economics. An economy is in equilibrium when there is an optimal match between what producers produce and what consumers consume across the full range of products. When demand exceeds supply, prices will rise and quantities sold may fall. *Partial equilibrium theory* was developed to explain mathematically the adjustments that eventually restore the equality between supply and demand. Clearly, however, markets are interconnected, so price increases will also cause consumers to cast about for substitute products. Under Marshall's second law of demand, the move toward substitution will be greater the more time the market has to adjust. It was the task of *general equilibrium theory* to explain changes across the entire economy. Leon Walras had begun the analysis of equilibria at midcentury, and Marshall was able to articulate the model to a larger audience.

Equilibrium theory was important for addressing the allocation of labor as well as consumer products. Here, the theory held that capitalist economies could be in equilibrium only under full employment, which was taken to mean that the only people who would be out of work would be the idle rich and the lazy poor (both classes deplorable) or those who were changing jobs (frictional unemployment—a wholly laudable exercise in which the marketplace was merely reallocating its resources).

Finally, equilibrium theory provided an ethical justification for the pursuit of self-interest. Vilfredo Pareto was able to prove mathematically that in an economy in perfect equilibrium, it would be impossible to improve the "welfare" of one consumer without making some other consumer worse off. Even though acting selfishly, producers and consumers were also acting to improve the lot of all people in society.

It was in proposing an appropriate role for government that the fragmentation among neoclassical economists was clearest. There was some acceptance of intervention in the mathematical formulations of Pareto, who approved of it as long as the gains of those who benefited would outweigh the losses of those who lost. Others were willing to accept a range of governmental activities: providing public goods like roads, education, parks, and playgrounds; providing a national defense; enforcing contracts; perhaps even supplying a medium of exchange. But still others were believers in laissez–faire and could use economic theory to limit governmental regulation.

It was difficult to criticize neoclassical economics in the 1920s. Like physics thirty years before, all of the main questions had been solved and only a few details near the edge needed to be worked out. What turned the world of physics upside down in the 1890s were the discovery of radioactivity and the development of relativity theory. For neoclassical economics it was a problem with equilibrium theory. As Keynes was to demonstrate, it simply did not work.

The Keynesian model

The writings of John Maynard Keynes and his disciples, plus a number of policy prescriptions about what government should do to regulate the business cycle, constitute Keynesian economics. Calling for a government that actively manages economic life, it came to the foreground during the Great Depression and was legitimized in the United States by the Employment Act of 1946. In *The General Theory of Employment, Interest and Money*, Keynes (1935) began by destroying an axiom of neoclassical theory— that it was impossible for a capitalist economy to be in equilibrium at anything less than full employment. Instead, he argued, large numbers of chronically unemployed people crying out for jobs might be a permanent feature of capitalism. Certainly it seemed to be so in the 1930s. From his rejection of the crucial neoclassical belief in a self-adjusting marketplace, Keynes developed a chain of axioms and corollaries of his own. First, capitalist economies were seen to be *demand–driven*. As national income rises, he wrote, so will consumption, although increases in consumption always will be less than increases in income. The ratio between changes in income and changes in consumption is called the *marginal propensity to consume.*

A second principle concerns the role of investment. Since income increases with improved employment opportunities, and if those opportunities are the result of investment, then how can flagging rates of investment be increased during hard times? The *inducement to invest* will be positive as long as the marginal efficiency of capital, when discounted against anticipated future earnings, is equal to or greater than the rate of interest that is paid to finance new plant and equipment. Since a sour outlook dampens the entrepreneurial spirit, the optimistic note sounded by Franklin D. Roosevelt in his inaugural address—"The only thing we have to fear is fear itself "— is perfectly Keynesian, even though several years passed before Roosevelt sought to apply the Englishman's economic teachings.

A concern with the outlook toward interest rates is associated with his third concept: the *liquidity trap*. Even though interest rates might be brought down by monetary authorities, as they were in the early 1930s, the belief that they may go even lower will dissuade potential investors from borrowing. It was a problem of "pushing on a string "—simply lowering the discount rate would not ensure that business would take advantage of looser credit. For this reason monetary policy is seen as inferior to fiscal policy in economic management. During downturns, then, the government should increase its spending, lower its tax revenues, and borrow to make up the difference.

This is where a fourth principle—governmental investment with borrowed money—becomes important. Keynes showed that government spending could act like private investment to stimulate demand as long as (1) the money was not raised through taxes (which would diminish consumers' spendable money) or (2) the government's borrowing was not from consumers (who would only be underwriting the government rather than buying consumer goods). Instead, the borrowed funds should come from the central banking system, for example, from the Federal Reserve.

To deficit spending, or compensatory fiscal policy, Keynes added a fifth principle: Government deficits are permissible only when the economy cannot sustain "full" employment. If employment is high and demand seems adequate, governmental spending should be paid out of current revenues. With the return of prosperity, taxes should be increased to dampen inflation, spending should be reduced, and the debt should be paid off. In fact, it is more likely that the debt will be outgrown rather than retired, which is what occurred after World War II, when the national debt as a percentage of GNP went from 130 percent in 1945 to 35 percent in 1980. It was not paid off; the nation simply increased its capacity to carry it.

Keynesianism, taken to mean not only the extensive writings of Keynes himself but also the numerous emendations made by his expositors and extenders, is a formidable intellectual edifice.

Two generations of economists have measured such key concepts as propensities to consume, investment demand schedules, investment multipliers, marginal efficiency, and even the notion of unemployment itself and reestimated them under all sorts of varying conditions and industries. The need for reliable information to inform Keynesian policy choices has spawned the development of hundreds of economic indicators that are reported at frequent intervals by agencies both public and private. Among the important original contributions are Alvin Hansen's IS-LM model and the Phillips curve, which expresses the relationship between inflation and unemployment. The Phillips curve relationship between inflation and unemployment is shown in Figure 2-1.

Keynesianism is subject to a number of criticisms, some political and some economic. Politically, the time needed to respond with new tax or expenditure legislation during hard times can be painfully long. As someone has said, Congress is not quick on its 1,070 feet, as can be seen in the enactment of a countercyclical "jobs" bill for the unemployed in transportation in 1991. Keynesian solutions are also asymmetric. It is easier to lower taxes in hard times than to increase them during prosperity; and as President Reagan discovered, it is more difficult to reduce spending under good conditions than to increase it during a recession. Speaking economically, the

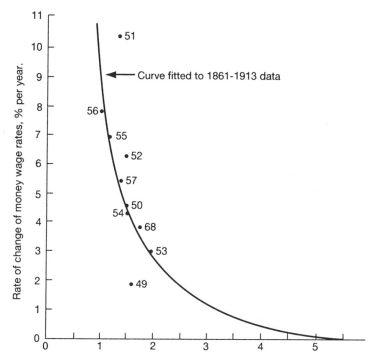

Figure 2-1. 1948-1957, with unemployment lagged seven months. Source: A.W. Phillips. 1958. "The Relation Between Unemployment and the Rate of Change of Money Wage Rates in the United Kingdom, 1861-1957." *Economica,* 25 (November, 1958), 283-299.

sorts of indicators needed to inform Keynesian policy need constant fine tuning. This need was apparent in the breakdown of the Phillips curve during the 1970s, when America encountered both high inflation and high unemployment at the same time. As an economy changes from manufacturing to service, the use of appropriate measures becomes clearer. Economically too, Keynesianism has been linked with a tendency toward inflation since the end of the Great Depression. The upwardly sweeping trace in the consumer price index since 1945 contrasts sharply with the 150 years that preceded it. Finally, those who prefer market mechanisms to governmental management harbor an opposition to Keynesianism that seems genetic, especially in the United States, where so much of politics is, at its core, economic in nature.

Keynesianism was controversial because of its perceived radicalism; but Keynes's goal was to save capitalism, not to abolish it. Although it was used only half-heartedly during the New Deal, an activist economic role for government was prescribed in the Employment Act of 1946, in which Congress charged the president with the role of being chief economic manager. As the pendulum has swung to the right, however, and as government has come to be regarded by many as "the problem, not the solution," undiluted Keynesians are more difficult to find, although James Tobin (1918—) and Robert Eisner (1922—) might be counted among them.

Neoclassical post–Keynesianism

After more than 200 years of analysis, economic orthodoxy in America today might be called neoclassical post-Keynesianism or *democratic capitalism*. Sir John Hicks has contended that Keynes's "general theory" was really only a special case of the old classical formulations of market equilibrium. In the years since the Great Depression, mainstream economists have refined the older notion of a single principle of utility by recognizing the importance of dual incentives: utility maximization for the consumer on the demand side of the equation and profit maximization for the seller on the supply side. Paul Samuelson's great contribution has been to assimilate Keynesian demand side economics, classical supply-side views that descend from Say's law, and monetary theories; and it is this synthesis that is taught in most of our classrooms today.

Economic schools on the left

Protests against concentrations of wealth and economic unfairness were raised as early as the seventeenth century by the Levellers and Diggers. As a well-argued economic doctrine, however, *socialism* emerged much later with the realization that the French Revolution had stopped short of attaining its goals of liberty, equality, and fraternity. Claude-Henri St. Simon (1760–1825) recognized that although the Revolution had removed the old noble class from government, it had not ended the economic privileges that birth continued to grant. His notion of a "new Christianity" as a means for ending exploitation won for him a wide following after his death. The term *socialism*, as opposed to individualism, was used by Pierre Leroux in 1838 in his attack on the *laissez-faire* capitalism that was spreading misery among the working classes of Europe. His remedy was the regulation of production and distribution by society as a whole. In England, Robert Owen (1771–1858) promoted communal societies grounded in religious belief, but his experimental American settlements in New Harmony, Indiana, and elsewhere were less successful than the Shaker communities of the nineteenth century. Because the success of socialist ideas requires levels of employer depredations and working class consciousness that have never been fully realized in the United States, socialism has never been popular in America. The high tide of American socialism was reached by the Socialist party of Eugene V. Debs (1855–1926), who was defeated in five presidential elections between 1900 and 1920—the last coming when he received 900,000 votes while in prison for violation of the World War I-era Espionage Act.

A far more virulent line of protest from the left was Marxism. Karl Marx (1818–1883), a German expatriate from a background of socialist activism, wrote what may have been the most important political tract of the nineteenth century, the *Communist Manifesto*. Marx, who had great knowledge of earlier economic writers and borrowed from Hegel's dialectical method of argument, contended that civilization progressed through a series of stages that culminated in a postrevolutionary "classless, stateless society." His rejection of organized religion, call for bloody revolution, and posthumous role in the East-West power struggle have made unbiased evaluation of his economic prowess nearly impossible. Marx developed the model of economics as a circular flow from producers to consumers and back again; and by calling attention to the plight of the working classes, he aroused righteous indignation in a way that was unmatched by other writers. Marxist economists in the United States are relatively scarce. One of them, Paul Baran (1910–1964), was concerned with the linkage between advanced, colonialist, Western capitalist countries and the plight of the underdeveloped Third World. Paul Sweezy (1956–), editor of *Monthly Review* magazine, has focused on what he considers to be American capitalism's final stage in the Marxist dialectic—the stage of monopoly imperialism.

Another school that challenges the status quo from the left is *institutional economics*. It is the product of a number of writers who have noted the gap between neoclassical theory and human reality. On theoretical grounds, institutional economists objected to models of perfect competition; the concept of rational, calculating economic man; and the belief that firms or individuals truly are profit or utility maximizers. Returning to the holistic spirit of classical analysis, they emphasized the importance of economic and social organizations, operating through the political process, in determining public policy. Thorstein Veblen (1857–1929) used humor and derision in a scathing analysis of the power of the rich in his *Theory of the Leisure Class* (1912), and Thurman Arnold's (1937, 1964) *The Folklore of Capitalism* expanded Veblen's insights for the 1930s and 1940s. Wesley C. Mitchell (1874–1948) and John R. Commons (1862–1945) were concerned with the condition of organized labor and turned in the direction of wage determination analysis by the 1940s and 1950s. A Swede, Gunnar Myrdal (1940, 1962), forced us to see ourselves as others see us with his analysis of the conditions of black Americans in *An American Dilemma*. This school, typically critical of the establishment, remains active among those who style themselves labor economists; and the work of John Kenneth Galbraith fits into the institutionalist school as well.

Schools on the right

The political right is associated with a defense of the status quo or with returning to some golden age of the past. Economists on the right typically defend the interests of those who hold positions of power and privilege as well. The archetypical economic right in America is the *laissez-faire* school associated with the writings of Herbert Spencer (1820–1903). Extrapolating from Charles Darwin, Spencer devised the term *survival of the fittest* in describing the conflict between the wealthy in society and those at the bottom of the economic pyramid. Charity, he felt, should be dispensed sparingly because it only perpetuated society's least competitive members. His view that government would wither away with the progress of society became so pervasive in arguments against the regulation of business that Justice Oliver Wendell Holmes, Jr., felt compelled to dissent in a case that had overturned New York's limitation on the maximum number of hours bakers could work: "The Fourteenth Amendment does not enact Mr. Herbert Spencer's *Social Statics.*" [1]

Recent decades have seen the appearance of others who share an aversion to governmental involvement in the economy. *Monetarism* has been developed through the work of Karl Brunner (1916–), Allan H. Meltzer (1928–) and especially by the writings of Milton Friedman (1912–), who expanded the Fisher equation by including variables like wealth, interest rates, and anticipated rates of inflation. Monetarists contend that economic stability can be brought about best by a slow, steady expansion of the money supply in concert with the rate of growth of the economy as a whole. Friedman's faculty position at the University of Chicago, together with a number of other conservatives, has given the appellation "Chicago school " to those who would marketize most of the public sector and who see government as the problem, not the solution, to most economic ills.

There are others on the right who have grown out of a neoclassical base. *Supply-siders*, best symbolized by the Laffer curve, are concerned with stimulating production rather than with promoting consumer demand, as the Keynesians would emphasize. They have historical roots in Say's law. It is the premise of people like Arthur B. Laffer, Norman Ture, and Paul Craig Roberts that high tax rates harm the economy by diminishing individual incentive and, consequently, reduce revenues to the Treasury because of their burden on individual endeavor. Supply-siders can be attacked by those who demand to see proof that tax savings will be invested and will create new jobs, and they also suffer from charges that they are little more than rationalizers for the rich in ways reminiscent of Herbert Spencer. *Rational expectations* analysts believe that in today's society, where economic information travels instantaneously, insightful people will have foreseen and discounted any governmental actions even before they occur. People like Robert E.

---

[1] (*Lochner* v. *New York*, 198 U.S. 45 1905). Useful biographies of many economists can be found in Pass and Ehrlich (1991) and in Pearce (1983).

Lucas, Jr., Robert J. Barro, and Thomas J. Sargent feel that only unexpected governmental actions will have an effect on the economy. Decisions by the Federal Reserve system to loosen credit by lowering the discount rate, for example, are said to have little specific impact because the marketplace will have already factored them into its behavior. The *Austrian school* of economics can be traced to Carl Menger (1840–1921), Friedrich von Wieser (1851–1926), and Eugen von Bohm-Bawerk (1851–1914). Most recently Friedrich A. von Hayek (1899–) enjoyed a following among young disciples who have argued that a laissez-faire system would be "an incredible bread machine."

PERCEPTIONS OF POLITICS: WHO GOVERNS?

The "schools" of political science must be conceptualized quite differently than those of economics. Indeed, the greatest divisions within the discipline have concerned the best way of studying political phenomena. The *traditionalists* mentioned at the beginning of this chapter were heterogeneous scholars whose only common feature was that they worked in ways that were well established before the middle of the present century. Some were institutionalists, meaning that they specialized in the lore of particular governmental institutions like legislatures or courts of specific agencies. Others were historical-descriptive in the manner of political historians, but different from them in that political scientists are more likely to proceed by testing hypotheses. Traditionalists were also legalistic in ways that emulated jurisprudence, as well as reformist and philosophically normative. By 1950, the *behavioral* approach elbowed its way into the study of politics by making a conscious attempt to apply the methods of the natural sciences to the study of politics. Facilitated by the development of the computer during World War II, behavioralism was characterized by a focus on the individual as the unit of analysis, the use of quantitative data that were often gleaned from survey research, the use of descriptive and inferential statistics, and an uneasiness about basing normative judgments about matters of right and wrong on objective data. And guiding all was the search for empirical, self-correcting explanatory theory.

By 1969, protests over the Vietnam War and the ascendancy of "value-less" scientism spawned a backlash that took the form of the Caucus for a New Political Science, the members of which tended to be an alliance of younger radicals and older traditionalists. A decade later, however, personal retooling, emphasis on quantitative methods in graduate training, and generational replacement allowed a synthesis of behavioralism and a renewed appreciation for traditional scholarship. This was the *new institutionalism*, which now constitutes the mainstream of political science.

Although there was some tendency for traditionalists to be liberal and behavioralists to be conservative, the correlation between methodological approach and economic ideology must have been small. Instead, where political economy is concerned, the appropriate analogy to economic schools lies in the differing perspectives of how America is governed. Three important perspectives are majoritarianism, elitism, and the pluralist model[2].

The classical democratic model

"Here, Sir, the people govern." Attributed to John Adams so very long ago, this statement summarizes the normative view of most Americans about how their country is (or ought to be) governed. This expectation about popular sovereignty is found also in the word *democracy*—which literally means "rule by the people." But although popular rule and "democracy" seem such simple notions, neither of them says anything at all about just how this self-rule will occur.

The model of governance internalized by most Americans can be called the classical democratic paradigm. It sees government as responsive to the will of the people—or at least to the will of a majority of them. As we see in the expression "one person, one vote," each person is expected to carry equal political weight. There should be a high level of mass knowledgeability, as well as a high degree of popular participation that can bring such knowledge to bear politically. The citizenry is expected to make rational choices among alternative candidates and policies through the electoral process; elected officials, for their part, are expected to be responsive to voters, who will be aware of their behavior. Present throughout this system is a reliance on individual responsibility and activity. In all, the classical democratic model presents an attractive and demanding picture of citizen governance.

Although this majoritarian model might be attainable in some idyllic community, special institutional arrangements for it would be needed in a large republic like the United States. Classical political philosophers like Hobbes, Locke, and Montesquieu recognized the role of a legislature in giving voice to the public will; and the framers of the Constitution (most certainly not a collection of democrats) crafted the U.S. House of Representatives as "the people's house." Particularly important as an institution of popular control was the creation of the modern, mass-based political party, which developed between 1791 and 1840 as a device to link the governed with their government. Also especially important is the place of a free press for supplying information that is essential for rational choice. From

2 Although the juxtaposition of elite rule, majoritarianism, and pluralism occurs widely in political science, this section acknowledges its treatment in Kenneth Janda, Jeffrey M. Berry, and Jerry Goldman, *The Challenge of Democracy: Government in America*, 3rd ed. (Boston: Houghton Mifflin, 1992), pp. 44–58.

the very beginning, classical democracy has required special institutions to sustain it.

By the last third of the nineteenth century it became clear that this classical democratic model did not depict reality. Between 1900 and 1917, the Progressive movement was important in trying to restore popular control through a series of reforms that remain in place today. Circumventing recalcitrant legislatures through the initiative, referendum, and recall; overriding the ills of party through municipal nonpartisanship; and reforming voting through such practices as the Australian ballot were all attempts to return power to the people. At the time of World War One, James Bryce (1916, II, 261) thought he could see new developments in opinion polling as a brave new way for the people to govern. And in our own time, Ross Perot would amalgamate computer, telephone, and video technologies to conduct electronic town meetings, which would yet again promise to return power to the people directly. Any flaws in such a system (such as verifying just who it is that is voting) can all be worked out, he assures us.

For all its attractiveness, the classical democratic model is a flawed one. Its fundamental tenet of equal political weight for all is undermined by the knowledge that social advantages and lobbying skills make some segments of society significantly more equal than others. Anyone who believes in equal political weight for all would be hard pressed to defend a system of voter registration that consistently dissuades millions of Americans from voting. Opinion polls have always reported low levels of knowledgeability about who our officeholders are or how to approach the tough issues of the day. Levels of voting participation range from the teens in many local elections to just over 50 percent for presidential elections. The proven effectiveness of negative campaigning and the persistence of election coverage that devotes more attention to the "horse race" nature of elections than to substantive policy discussions lend little credence to the requisite of rational choice. Unresponsive elected officials and an independent bureaucracy have given rise to demands for term limitation. Taken together, it is impossible to sustain the classical democratic model as a valid depiction of how America is governed.

There are two other major problems with this majoritarian view. First, seldom is there any single majority position for or against any important public issue. In the increasingly heterogeneous society that is the United States, the search for numerical majorities becomes an exercise in coalition building. Second, as James Madison would have put it, the truest test of constitutional politics is whether the government (especially one that reflects majority will) is obligated to control itself. In other words, the protection of minority rights is as important for the maintenance of a democratic system as is majority rule. For all its apparent simplicity, the classical democratic model is heavily flawed.

The elite rule model

Quite a different view of governance is held by those who believe that a small group of political elites actually runs the country. The elitist, stratificationist model can be envisioned as a pyramid, with power concentrated among a tiny few at the apex, with a wide base consisting of the masses on whom it rests, and where social stratification limits vertical mobility from the top down or from the bottom up. Admission to elite status, in this view, comes from family connections, inherited wealth, and institutional position. Estimates of the size of the political elite vary from one commentator to the next and range from the high hundreds to about 7,000 in the view of Thomas Dye (1983, p. 267). Community power studies, which first sensitized social critics to the "reality" of elite rule, find analogous conditions of socially stratified governance at the local level.

Just as the implementation of classical democracy requires a set of institutions, so too would a system dominated by elites. One requirement would be a shared social milieu of old school ties, common religious institutions and club affiliations, and shared control of major corporations and financial institutions. The ability to dominate the media would also be essential if the minds of the masses were to be molded to the will of the elite. The rudiments of most of these elements are present in the eyes of many critics of American governance. The notion that "they"—the wealthy, the wellborn, the career bureaucrats—really run things is appealing to many who believe their own wishes are seldom taken into account.

As tempting as it may be, the elite model is also flawed. It sings the siren's song of envy, but to the extent that power comes with corporate position, it is more associated with the job than with the person who holds it. How influential is a *former* CEO of a Fortune 500 corporation once he or she no longer occupies an executive suite on the forty-seventh floor? If there is institutional turnover, doesn't the infighting that often accompanies the selection of new leadership usually suggest the reality of vertical social mobility? And just where do these governing elites meet to work out their plan of control? Aren't there socially elite people who care little for politics and politically influential people who come from humble family backgrounds? And what about elite dissent? Opinion leaders who promote an activist governmental economic policy are sure to be confronted by others espousing a hands-off policy of laissez-faire. For every elite leader who seeks a Western Hemisphere- free trade zone there are others who are promoting trade protectionism for the glass or automobile industry.

Despite its flaws, elite theory has a firm grip on the minds of many Americans. Its roots antedate the Middletown study of Robert and Helen Lynd, who suggested that Muncie, Indiana, was a typical middle-American city in the way that it was dominated by a small, relatively stable social set.

During the cultural restiveness of the 1950s and 1960s, C. Wright Mills (1956) wrote that America was dominated by an elite consisting of the heads of major corporations, military leaders, and political officeholders. Most recently, elite theorists like G. William Domhoff (1983), John Manley (1983), and Thomas Dye (1983) continue to see government as being under the control of small numbers of people. Domhoff and Manley see elitism as reprehensible, whereas Dye, William F. Buckley, and others view it as a source of stability. At bottom, however, the elite paradigm stands as a refutation of the American dream.

The pluralist model

The most complex theory of how America is ruled is the pluralist model. The work of Robert Dahl (1982, 1990), its best-known proponent, and the contributions of his many disciples, make it the consensual favorite among political scientists.

If the pyramid portrays elitism, then the trapezoid (or rather, a series of overlapping trapezoids) represents pluralism. This view suggests that there are more influential people at the figure's top who can participate effectively and that there are as many sets of power holders as there are domains of public policy. Those who are influential in economic policy, for example, may be quite different from the players in civil rights, women's issues, or defense. Especially important is the vertical mobility that is a component of pluralism—something that attenuates the link between personal wealth and political influence.

The central importance of political groups is a different facet of pluralism. Alexis de Tocqueville had remarked on the American affinity for forming social groups of all kinds; and in pluralist theory the periodic entry of groups into political conflict is crucial. Few groups are organized for avowedly political purposes, according to pluralist theory; instead they enter politics only occasionally in order to obtain their more central interests. When they do so, however, they and their leaders displace as decision makers that uninformed electorate that so troubles the majoritarian paradigm. It is among the smaller universe of pressure-group leaders, then, that we find political actors who are indeed informed, rational, and highly participatory.

According to pluralist thought, governance becomes rule by coalitions of minorities and politicians become responsive to group demands. Many studies show that a majority of the groups that enter the political arena have some economic basis for their existence. Often they are trade associations like the American Petroleum Institute, large pressure groups like the U.S. Chamber of Commerce, or labor unions. Pluralists see public policy as largely, though not entirely, the product of interest-group interaction.

Institutional arrangements are no less important for the pluralist view of governance than for majoritarianism or the elite view. One of them is the decentralization that distinguishes American government from parliamentary systems. Acting through the separation of powers among the three branches of government, as well as through federalism, it provides a multitude of decisional points that offer many routes to exercising influence, as well as multiple veto points where threatened action can be brought to a halt. The pluralist perspective on political parties is one in which they are viewed as coalitions of group interests that undergo major reconfigurations periodically through critical, realigning elections. Electorally, the political action committees (PACs) that have become so very important since the campaign finance changes of 1974 further enhance the importance of pressure groups in political life.

Any empirical theory should seek to reflect reality. In the last ten years Dahl (1982, 1990) has reformulated *neopluralism.* Having moved somewhat closer to the elite model, he feels that business corporations have become considerably more powerful during the 1970s and that the American public has developed a nature that is more avaricious and less public-minded.

ACADEMIC SCHOOLS: THEIR DISTINCTIVENESS AND IMPACT

Thomas Kuhn (1970) has suggested why there are so many schools of economic or political thought and why their popularity ebbs and flows over time. Usually there is a predominant orthodoxy in any scientific community—a dominant scientific paradigm. It is constructed incrementally as many researchers piece together an explanation that can account for the motion of planets, the structure of matter, or the nature of economic and political life. In the physical sciences, dominant paradigms are replaced when an important flaw is recognized that can be rectified only by adopting a new theoretical system. In the social sciences there is also the fact of changing social conditions. Although an explanatory model like early Keynesianism or classical democratic theory may have matched conditions at one time, a restructuring of behavior can drain it of its usefulness at another. It is when the models fail to work, as in the breakdown of the Phillips curve during the late 1970s, that competing explanations like the Laffer curve attract new adherents.

Economically, why do we hear so little about schools other than neoclassical post-Keynesianism? Why is this one approach singled out as the pedagogical framework for economics in America? Here again, Kuhn's (1970) approach suggests that a consensus will hold some scientific explanations in higher regard than others, purely on scientific grounds. Politically, why do Americans long for a classical democratic world that never existed or turn cynically to an elitist model that is equally flawed? In fact, the major conflict in American political economy today is being waged in a neopluralist arena among Keynesian interventionists, neoclassical free marketeers, and monetarist managers of the money supply.

DISCUSSION QUESTIONS

1. In what ways are politics and economics different from each other and in what ways are they similar? Which is the more usual view in the United States—that they are different or similar?

2. What are some of the "schools " within economics, and how do they differ from one another? Which ones prescribe the greatest amount of governmental intervention in the economy? Which prescribe the least involvement?

3. Distinguish between the traditionalist and behavioralist approaches to the study of politics. What is meant by the "new institutionalism?"

4. What differences are there among political scientists concerning how the United States is ruled?

5. In what ways are the academic disciplines of economics and political science different from each other? How are they similar?

6. Americans usually see competition as a good and healthy thing. How would you compare the level of competition in our political system today with the degree of competition found in our economic markets?

REFERENCES

Arnold, Thurman W. 1937, 1964. *The Folklore of Capitalism.* New Haven, CT: Yale University Press.

Chydenius, Anders. 1765. *The National Gain.* Translated by Georg Schauman. London: Ernest Benn, 1931.

Commons, John R. 1934. *Institutional Economics: Its Place in Political Thoery.* New York: Macmillan.

Commons, John R., et al. 1926–1935. *History of Labour in the United States.* 4 vols. New York: Macmillan.

Dahl, Robert. 1990. *After the Revolution: Authority in a Good Society,* rev. ed. New Haven, CT: Yale University Press.

_____. 1982. *Dilemmas of Pluralist Democracy: Autonomy vs. Control.* New Haven, CT:

Yale University Press.

Dye, Thomas R. 1983. *Who's Running America? The Reagan Years*, 3rd. ed. Englewood Cliffs, NJ: Prentice-Hall.

Hayek, Friedrich A. von. 1944. *The Road to Serfdom.* Chicago: University of Chicago Press.

Janda, Kenneth, Jeffrey M. Berry, and Jerry Goldman. 1992. *The Challenge of Democracy: Government in America*, 3d ed. Boston: Houghton Mifflin.

Keynes, John Maynard. 1935. *The General Theory of Employment, Interest and Money.* New York: Harcourt, Brace and World.

Kuhn, Thomas. 1970. *The Structure of Scientific Revolutions*, 2d ed. Chicago: University of Chicago Press.

Manley, John F. 1983, March. "Neo-Pluralism: A Class Analysis of Pluralism I and Pluralism II." *American Political Science Review*, 77 368-383.

Mills, C. Wright. 1959. *The Power Elite.* New York: Oxford University Press.

Myrdal, Gunnar. 1940, 1962. *An American Dilemma: The Negro Problem and Modern Democracy.* New York: Harper and Row.

Pass, Christopher, Brian Lowes, Leslie Davis, and Sidney Kronish. 1991. *The Harper-Collins Dictionary of Economics.* New York: HarperCollins.

Pearce, David W., ed. 1983. *The MIT Dictionary of Modern Economics*, rev. ed. Cambridge, MA: The MIT Press.

Phillips, A.W. 1957, November. "The Relation between Unemployment and the Rate of Change of Money Wage Rates in the United Kingdom, 1861-1957." *Economica*, 25, 283-299.

Schumpeter, Joseph A. 1954. *History of Economic Analysis.* New York: Oxford University Press.

Spencer, Herbert. 1861. *Social Statics.* London: Chapman.

Sweezy, Paul. 1956. *Principles of Marxian Political Economy.* New York: Monthly Review Press.

Veblen, Thorstein. 1912. *Theory of the Leisure Class: An Economic Study of Institutions.* New York: Macmillan.

PART TWO

A HISTORICAL OVERVIEW

To some, the usefulness of historical narrative is questionable at best; to others, it is a dire necessity. For every Matthew Arnold who proclaims the uselessness of history or every Hegel who contends that humankind never learns from its past mistakes, there are others who side with Churchill—that those who learn nothing from history are condemned to relive it. This group of three chapters examines the historical development of the American political economy through three degrees of magnification. Chapter Three applies the longest focus—from the country's colonial beginnings through the Great Crash of 1929. Much of the American political culture was fixed during this vast period, as were many of its economic and governmental institutions. By collapsing time so dramatically we can recognize the flow of economic intelligence as it moves from mercantilism through the classical period and on into neoclassical economic thought, and we can develop a feeling for how each of them related to the issues of the day. A far shorter period, the half century from 1932 to 1980, is described in Chapter Four. This is the age of Keynesianism—of its cautious application during the New Deal, its ascendancy in the Employment Act of 1946, and its descent from glory with the stagflation of the 1970s. Chapter Five recapitulates the events of the shortest period, the era of Reaganomics and of the Bush sequel, and is most closely associated with today's issues of political economy.

There are several reasons for this tour of history. One is to describe to an audience whose strength may not lie in detailed knowledge of American history just how today's system has evolved. Another justification is that more misinformation may abound about American economic history than about any other topic. For example, we will see that our particular brand of mixed capitalism was not accidental but in large part is the result of our political culture, constitutional arrangements, and experiences with the twin caldrons of war and depression. We will see that government from the early national period to almost the Civil War served as an investment banker and even as a direct entrepreneur in the world of business and that regulation often was sought as much by the regulated as by reformers. Contrary to what many believe, governmental intervention in the economy long antedated Franklin D. Roosevelt.

Finally, a sense of history can help to reveal how behavior can be examined, how data can be arranged, and how longitudinal hypotheses about political economy can be developed and tested.

CHAPTER THREE

AMERICAN POLITICAL ECONOMY: COLONIAL TIMES TO 1932

This chapter, together with the two that follow, provides a historical overview of government's involvement with the economy throughout American history. The purpose of this chapter is to sketch the broad outlines about policies and institutions rather than to provide fine details. It begins with America's colonial origin and early experiences with British-style mercantilism and concludes with the social carnage that was the Great Depression. This period of more than three centuries was not characterized by smooth, easy transitions of development but rather by fits and starts that created first one pattern of relationships then yielded to major changes after some cataclysmic set of events. The description will focus on seven periods of unequal length: (1) the colonial era and the age of mercantilism, (2) the formation of the Constitution, (3) the antebellum era, (4) the age of industrialization, (5) agrarian and Progressive protest, (6) the explosion of governmental activity during World War I, and (7) normalcy and the boom and bust of the 1920s.

COLONIAL AMERICA

The age of exploration, the era of Columbus, da Gama, Cabot, and hundreds of others, was soon followed by the development of colonial empires by the European powers. Spain, Portugal, France, Holland, and other European nations staked out colonial territories in the newly discovered worlds beyond Europe. Soon, too, the new pattern of mercantilism evolved. Actually more of a "shared perception," in the opinion of McCusker and Menard (1985), than a specific doctrine, mercantilism involved the use of the economy—particularly in colonies in the Far East and the New World— to enrich the state. Colonies supplied raw materials to encourage the production of finished goods in the mother country. These goods would be exported back to the colonies, as well as consumed in the home market, as part of an overall goal of national self-sufficiency. The mechanisms of mercantilism included subsidies to the new industries, tariffs and embargoes to protect manufacturing, regulation of trade with other colonial empires, and limitation of the outflow of gold and silver specie. Overriding all other considerations was a fetish for gold; for in the time long before national income statistics like GNP or per capita income and given the lack of nonmonetary measures of quality of life, the abundance of specie was the one crucial test of a nation's economic well-being. Mercantilism persisted until the nineteenth century, when increasing world trade destroyed it.

Britain may have explored North America in some hope of finding the fabulous riches in silver and gold that Spain was then plundering from the Aztecs and Incas, but the results were quite different. Under the tutelage of John Rolfe, the first English settlements in Virginia were able to produce tobacco for export as early as 1612—a development that was especially well fitted for a mercantilist economy (McCusker and Menard, 1985, p. 118). The colonies in New England and Pennsylvania, however, developed more into destinations for social and religious dissenters than as sources of wealth for the mother country. Nevertheless, British North America was a valuable source of strategic naval stores (trees for masts and yardarms, tar, pitch, and turpentine) as well as a source for the sugar, fur, indigo, and tobacco that other nations would pay for in specie—hard gold or silver. By the mid-1700s, however, Britain imported very little cattle, salt, or wool from her own North American possessions (Smith, 1937, p. 420).

In comparison with other European powers, Britain was a modest mercantilist nation until the 1760s. Laws like the Navigation Act of 1660, passed by the Restoration Parliament, required that only British-built ships could carry on trade with England. "Enumerated" exports of sugar, tobacco, indigo, furs, and naval stores could be shipped only to England or other British colonies. But then, the American colonies were very much English, too, and the statute worked to stimulate the American shipbuilding industry. Britain also provided incentive payments to encourage agricultural productivity, and the six-pence-per-pound subsidy on indigo production created that entire industry in South Carolina. But if government could give, it could also take away, and there were prohibitions on economic life as well. Americans were forbidden to erect iron foundries, for example, or to cart finished products overland from one colony to another. Many imported goods, including those produced in the Spanish and French possessions of the Caribbean, first had to come through English ports. The intent of this law was to reduce the opportunity for smuggling, but the long-range effect was to increase the volume of shipping, much as the regulation of trucking was to do during the Great Depression of the 1930s. On the whole, however, British regulations were only sporadically enforced in North America, and illegal smuggling with the French and the Dutch West Indies in sugar, molasses, and rum was encouraged by lax law enforcement.

The colonial governments regularly sought to influence economic life, although the extent of their actual impact is difficult to assess. Because the government regularly looked out for the good of the state and its subjects, it should not be surprising that it would become involved with the economy, too. There were differences in provincial involvement among the three regions. In Massachusetts, for example, the government organized migration; attempted to regulate wages and prices; and supported the construction of bridges and roads, mills, ferries, harbors, wharves, and other transportation structures. Similarly, in Maryland, when hard times occurred periodically during the 1700s, the legislature intervened in the tobacco market by regulating selling prices and production quantities and even monitored product quality through an inspection system.

Few areas of private economic behavior were outside of the government's scope during the colonial period: land sales; licensing; construction of roads, harbors, and schools; or public lending institutions—land banks—allowed people to become established in farming or business. New York promoted a sugar refinery, and Pennsylvania inspected its exported flour in an attempt to enhance its reputation in overseas markets (Perkins, 1988, p. 193).

A major change in British policy occurred with the end of the French and Indian War, known as the Seven Years' War in Europe (1756-1763), when its benign neglect of North America was replaced with more invasive involvement. For at least a century, Parliament had been concerned almost exclusively with trade regulations rather than with direct taxes on the internal activities of the American colonies. All that changed abruptly after 1763, when Chancellor of the Exchequer George Grenville thought that the colonies should shoulder their share of the costs that had been borne on their behalf. First, new "external" taxes in the form of tariffs were levied by the Navigation Act of 1763. The Sugar Act of the following year was the first law ever passed to raise money in the colonies for the support of the crown, or the first "internal" tax. The Currency Act, also in 1764, prohibited the further use of the paper money that Virginia and other colonies had found to be useful because of the chronic shortage of coin. It was at this time that England also became more vigorous in enforcing its mercantilist policies. An outcry went out across the land, and Americans saw all this action as unjustifiable British interference. Settlement west of the Alleghenies was prohibited after 1764 in the interest of maintaining peace with the Indians. The following year, the Stamp Act imposed taxes on all newspapers, pamphlets, "broadsides," and legal documents to pay for the maintenance of British troops in America. These levies were repealed after angry outbursts, only to be replaced by the Townshend Act's import duties of 1767, which in turn was answered by a revival of a policy of nonimportation of goods from Britain. The escalating series of regulations from Britain, then renewed hostility toward it, reached an intolerable stage in the next decade. After more than a year of armed hostilities the Declaration of Independence provided for legal separation from Britain on July 4, 1776. In fairness, however, Robert Thomas (1965) has shown that Americans were among the least taxed people in the known world, and all of the regulations probably added less than 1 percent to the costs of American consumers.

The American Revolution was different from the class-based revolutions of our own time. Patriots and Loyalists alike were drawn from the ranks of both landed aristocrats and small farmers, from merchants and simple laborers, from shopkeepers and mechanics, and from day laborers and tenant farmers. Also, the issues that divided colonists from the mother country were perceived to concern civil liberties—the freedoms of speech, thought, press, and religion—and political autonomy more than economic values. Because sides were not chosen along social and economic class lines, the country was not engulfed in the bloody scenes that accompanied the French, Russian, or Chinese revolutions that we know so well.

The year 1776 was noteworthy not only for the Declaration of Independence but also for another seminal work, Adam Smith's masterful *The Wealth of Nations*. The book was a wide-ranging explication of how market-based systems offer great advantages for producers and consumers alike and why interference by governments was always counterproductive. Book IV in particular was a critique of the "commercial or mercantile system," and it deplored the British folly of limiting the contributions of America rather than offering the opportunity of participating in a wider market: "A new set of exchanges ... should have proved as advantageous to the new, as it certainly did to the old continent. The savage injustice of the Europeans rendered an event, which ought to have been beneficial to all, ruinous and destructive to several of those unfortunate countries" (Smith, 1937, p. 416). The core of Smith's theory of markets was that individualism, epitomized by "the propensity to truck, barter, and exchange one thing for another" (p. 13) gives rise to the division of labor. Individuals acting out of their own self-interest unwittingly are the true basis of national wealth: "He intends only his own gain, and he is in this, as in many other cases, led by an invisible hand to promote an end which was no part of his intention" (p. 423). Particularly important in Smith's view was the extent of the market—the larger the better. If not for the governmental interference that had driven them away, the American colonies would have been of great future benefit for Great Britain.

.

THE CONSTITUTION: A PETRI DISH FOR CAPITALISM

The years immediately following the Revolution are often called "the critical period." In the orthodox view, a distressing litany of wrongs is recited about the 1780s. There were commercial rivalries among the newly independent states that manifested themselves in actual or threatened restrictions against trade. There was no dependable medium of exchange. The Continental currency that had been issued by Congress during the war for independence was worthless, and there was a lack of gold and silver coin. The unpaid debts of both the state and national governments were an embarrassment or worse to creditors both at home and abroad. European nations smugly wondered aloud whether the United States, under the Articles of Confederation, was a single nation or a thirteen-headed hydra. Independence, for all of its benefits, also brought an end to the protection offered by the Royal Navy, with the result that U.S. ships and seamen were seized by piratical North African states like Tunis, Algiers, and Tripoli. Freedom from the old Navigation Acts also brought an end to freedom to trade with the British West Indies, though this prohibition prompted American merchants to begin the profitable trade with China in 1784. With the reintroduction of paper money by the Rhode Island legislature and the specter of Daniel Shays's 1786 Rebellion in Massachusetts on behalf of debtor interests, the abuses seemed to the more stable elements in society to have reached crisis proportions. The Annapolis Convention in 1786 searched for a way out of the troubles and found it by calling for a Grand Convention at Philadelphia the following summer to revise the Articles of Confederation. That gathering, as everyone knows, went well beyond its charge by drafting an entirely new fundamental law.

There is more than one interpretation of the years 1783 to 1787, however, and a revisionist school makes the case that the times actually were not so desperate after all. First, a number of very positive events occurred in those four years. Several of the newly autonomous states abolished their established churches, and others created new colleges. Frequent elections, typically held annually, were instituted; and most states adopted bills of rights. Nationally, the Northwest Ordnance of 1787 was remarkable for setting the groundwork for bringing in new territories on an equal footing with the original states. Second, the litany of evils that propelled the drive for the new constitution seemed to dwell more on the concerns of the wealthy, or of the merchant class, than on those of the farmer-freeholder. The argument that the framers were motivated by economic self-interest was present during the politics of ratification but was generally forgotten until it was reasserted by Charles A. Beard in 1913. Finally, the very term *critical period* was not a contemporary one but rather was coined by John Fiske in 1888. In the minds of revolutionary leaders such as Patrick Henry, John Hancock, George Mason, and others, the period was a promising launch of a new experiment in self-governance. Theirs was the losing side, the Antiffederalist side, in the politics of ratification.

The new Constitution contributed to the growth of the nation's economy. Given the largely agrarian character of the country, it was hardly a capitalist plot. It could, however, be called a petri dish for capitalism—something that provided an environment in which America's economic development could move forward. European influences on the Constitution included the writings of Montesquieu, Locke, and Harrington and the lessons of Greece and Rome, as well as a century and a half of governmental experience here in North America. But a number of provisions in the document, and the legislation that soon implemented it, bear the imprint of Adam Smith:

> **1. Limited representative government.** The only officials of the new government who were directly elected by the voters were members of the House of Representatives. Congressional districts were to be large in order to mute radical voices that might succeed in smaller constituencies. All other officeholders were selected indirectly — the Senate by state legislatures, the president by the Electoral College, and the Supreme Court free from election at all. Shaysite radicalism would have a difficult time gaining a foothold nationally.

> **2. Limited democracy.** Those who could vote for president were those who could vote for the "more numerous branch," their state legislature. Since this franchise was established by the states themselves, its breadth varied from wide in New England to extremely narrow in the South.

> **3. A large national market.** By granting to Congress alone the power to regulate the flow of goods across state or national boundaries, the Constitution made possible the large national market that Smith saw as necessary to realize the benefits of the division of labor. The full "faith and credit clause," which required each state to enforce the commercially important civil law judgments of other states, further protected against economic Balkanization.

> **4. Reliable money.** The growth of national markets is greatly enhanced by a reliable medium of exchange. There were frequent shortages of specie in America, so people circulated Spanish dollars and various English and Dutch coins. The paper money issued by the states was in bad favor, and bank notes issued by commercial banks did not become useful until the next century. Thus, this authority vested in Congress became important as the new government strove to make the money supply sound.

5. Patents and copyrights. Rewarding creativity by granting monopoly rights to inventors for limited periods of time became a popular idea among the French *philosophes* during the middle of the eighteenth century. Yankee ingenuity could be rewarded by the government, with the agreement that all rights to use the process or patent would pass to the general public after a fixed period of years. Although this cornerstone of economic life remains today, it is often seen as anticompetitive by the Japanese and others.

6. Sanctity of contract. Under Article I, Section 10, neither the new national government nor the states could abolish the obligations of contract. This provision was to end the threat of debt abolition that had occurred in Rhode Island and that Shays had sought to bring about in Massachusetts. Although this provision remains steadfast, state laws calling for temporary moratoriums on mortgage payments during the Depression were not found unconstitutional during the 1930s.

7. Limited taxing power. Although power to tax under the new governmental system was far greater than it had been under the Articles of Confederation, Americans then, as now, were wary of the burdens of taxation. In the decade before the Revolution the Americans had sought to distinguish between "internal" and "external" taxes and to argue that Parliament had authority over the latter but not the former. In the Constitutional Convention, the ability to levy a "direct" tax, which meant either a property or a poll tax, was arranged in a way that would make it politically unlikely to be used. As a result, property taxes have been left virtually exclusively to the state and local governments. Perhaps even more significant was the prohibition against taxes on exports. Included because of the insistence of southern tobacco and exporting interests, the United States remains one of the few nations not to impede its own ability to compete in international trade by taxing goods as they leave the country.

8. Protection of private property. The idea that property cannot be taken without due process of law was incorporated in the Fifth Amendment to the Constitution. The expansion of that guarantee in the Fourteenth Amendment so that it also guards against state action, plus the doctrine of substantive due process of law, became the single greatest barrier against governmental regulation of business between 1882 and 1937.

The new government that assumed power in 1789 was anything but laissez-faire. Given its mercantilist heritage, we would expect it to take an interest in economic well-being; but given the distrust of greater national authority, one would not be surprised to find the preponderance of governmental action in the economy to come at the state level. Alexander Hamilton, the first secretary of the Treasury, quickly developed plans for *assuming* the unpaid Revolutionary War debts of the states by the national government and then for *funding* that entire debt load in order to reestablish the credit of the nation in overseas financial centers. In addition to an excise tax, he also proposed an import tariff that, although modest at first, moved toward protectionism by 1792. Tonnage taxes were used to support the employment of American-built ships. A national bank, federally chartered and with a number of presidentially appointed directors, was to provide a vehicle to handle government accounts — something to which we will return later. Hamilton was a conservative at a time when conservatism meant supporting domestic manufacturing, strengthening national self-sufficiency, and increasing military capability.

ANTEBELLUM AMERICA

The years between the end of the War of 1812 and the Civil War saw considerable governmental involvement in the economy. The precise degree of that involvement is difficult to assess, however, because of two ideologically conflicting historical schools. The orthodox interpretation is what Louis Hartz (1948) once called the "*laissez-faire* cliché," which sees Yankee ingenuity putting forward a series of inventions that were as crucial to economic development as they were free of governmental influence. Others, like Hartz himself, have unearthed far greater amounts of governmental involvement. In his view, elected officials were important capitalist figures, as in the case of Henry Clay's American System. Community purpose outweighed personal ambition in selecting goals for local economic activity. It was the public treasury, as much as private saving, that was a major source of venture capital. Mixed public-private enterprises also were customary institutions for the support of important innovations.

A wide range of governmental involvement can be found at the state level. At one extreme was Pennsylvania, where something very much like mercantilism continued well after the Revolution. State policy affected nearly every phase of business, with important interest-group struggles as a consequence. The state's chartering policy influenced the character and shape of banking, transportation, and new manufacturing. Pennsylvania was an investing partner, in the amount of $6 million, in 150 corporations in 1844. The state had invested $102 million in the Main Line canal and railroad by 1860 —the same year that it abolished child labor. Missouri was in an intermediate position, having pledged $23 million for internal improvements in 1806, an amount that was twenty-five times the territory's annual income. At the other extreme, however, New Jersey remained almost entirely out of what has been called the "public aid" movement (Lively, 1955). State-level activity diminished after the Civil War, perhaps because Republican activity in Washington moved the federal government into economic policy areas, displacing statehouses from the field.

The Civil War remains the most cataclysmic event in the country's history. Although its causes were grounded in part in life-style and moral outlook, it was both the result of preexisting economic forces and the catalyst for new ones. A number of causes of the war have been identified, including the fight over the abolition of slavery, opposition to high import tariffs from southern planters, preservation of a "way of life," a plantation economy that had proliferated after the introduction of the cotton gin after 1800, and the classic confrontation between farmer-consumers and manufacturer-suppliers. The seeds of the conflict had been sewn in the mercantile past—in the indigo, tobacco, and cotton trade—and had surfaced in the Constitutional Convention in the guise of the Three-fifths Compromise, the prohibition of export taxes, and the resumption of slave importations until 1808. But it was Eli Whitney's cotton gin, a simple device for efficiently separating the worthless cotton seeds from the useful strands of cotton fiber, that made American cotton competitive with Egypt's. And that in turn stimulated the development of a plantation society, a new power elite, and required more human capital for the South's "peculiar institution."

The outcome of the war was as much determined by economic forces as was its cause. The superior generalship and battlefield skills of the Confederacy eventually were outweighed by the foundries of the North. The dissimilarities in railroad track gauges in the South meant that goods and troops could not be moved about as easily as in the North. But perhaps the most important thing to remember about the impact of any war is that it compresses social trends that are already under way.

THE INDUSTRIAL AGE

The levels of industrial growth that followed the Civil War were unprecedented. Railroads led the way. George Pullman built the "Pioneer," the first railway sleeping car, in 1864, and soon organized the Pullman Palace Car Company. In 1869, George Westinghouse's air brake greatly enhanced rail safety, and later his electrical switching and signaling devices and transformers for alternating current put him in the first rank of inventors. The modern railroad knuckle coupler was patented by Eli Janney in 1874, and the first electric streetcar appeared in New York City that same year.

There were inventions on other fronts as well. There was Thaddeus Lowe's compression process in 1865 for making artificial ice, which allowed year-round food preservation. Two years later, Christopher Sholes built the first practical typewriter, marketed after 1873 by the new firm of E. Remington & Sons. A machine for sewing shoe soles to uppers had been patented in 1858 by Lyman Blake and was in general use by 1876. Later, ownership of virtually all this shoemaking machinery became centralized under the United Shoe Machinery Company monopoly in 1899. Melville Bissell's carpet sweeper was patented in 1876, and the cash register by James

Ritty in 1879. Lewis Waterman created the fountain pen in 1884, and William Burroughs made the first practical adding machine in 1888. But the greatest inventions of the age may have been Alexander Graham Bell's telephone, exhibited at the Philadelphia Centennial Exhibition in 1876, or Thomas Edison's first practical incandescent electric light bulb in 1879. Or as the century drew to a close, perhaps the greatest breakthrough of all was in the contributions of hundreds of individual inventors who were developing the automobile.

If the late nineteenth century was a time of invention, it was also the Gilded Age of abuse—the era of the swindler and boodler. Railroads again set the pace, either with monopoly power that gouged farmers and shippers with exorbitant freight rates or with manipulations that robbed shareholders. Col. Jim Fiske of the Erie Railroad was a master of both. Not all inventions were mechanical: The creative mind of John D. Rockefeller perfected the trust agreement in 1882 as a way to monopolize the emerging oil business. Within a few years, monopolies had come to control significant supplies of rope, cotton oil, linseed oil, lead, whisky, and sugar. This was also a time of the development of vast fortunes—Vanderbilt, Morgan, Carnegie, and Stanford.

Into this milieu came Herbert Spencer (1820–1903) with a philosophy that explained why there could be so much wealth along with such abject poverty in America's cities and countryside. His answer: The rich were rich because they deserved it. Spencer produced a ten-volume corpus of "synthetic philosophy," contending that society grows from the simple to the complex, from the homogeneous to the heterogeneous. This growth provides criteria for distinguishing the obsolete from the robust and the socially and economically fit from the unfit. Years earlier (1859), in *The Origin of Species*, Charles Darwin had argued that evolution occurred through natural selection for variations that increased an organism's ability to survive and reproduce. Whereas Darwin saw competition between one species of animal and another, Spencer focused on competition between individuals of the same species. As society became more complex, the private sector would prosper and assume the functions of government, which would become obsolete. At the same time, Spencer opposed regulation of industry and public health, safety devices, and even public support of education. He saw charity as something that would only prolong the suffering of the poor. Here was a philosophical justification for minimalist government—the laissez-faire model—and for the concentration of power in private hands. It was Spencer, not Darwin, who coined the term *survival of the fittest*, and the phrase had a popular ring to it. Notably, when Associate Justice Oliver Wendell Holmes, Jr., observed in *Lochner* v. *New York* (1905) that the Fourteenth Amendment had not enacted Spencer's ideas, his was a dissenting opinion.

AGRARIAN AND PROGRESSIVE PROTEST

With the emergence of a newly wealthy economic elite, pressures for limiting the excesses of the marketplace welled up after the Civil War. Reactions to excessive rates charged by railroads, who exerted control by virtue of their geographic monopoly, were the first to occur. Farmers initially, and then minor political parties like the Grangers, Greenback party, and the People's party (known as the Populists), attempted at the state level to regulate freight rates for years but had been hamstrung by two arguments. One was applied by the Supreme Court in *Wabash, St. Louis & Pacific R.R. Co. v. Illinois* (1886) and held that railroads operated in *interstate* commerce and thus were beyond the reach of state-level authorities. The other was that state regulation by its very substance could be unconstitutional. In *Chicago, Milwaukee & St. Paul R.R. Co.* v. Minnesota (1890), regulatory action was interpreted to be a deprivation of corporate property without due process of law—a violation of constitutionally guaranteed property rights that had been extended beyond the Fifth Amendment by the Fourteenth Amendment. When federal legislation was instituted with the Interstate Commerce Act of 1887, it included the wishes of the railroads as much as those of the reformers. Gabriel Kolko (1965) has argued that the corporations preferred uniform national regulation over more fragmented, and more vigorous, regulation by the states.

Another feature of the post-Civil War period was the long-term deflation that spawned political protests and third-party movements and that drove farmers off their land and into the cities. A series of droughts that began in 1887 gave rise to associations that merged into the Northern and the Southern Farmers' Alliances. Agrarian anger was directed at eastern monied interests, as well as at railroads and the monopolies that quickly emulated Rockefeller's Standard Oil Trust. The problem was a lack of a sufficient supply of money at a time when silver was being mined at record rates in the West. The 1890 Sherman Silver Purchase Bill called for the Treasury to buy virtually all the annual production of silver and to pay for it by issuing legal tender Treasury notes redeemable in either gold or silver. Prosilver forces were centered in the Senate (where sparsely populated western states enjoyed relative overrepresentation) but were aided by Populist representatives in the House. Together, they were able to pass the bill by threatening to oppose the protectionist McKinley tariff. The new law did increase the amount of currency in circulation but not enough to satisfy the Populist party, which led the campaign for more and cheaper money. Then, in 1893, with Grover Cleveland and the eastern wing of the Democratic party again in control of the White House, the president used heavy-handed tactics to bring about the repeal of the Silver Purchase Act. The Democrats split into conservative and radical camps in 1894 with the publication of William

Harvey's *Coin's Financial School* and Ignatius Donnelly's *The American People's Money*. Despite the oratory of William Jennings Bryan in 1896, the front-porch campaign of Republican William McKinley carried the day. The gold standard was confirmed by the Currency Act of 1900, and the Democrats declined to the status of the minority party until their rescue by Franklin Roosevelt in 1932. Prosperity returned to cool the passions of the day and other concerns, particularly the trusts and the corruption exposed by the muckrakers, replaced monetary issues at the top of the public agenda.

After 1900, the Progressive Movement—arguably the most successful wave of reform in the nation's history—began to attack a succession of social ills. Looking beyond the old issues of business practices, however, it turned its attention to the political process itself. An upper-middle-class movement, it saw the control of political parties by city bosses as one root of the problem and legislative corruption as another. Nomination for office through the direct primary, and nonpartisan elections at the local level, were reforms aimed at abuses attributed to political parties. Bill drafting by the public through the initiative process and public reaction to proposed legislation through the referendum election were ways of circumventing legislatures that may have been in the pocket of one interest or another. Recalling politicians from office was the ultimate threat. Despite exposés like David Graham Phillips's series of articles entitled "The Treason of the Senate," the Progressives' prescriptions were adopted only at the state and local levels. Nationally, there are no provisions for citizen initiative, for referenda, or for the recall of federal officials from office.

For more than a decade, Progressives lashed out at the status quo and at figures like the Speaker of the House, Joseph G. "Uncle Joe" Cannon (R–IL). Although President Theodore Roosevelt lashed out at muckrakers for displaying all of society's ills, it was in his administration and that of William Howard Taft that the Sherman Antitrust Act was finally used successfully in the *Northern Securities, Swift & Co.*, and *Standard Oil* cases. In 1912, Woodrow Wilson was able to win only because the Republican party was divided between William Howard Taft (the incumbent president) and former president Roosevelt, who was running as a "Bullmoose" Progressive Republican.

The Wilson administration and an accompanying Democratic majority in both houses of Congress set about to enact a series of economic reforms. Even before the election of 1912, with the House of Representatives in Democratic hands for the first time since Grover Cleveland was president, a subcommittee of the House Committee on Banking and Currency headed by Representative Arsene Pujo (D–LA) began an investigation of the increasing concentration of wealth. Testimony from leading financiers, including J. P. Morgan, led to the conclusion that the nation's economy was becoming more concentrated in fewer hands because of banking trusts; takeovers of competing firms; and interlocking corporate directorates in railroads, public utilities, and manufacturing. Four major reforms soon grew out of the work of this committee: the Federal Reserve Act of 1913, the Federal Trade Commission Act of 1914, the Clayton Antitrust Act of 1914, and the Federal Farm Loan Act of 1916.

THE GREAT WAR

The Great War, the War to End All Wars, is now a little-remembered chapter of American history. It is odd, but not surprising, that this is so. World War I was the first American military involvement in Europe with the quarrels of the Old World. Millions of men were mobilized for military service only months after Wilson had won reelection with the promise to keep America out of the conflict, and soon a fever pitch of nationalism supported limitations on speech and press through the Alien and Sedition Act and the Espionage Act. But most important, from the perspective of political economy, the war resurrected governmental involvement with the economy to an extent that was not only remarkable but even unprecedented. Many of the regulatory innovations of the New Deal, for example, had their roots in the prototypes that were created between 1914 and 1920.

If the effects of World War I were so dramatic, why are they so ill remembered today? Partly because today "the war" now means World War II or even Vietnam. Whatever came afterward, especially in this logarithmic century, must by nature be bigger, better, and more worthy of recollection. But it is also little remembered because in its impact on political economy, it was such a poor fit with neoclassical economic thinking. Rationing, price and quantity controls, and direct governmental control of railroads were such anathemas that it was easy to put them out of mind once the war was over.

World War I began in Europe in August 1914, and it began in the United States with the preparedness movement. Belgium was an example of what happened to unprepared nations, so a Council of National Defense was created to coordinate industrial war efforts. An Advisory Commission headed by Daniel Willard developed plans for education, labor, manufacturing, mining, medicine, transportation, and other endeavors. The U.S. Shipping Board became the parent of the Emergency Fleet Corporation, which appropriated $50 million to buy or lease transport vessels. The Smith-Hughes Act of 1917 moved the federal government into the promotion of agricultural training and manual training in the nation's schools. Once war was declared in 1917, a War Industries Board was created with broad powers in production and pricing. Particularly far-reaching was the Lever Food and Fuel Control Act. It empowered the president to ensure the availability of food and fuel needed for the war and to fix wheat prices at not less than two dollars per bushel. Also among the regulatory agencies created were the offices of food administrator (Herbert Hoover) and fuel administrator (Harry Garfield), as well as the U.S. Grain Corporation and the Sugar Equalization Board.

As a result of three converging factors, the war also fostered Prohibition. Wartime is often accompanied by a good deal of moralizing—in this case to heightened receptivity to the temperance movement and the Anti-Saloon League of the nineteenth century. Then there was the "patriotic" condemnation of those of German birth or ancestry who were leaders in distilling and brewing. The final element was the Lever Act's prohibition on the use of foodstuffs to manufacture distilled liquor. The "noble experiment" of Prohibition was established through the Eighteenth Amendment, which authorized Congress to regulate alcoholic beverages. It was ratified on January 29, 1919, just as "the boys" were returning from Europe, and the Volsted Act was passed over President Wilson's veto on October 28, 1919. Together, they were a windfall for bootleggers and provided the medium in which organized crime could gain a foothold in America.

Three areas of government-industry relations suggest the spirit of the war years. One was transportation, where the U.S. Railroad Administration, headed by Secretary of the Treasury William G. McAdoo, came to control 397,000 miles of track operated by 2,905 companies. The administration enjoyed far-reaching powers, for example, fixing the compensation of employees. Eventually it also controlled inland shipping and railroad express companies.

Labor relations were a second area of new governmental action. Organized labor's lot had been hard for decades, and many of its leaders were of Irish or German heritage—a daunting fact not only because of the German enemy but also because of the Soviet Revolution. With labor peace seen as crucial for war production, first a Mediation Commission and then the National War Labor Board were created. The federal government decreed that anyone wanting to do business with it would have to make collective bargaining available to any employees who might want it. The result was not particularly a growth in real unions but rather in company unions, which were under the domination of management. The Wilson administration's posture toward labor was hardly benevolent. The American Federation of Labor, led by Samuel Gompers, approved of America's entry into the war; but the International Workers of the World (the "Wobblies") and the Socialist party opposed it because, as Eugene V. Debs said, "The master class has always declared war, the subject class has always fought the battles. The master class has had nothing to lose, while the subject class has had nothing to gain and all to lose—especially their lives."(Quoted in Ronald L. Filippelli, *Labor in the USA: A History*, New York: Alfred A. Knopf, 1984, pp. 144-145.) For this statement, despite the First Amendment, Debs was found guilty of sedition and sent to federal prison in Atlanta. While there, he received 912,000 votes for president in 1920.

Another area of governmental activity was energy. As David Howard Davis (1982, pp. 65–66) has written, the future direction of the oil industry was largely shaped by the war. The industry, given the early phases of the automobile's development, was only coming into its own in 1917. The British Navy was a very major consumer of Texas and Louisiana oil even before American entry into the war, when the Petroleum Advisory Committee, dominated by major producers, began to allocate production between American domestic use and that destined for the war in Europe. In 1917, renamed as the National Petroleum War Service Committee (NPWSC), the members "forged a cartel greater than the old Standard Oil Company" (p. 66). One part of the U.S. Fuel Administration, the Oil Division, was headed by Mark Requa, who championed the interests of the participating firms in conflicts with the Federal Trade Commission. At war's end, the NPWSC transformed itself into one of the nation's premier interest groups, the American Petroleum Institute, with Requa at its head.

NORMALCY, THE ROARING '20s, AND THE GREAT CRASH

With the end of war, the Roaring '20s became one of the most singular decades in American history. It began with a nasty business depression in 1920–1921 which yielded to prosperity in many sectors of the economy. There was a runaway boom in Florida land prices. Often property that was worthless swampland was bought on option, then sold to others, then resold again in the belief that northern "snowbirds" would flock to the state because of its climate and ambiance. People as diverse as Henry Ford and William Jennings Bryan loaned their names to the speculation, but a diminution in new buyers began by mid-decade. Then on September 18, 1926, a powerful hurricane ended the speculation dramatically as over 400 people lost their lives and much of the state's infrastructure lay in ruins. But if Florida went bust, other ventures filled the void, for this was also the decade of the holding company. Samuel Insull's Chicago-based empire and companies like Commonwealth and Southern bought up public utilities, railroads, and entertainment businesses. It was also the seedtime of the corporate chain store in retailing, and for Montgomery Ward, American Stores, and F. W. Woolworth, the future seemed unbounded. Radio, not the electric marvel of the age itself but the nickname of the Radio Corporation of America, was the hottest stock of the decade. Indeed, notwithstanding the temporary ups and downs of Wall Street, the only worrisome economic blot seemed to be the agricultural depression. Farm prices had never recovered from the 1920 downturn, and farmers' production costs were unduly high. As Americans continued to migrate away from the farm, however, "out of sight" was also "out of mind" for the majority of Americans.

If the 1920s were a time of "get rich quick," then the quickest pathway to that goal ran through the stock market. The flames of stock speculation, fanned by a rising market, were fueled by the ability to buy stocks on margin—25 percent down now, borrow the rest, and pay off the balance later when the shares were certain to have doubled in price. The market's drive upward began in 1924, or perhaps as late as 1927, and the self-deception that share prices could only increase convinced even average Americans that there was easy money to be made. The interest on borrowed money for margin trading was low because of an easy-money policy adopted by the Federal Reserve at the urging of British, French, and German central bankers in 1927. And even if there were some very large traders who could manipulate the market, the "little guy" could still ride their coattails to prosperity.

Although the 1920s were a time of laissez-faire, there were still options that the government could and did take. A tighter money policy, achieved by selling government securities in the open market by the Federal Reserve, did help to diminish somewhat the pool of cash that was available to feed the speculatory borrowing. Surprisingly, however, little federal debt was held by the Federal Reserve system at that time. Indeed, it did sell much of what it had, and its holdings fell from $617 million in January 1928 to $228 million by the end of year; however, John Kenneth Galbraith (1962, p. 34) has assessed the impact of that action as marginal. Again, the Federal Reserve board could have asked Congress for the power to increase margin requirements to 50 or 75 percent, although the Republican Congress would not have agreed to such a proposal, given the opinion of the public and the financial community at that time. (The board finally did obtain such powers in the Securities Exchange Act of 1934.) There might have been more vigorous warnings from the government, the Federal Reserve board, the Treasury, or even the president himself; but again, given the market-oriented opinions of the time and pressures from Durant, Mitchell, and other financial elites, this did not occur. If the "business of America [was] business," as Calvin Coolidge had said, then the business of the government was to stay out of the marketplace.

All this euphoria came to a grinding halt on Black Thursday, October 24, 1929. There had been statistical signs during the preceding summer that a business slowdown had begun. In hindsight, the great bull market of the 1920s reached its apex on September 3, 1929. Then, after several days of marginally falling prices, the bottom fell out in the third week of October. Despite attempts by National City Bank, Chase National Bank, Guaranty Trust, Bankers Trust, and Thomas Lamont of Morgan's to buoy up the market by coordinated buying, the nosedive worsened on the following Monday. But unlike past panics, there seemed to be no bottom to this sell-off.

> The singular feature of the great crash of 1929 was that the worst continued to worsen... .Even the man who waited out all of October and all of November ...

and who then bought common stocks would see their value drop to a third or a fourth of their purchase price in the next twenty-four months. (Galbraith, 1961, p. viii.)

From all around the country the news worsened for the rest of the year. Railroad freight car loadings were off, agricultural prices were down, and by July 1932 steel production was at only 12 percent of capacity. By 1933 there were 13 million people out of work—about one American in every four. The political importance of the period lay not only in the causes of the Great Crash but also in the duration of the Great Depression that followed it. In the great panics of the past—1819, 1873, 1907, or 1920–1921— the bottom lasted for only a number of months until recovery set in. But the post-1929 problems continued year after year because of: (1) the unequal distribution of income among Americans, which made the economy dependent on a high level of investment and luxury spending; (2) a structure of corporate holding companies that relied on borrowed money or dividends from their operating units; (3) banking problems that included bad loans and an organizational structure that promoted runs on banks; (4) diminished international trade from the protective Smoot-Hawley Tariff of 1930 and the inability of debtor nations to make payments to American interests; and (5) poor economic intelligence (Galbraith, 1962). Both political parties called for neoclassical remedies: balanced budgets, spending cuts in the public sector, and a tight money policy.

Marketplace decision making and neoclassical economics had failed. Now it was time to search for new economic solutions and to turn to the world of politics.

DISCUSSION QUESTIONS

1. Why was Great Britain only a limited mercantilist before the Seven Years' War (1756–1763)? What caused it to take an interest in American affairs after 1760?

2. Many inventions affected the economic lives of early Americans, among them better ships, advances in navigation, the cotton gin, steam power, and the Jacquard loom. But what innovations made a major impact on the *political* aspects of American history?

3. Were the American colonists more angered by issues of civil liberties and self-government or by economic issues?

4. What were the backgrounds of the men who met at the Constitutional

Convention? Can the Constitution be called a rich person's document?

5. To what extent did Adam Smith's *The Wealth of Nations* affect the outlines of the Constitution?

6. There were many governmental supports for the private economy during the first half of the nineteenth century. What were some of them? Why aren't they better known?

7. The post-Civil War decades (1865–1900) were characterized both by rapid economic development and by political corruption. Was there any causal linkage between them?

8. How sincere was government about regulating corporate predations during the 1880s and 1890s? Why was there an apparent change during the first decade of this century?

9. What were the differences between the Populists and the Progressives? The similarities?

10. Why were the Progressives able to obtain so many of their reform objectives when the Populists were not? Were the Progressives more interested in reforming political or economic malfeasance?

11. How was it possible for the federal government to intervene so rapidly in the private sector during World War I? How many of those agencies and programs were reincarnated during the New Deal after 1933?

12. What steps could the government have taken to avoid the Great Crash of 1929? Why wasn't anything done?

13. Which of the historic periods described in this chapter was the most influential on political economy today? Which were the least influential?

REFERENCES

Beard, Charles A. 1913. *An Economic Interpretation of the Constitution of the United States,* rev. ed. New York: Macmillan, 1935.

Davis, David H. 1982. *Energy Politics,* 2nd ed. New York: St. Martin's Press.

Filippeli, Ronald L. 1984. *Labor in the USA: A History.* New York: Alfred A. Knopf.

Fiske, John. 1886. *The Critical Period of American History: 1783–1789.* Boston and New York: Houghton Mifflin.

Galbraith, John Kenneth. 1961. *The Great Crash: 1929.* Boston: Houghton Mifflin.

Handlin, Oscar, and Mary F. Handlin. 1947. *Commonwealth: A Study of the Role of Government in the American Economy, 1774–1861.* New York: Studies in Economic History.

Hartz, Louis. 1948. *Economic Policy and Democratic Thought: Pennsylvania, 1776–1860.* Cambridge, MA: Harvard University Press.

Kolko, Gabriel. 1965. *Railroads and Regulation, 1877–1916.* Princeton, NJ: Princeton University Press.

Lively, Robert A. 1955, March. "The American System: A Review Article." *Business History Review,* 29, 81–96.

McCusker, John J., and Russell R. Menard. 1985. *The Economy of British America, 1607–1789.* Chapel Hill, NC: Institute of Early American History and Culture/ University of North Carolina Press.

Morris, Richard B.,(ed.). 1982. *Encyclopedia of American History,* 6th ed. New York: Harper & Row.

_____, and Jonathan Grossman. 1938, March. "Wage Regulation in Massachusetts." *New England Quarterly,* 12, 470–500.

Perkins, Edwin J. 1988. *The Economy of Colonial America,* 2nd ed. New York: Columbia University Press.

Smith, Adam. 1776, 1937. *The Wealth of Nations,* ed. Edwin Cannan. New York: Modern Library.

Thomas, Robert P. 1965, December. "A Quantitative Approach to the Study of the Effects of British Imperial Policy Upon Colonial Welfare: Some Preliminary Findings." *Journal of Economic History,* 25, 615–638.

CHAPTER FOUR

THE AGE OF KEYNESIANISM: 1932–1980

The modern age of American politics began in 1932. The election of Franklin D. Roosevelt was the last truly realigning election that political observers can agree on—a critical election in which substantial groups of voters deserted the party of their old allegiance and crossed over, more or less permanently, to join the old opposition. For most, it was a migration to the Democrats; and serious students of political parties still speak of the great Roosevelt-inspired New Deal coalition, even though chunks of it have been breaking away since about 1965. The modern presidency also is a creature of the 1930s—a presidential team in which the chief executive is aided by an institutionalized staff that has grown to imperial proportions. Congress has long since become a full-time career, not only for the members, but also for the 25,000 men and women who fill a myriad of professional staff positions on the Hill. The 1930s also saw the end of the federal judiciary as a major determinant of economic policy, although this end did not come about without a struggle. The fifteen years at the beginning of the period addressed in this chapter contain the two great formative experiences of twentieth-century America: the Great Depression and World War II. The years that marked its end contain the decline of faith in the Keynesian prescription and in a belief that an activist government is best for the economy.

Any period of fifty years harbors great variation, and the years between the election of Franklin D. Roosevelt and the defeat of Jimmy Carter are no exception. Demographically, the country was changed by migration both within its borders and from abroad. Regional realignments resulted in the relative decline of the Midwest, both economically and politically, and the absolute growth of the sunbelt states of the South and West. Ethnically and in matters of life-style, the nation became more diverse than at any time in the past. Sociologically, woman-as-homemaker became supplanted by woman-as-employee. Shorter workweeks and increased leisure hours, once seen as signs of progress, have been replaced by demands for efficiency and competition that make shorter hours seem wasteful and un-American. Economically, a confidence in America as the "arsenal of democracy" has become a concern that the nation, with three-fourths of all jobs in the service industries, is under siege by manufactured imports from the Third World.

This chapter will focus particularly on five periods: (1) the Depression and the "New Deal for the American people" that sought to end hard times, (2) the stimulus of World War I, (3) America as postwar leader of the free world, (4) the New Frontier and Great Society of the 1960s, and (5) the troublesome stagflation of the 1970s.

A NEW DEAL FOR AMERICA

Good men out of work; dust bowl farms dried up and blown away; businesses closed down and shops boarded up—for one American family in three this described the 1930s. There had been depressions before—the 1870s and again in the 1890s, 1907, and 1920–1921—but this one was unique. Most of the people who were unemployed had never been out of work before, so it seemed clear to many that the fault was with the system itself. Herbert Hoover, the prisoner of the White House, agonized for long hours in pursuit of solutions, all the time convinced that Americans were above any demeaning handouts from welfare agencies. With direct governmental intervention an unacceptable solution, little "Hoovervilles" multiplied on the outskirts of cities across the nation. In literature, which so often mirrors life, cynicism gave way to despair—to the squalor of the Irish in Chicago (James Farrell's *Studs Lonigan*), the poverty of the rural South (Erskine Caldwell's *Tobacco Road*), and the hypocrisy of American business (John Dos Passos's *USA*). By the end of the decade the overall image was captured best in John Steinbeck's *Grapes of Wrath*.

The election of 1932 was a turning point in American politics. Roosevelt was the early favorite, but the Democratic party's historic rule requiring two-thirds of the delegates' votes nearly kept him from getting the nomination. His unprecedented airplane flight to Chicago to address the convention, despite the paralysis caused by polio, was a dramatic demonstration of his mobility. As the campaign wore on through the autumn, the two party platforms did disagree on some issues: the protective tariff and maintenance of the gold standard (the Republicans in favor); and the regulation of monopoly, an end to Prohibition, and the notion of a social security pension system (the Democrats in favor). Still, the differences were not major, and remarkably, both parties pledged to reduce governmental expenditures and to balance the budget.

Where the candidates personally were concerned, however, the contrast was one of night and day. "I pledge you, I pledge myself, to a new deal for the American people." The words were those of Roosevelt, the "champion campaigner." Hoover, steeped in the notion that those who worked hard would always be rewarded, reiterated that "prosperity is just around the corner," but it was the marketplace, rather than governmental planning, that would take the nation there. As James D. Barber (1985, p. 40) has observed, Hoover was shocked by the outcome in November: Roosevelt won in a landslide with 59 percent of the two-party vote.

What made real change possible was the outcome of the congressional races, which gave the Democrats a majority of 315 to 117 in the House and of 61 seats in the Senate. It was this election of 1932, plus some additional shifts among organized labor four years later, that constituted the great Roosevelt coalition—the basis for the Democratic domination of national politics (except for the presidency) for two generations. Since that time the Republicans have controlled the House for only four years—the 80th Congress in 1947–1948 and the 83rd Congress in 1953–1954, and the Senate for the same years plus the first six years of the Reagan administration.

Things worsened during the four months from the November 8 election to the March 4 inauguration. The economy drifted while Roosevelt, for symbolic reasons, had no contact with the discredited Hoover administration. "Brain trusters" from Columbia, Harvard and other universities descended on Washington with designs for planning America's future—people like Raymond Moley, Harry Hopkins, and Felix Frankfurter. Meanwhile, industrial production declined and there were runs on banks and currency hoarding. In Louisiana, Michigan, and New York, state authorities declared "bank holidays," closing financial institutions briefly in the hope that public nervousness would abate. In many circles the idea was put about that banking should be taken out of private hands through nationalization.

The crisis in banking was the most immediate problem confronting the new administration, and the day after assuming office Roosevelt invoked emergency powers under the World War I "Trading with the Enemy Act" to declare a four-day, national bank holiday. He called a special session of the 73rd Congress. The Glass-Steagall Act, passed in June 1933, created the Federal Deposit Insurance Corporation (FDIC) to build depositors' confidence by ensuring accounts in national banks up to $5,000. It also removed banks from stock speculation by forbidding them from offering stock and bond brokerage services—a prohibition that remained in place until 1985. Later, the Banking Act of 1935 restructured the Federal Reserve system to enhance its independence.

The Depression was not new to America's farms, where it had arrived as early as 1921. The increased production of World War I had given way to glutted postwar markets and declining prices. Those who had borrowed to purchase more land during the boom years were in deep trouble by 1932, when farm receipts were one-third of those in 1918; the value of farms had declined by one-half, and farm foreclosure sales were up more than 450 percent. There had been political efforts to help. Bills to control prices and reduce the surplus were sponsored by Senators Charles McNary (R–OR) and Gilbert Haugen (R–IA) between 1924 and 1928, but they were vetoed by President Coolidge. An administration-sponsored Agricultural Marketing Act in 1929 attempted little and generally failed to accomplish even that. With these efforts in the background, the New Deal aimed a dozen laws and more at directly bolstering the finances of farmers through refinancing farm mortgages and controlling the amount of acreage under cultivation. Despite a severe drought that was at its worst in 1934, the production-control programs of the Agricultural Adjustment Act managed to limit the surpluses, and farm receipts rose from $4.7 billion in 1932 to $7.7 billion three years later. Although the 1937 recession was a significant setback to the farm program, farm foreclosures finally returned to their prewar level by 1940.

Trade and tariff issues have separated the two major parties since the beginning of the Republic, and the years of the Depression were no exception. The Republican high-tariff policy culminated in the Smoot-Hawley law of 1930, which on average levied an import tax of 49 percent on agricultural products and 34 percent on manufactured products. As E. E. Schattschneider (1935, 1963) was able to show, it was a triumph of special-interest pleading and congressional logrolling. The final rates were higher than any one person might have wished; and together with similar trade barriers in other countries, Smoot-Hawley was blamed for the general collapse of trade all around the world.

Freer trade, though not high on Roosevelt's personal agenda, became another New Deal prescription for recovery. During his service as a member of Congress from Tennessee, Cordell Hull had championed the South's traditional preference for low tariffs. In addition, he also came to believe that interruptions in international trade and attempts at national self-sufficiency like Germany's movement toward autarchy would surely increase the likelihood of war. As Roosevelt's Secretary of State from 1933 to 1944, Hull was the leading proponent of the Reciprocal Trade Agreements program. Adopted in 1934 and renewed periodically, the law empowered the Department of State to enter into bilateral negotiations to raise or lower import rates by as much as 50 percent on selected commodities. In fact, since tariff rates were only reduced, bilateral reciprocal trade was the beginning of the movement to free trade that has continued unabated even today, although the position of the two parties toward it has been reversed.

The New Deal was a whirlwind of legislation and administrative rule making not only during the First Hundred Days, but in the second New Deal after 1935 as well. It included policy innovation and reform in many corners of the economy. The nation abandoned the gold standard, canceled gold clauses in all contracts, and devalued the dollar. Public power became an intense battleground between private power companies and the advocates of publicly generated electricity. The creation of the Tennessee Valley Authority and of the Rural Electrification Administration (REA) brought electric lights to isolated farms for the first time. Corporate bankruptcy law was liberalized. New regulations cut across many areas of activity, including public utility holding companies; the securities industry; truck, bus, and air transportation; and communications. The theme was to provide enough jobs so that there would be work for all.

Labor was dramatically affected by the Wagner Act, which finally gave governmental blessing to the right to organize and bargain collectively. Next in importance were minimum wage and hour standards enacted in the Fair Labor Standards Act of 1938. There were a number of initiatives in relief— either through indirect support to the states or through direct governmental programs like the Civilian Conservation Corps (CCC), which was aimed at employing young men between the ages of eighteen and twenty-five in reforestation and other projects. There was the Works Progress Administration, or WPA, which eventually employed 4 million people. A national employment system based on coordination with state agencies was one of many steps that eroded the division between national and state action and that evolved into the cooperative federalism of today. There were efforts to stimulate the house building industry and to put home ownership within reach of the average American, as well as to improve the standard of living for the poor.

There was opposition to large-scale commercial enterprise that was a legacy of populism. It took the form of the Robinson-Patman Act, an amendment to the antitrust law, which sought to protect small merchants from the threat of emerging chain stores by outlawing price discrimination, which tended to promote monopoly. Still, the Miller-Tydings Act allowed resale price maintenance agreements for nationally advertised brands. There were subsidies to stimulate the merchant marine and naval construction; and beginning in 1935, there was Social Security. A food stamp program to aid the poor and distribute surplus agricultural products existed from May 1939 until World War II, then was readopted in 1959. And, since man cannot live by bread alone, beer and liquor returned with the end of Prohibition.

Although, even today, Roosevelt remains a heroic figure, he was not universally beloved in his own time. Many Americans were well off during the 1930s. Three-fourths never lost their jobs, and many saw governmental planning and regulation as dangerous interference with individual liberties. Opposition to New Deal labor, tax, and economic policies came from members of the Liberty League, who were drawn from the worlds of industry and finance but who included a number of conservative Democrats as well. Political entrepreneurs and demagogues—people like Senator Huey Long (D–LA), Francis Townsend, Father Charles Coughlin, and Gerald L. K. Smith—offered radical critiques of the administration.

The Supreme Court presented a major barrier to the administration during its first four years. The justices represented the ideology of the 1920s and before. Newspaper columnist Drew Pearson singled out four of the most anti-New Deal justices as the Four Horsemen of the Apocalypse—Willis Van Devanter, George Sutherland, James McReynolds, and Pierce Butler. By 1937, thirteen pieces of New Deal legislation had been invalidated by the Court. A brief if contentious attempt to pack the Court with additional justices attuned to the New Deal backfired on Roosevelt; but soon afterward, retirements and death changed the roster of the Court. Nearly all of the invalidated statutes were easily revised by Congress and put back to work. The lone exception was the National Industrial Recovery Act, which had authorized the National Recovery Administration—the Blue Eagle code authority—which had become an embarrassment. It was allowed to die with little objection from the White House, with the hope that its administrator, General Hugh Johnson, would fade from the scene.

The ability of Roosevelt to lead Congress eroded significantly after 1936. By unsuccessfully seeking to defeat several members who had refused to toe the administration line, the president inadvertently brought about a conservative coalition of Republicans and southern Democrats that was to plague presidents and liberals to our own time. When called into a special session in November 1937, for example, Congress simply refused to move on new agricultural, wage-and-hour, and executive reorganization plans. By the second administration there were well-dressed swells, as drawn in *The New Yorker*, contemplating a night on the town: "Let's go down to the Trans-Lux and boo Roosevelt."

Evaluating the New Deal remains problematic even today. Roosevelt assumed office when Mussolini's fascism was swaggering in Italy, when Hitler was seizing power in Germany, and when Russian communism seemed appealing to some dissenters in American intellectual life. The New Deal at least attempted to do something, whereas Hoover had done little. The worst thing about the Great Depression was not its depth but its duration. It continued year after year—1934 wore on into 1935, then 1936. The recession of 1937 threw even more people out of work than had been unemployed before. Arguably, recovery did not occur until orders for war materials began to emanate from Europe in 1939. Why was recovery so long in coming?

One line of thought is that the New Deal was simply a case of too much government thrashing about in wasteful, unplanned ways. The National Industrial Recovery Act, that piece of First Hundred Days' legislation that created the National Recovery Administration (NRA), exemplified this charge. It was grounded on the belief that the Depression was the result of technological unemployment in some industries, overproduction in others, and predatory competition. It contended that increased collective economic control should be a guiding principle of economic life. In answer to just how the NRA might promote recovery, however, a contemporary account by a group from the Brookings Institution (1934) reported that there was disagreement among supporters of the program about "what was intended or exactly how the Act was expected to induce recovery" (Dearing, Homan, Lorvin, and Lyon, 1934, p. 23).

The NRA allowed voluntary agreements within the most important industries" concerning production and minimum wages and selling prices, with provision for multiple tiers of reviews and insistence that the agreements must be representative and not designed to increase monopolies or oppress small enterprises. "Codes" could be small, localized agreements or developed on a national scale. The automobile code was written in Detroit, for example, the oil code in Chicago, and the iron and steel code in New York City. Controversy arose over how far the NRA interfered with the antitrust laws, and the director, General Hugh Johnson, soon rubbed the president the wrong way. When, after two years of operation, the Schechter brothers argued that the NRA excessively delegated legislative power to the executive and that their Brooklyn-based poultry business was intrastate in character, the Supreme Court agreed. When the NRA was found unconstitutional, there was a collective sigh of relief from many in the administration.

Recovery was impeded also, E. Cary Brown (1956) argued, because the tools of fiscal policy were uncoordinated and were used only half-heartedly, partly as a consequence of federalism. Brown's analysis shows that although modest stimulative efforts were made at the federal level for every year of the decade, tax increases at the state and local levels counteracted many of these expenditures. Tax policy at the national level also applied the brakes to recovery. The Revenue Act of 1932, passed by a Democratic House and a Republican Senate, increased rates overall but had a special impact on the lower- and middle-income taxpayer by decreasing the personal exemption. Later, various processing taxes associated with New Deal programs and the Social Security tax further detracted from the stimulative effect of fiscal policy. Only in 1931 and 1936 was the combined impact of governmental policies markedly stronger than they had been in 1929; and ironically, it was Hoover who was president in one of these two years. Ironically, too, in both years the stimulative impact was due largely to payments to World War I veterans, which were opposed by the White House. It was not until the second New Deal that Keynesians like Marriner Eccles, Lauchlin Currie, and Alvin

Hansen began to win out over institutionalists like Rexford Tugwell, Adolph A. Berle, and Hugh Johnson, who wanted to reorganize the social structure.

Keynesian prescriptions were slow in coming. For all the problems that engulfed the nation in that spring of 1933, Keynesianism had a difficult time in making its way to Washington. Many of the brain trusters of the first New Deal were intellectual heirs of Thorstein Veblen and believed that the dreadful condition of the nation would finally bring about the fundamental institutional changes that were needed. Other New Dealers were Marxists — and even the occasional Communist — who believed that the inevitable breakdown of capitalism was then unfolding. To both groups, the promise of Keynes that a few simple repairs could minimize the need for fundamental change seemed unsound.

It was not until after 1937, that Keynesian prescriptions began to attract interest among the president's economic advisers. Social Security was designed so that benefits would be paid out of future contributions rather than from current taxes. The hope was to prevent increased taxes from dragging down the tenuous recovery. It wasn't until the war years that Keynesian prescriptions had taken center stage in the White House. Clearly, then, a major reason for the Depression's persistence was the half-hearted application of the economic prescriptions that were, for that time at least, widely needed.

THE STIMULUS OF WORLD WAR II

The other great formative event of today's political economy was World War II. Expansion occurred almost overnight. "The executive branch," as David Brinkley (1988) has written, "despite its expansion during the New Deal, remained relatively small, its employees more concerned with egg prices and post office construction than with the war clouds gathering in Europe and Asia" (p. xiv). After the outbreak of hostilities in Europe in 1939, the administration moved against great pressure from isolationist groups to aid the allied powers. With the fall of France in June 1940, Roosevelt acted to help Britain through both overt and covert aid. The Japanese attack on Pearl Harbor sealed American involvement in the greatest armed conflict the world had ever seen.

The war brought instant economic recovery. Production was stimulated as the United States became the "arsenal of democracy," and the index of productivity, which had been 105 in August 1939, then 125 in December, reached 235 by 1944. The 10 percent unemployment rate of 1939 was virtually erased with wartime mobilization and the draft.

The war also brought changes in U.S. political institutions. The "rally 'round the flag" phenomenon of public opinion gave Roosevelt such high levels of approval, with magnitudes of 70 and 80 percent, that they are omitted from most comparisons of presidential popularity today. Alphabet agencies proliferated, and the "planning" that had been so contentious a few months before was seen, as during World War I, to be a necessity. The War Manpower Commission (WMC) gained control over the Selective Service (the military draft) and the U.S. Employment Service. With the personnel demands for the military and war industries, unemployment was no longer a problem. A labor shortage developed, and an executive order of February 9, 1943, established the minimum work week to be forty-eight hours in areas where labor shortages occurred, although it required time-and-a-half pay scales for the additional eight hours.

Labor problems mounted during the war. Roosevelt had trouble with United Mine Workers (UMW) President John L. Lewis in 1940; and in 1943, 530,000 coal miners went on strike in the eastern states. The mines were seized by the Interior Department, and legislation was passed over the president's veto to broaden his authority to deal with wartime labor unrest. The army briefly seized the railroads late in 1943 to prevent a strike, and it did the same with a number of Montgomery Ward retail stores somewhat later.

The War Production Board, headed by Donald M. Nelson, prioritized allocations for strategic materials. The Office of Price Administration (OPA) had been created eight months before Pearl Harbor and was in place to manage rationing programs for tires, coffee, gasoline, and fuel oil, which concluded at war's end in 1945 except for the rationing of sugar, which continued until 1947.

After World War I, the United States had refrained from international participation and turned toward isolationism. This was not to happen again, and the multilateralism of the war effort carried over into planning for peacetime relations. Forty-four nations were represented at the United Nations Monetary and Financial Conference at Bretton Woods, New Hampshire, during the first three weeks in July 1944, and they created the International Monetary Fund to stabilize national currencies and facilitate world trade. The conference also established the International Bank for Reconstruction and Development, better known as the World Bank. Then, in late summer and early fall, a conference at Dumbarton Oaks in suburban Washington carved out the basic outline for the charter of the permanent United Nations organization. That act, together with the determination to occupy Germany after its defeat and the fact of America's postwar major power status, ensured that American participation in the world community after the war would be extensive.

One theorist, Adolph Wagner, formulated a "law" that regarded governmental growth in the twentieth century as a consequence of increasing costs of public administration, increased public demand for services, war, and depression. He concluded that growth in the public sector was inevitable (Pearce, 1983, p. 469). Certainly the trauma of the Great Depression, the New Deal experience, the can-do spirit of World War II, and the greatly strengthened administrative branch of government left as their legacy a habit of looking to Washington for money, solutions, and blame for the ills that bedevil us.

FREE WORLD LEADER: 1945-1960

The United States seemed to stand alone as World War II closed. The industrial might of Japan and Germany, our major trading partners today, lay in rubble, all broken and burned. As for Britain and France, and for the smaller European nations as well, it seemed that they might never regain their prewar status. And even when the Soviet Union emerged ominously with the outbreak of the Cold War, the countries of the Communist bloc counted for little in the economic circles in which America traded. For the United States, it was a time of limitless economic promise.

Still, two concerns lingered. The first was the fear that the United States might again withdraw into the isolationism of the interwar period. In hindsight, this concern seems unwarranted, for the majority of Americans had come to believe that turning away from the world community had allowed the return of world conflict in the 1930s. Many saw the Soviet threat that soon developed as a possible continuation of hostilities. The Vandenberg Resolution of 1948 supported American participation in regional security arrangements, set the stage for the North Atlantic Treaty Organization (NATO) and other alliances, and signaled an end to the threat of isolationism. Expenditures of military hardware became an important element throughout the Cold War, although the multiplier effect from defense expenditures is less than that for nonwar items.

A major part of U.S. involvement in Europe took the form of economic aid. At first, between the German surrender and 1947, the United States sent $11 billion in aid to Europe through the United Nations Relief and Rehabilitation Agency (UNRRA), much of it to eastern European nations. Thus, it was the Marshall Plan that was devised to assist the West. Overall, more than $82 billion in Marshall Plan aid was given between 1946 and 1961. But aid was not restricted to Europe; it was granted also to the French in Indochina—$10 million in 1950, $500 million the next year, and annual increases thereafter.

The other concern of the postwar world was that the Depression would return. One of the axioms of economics is that a return to peacetime inevitably brings about a recession in economic activity. With war's end, President Truman recommended a twenty-one-point program to Congress for increasing the minimum wage, constructing up to 1.5 million new homes annually, and supporting research. Out of this program grew one of the most significant statutes in economic history—the Employment Act of 1946. As recounted by Stephen K. Bailey (1950), the law made it the responsibility of the federal government to maintain "full employment" and production and to minimize inflation. Since these goals are mutually exclusive, the president was given the assistance of a new Council of Economic Advisers. The chief executive was also charged with being the chief manager of the economy and required to submit an annual economic report to Congress. For its part, Congress created a new Joint Economic Committee. Although the statute did not expressly call for unbalanced budgets to even out the business cycle, clearly this was one of its consequences.

Organized labor, which had enjoyed major gains during the New Deal, lost some of those advantages during the postwar period. The Taft-Hartley Act of 1947, a product of what Truman called "that do-nothing 80th Congress," sought to redress the balance between labor and management by banning closed shops, permitting employers to sue for damages suffered during strikes, and allowing a sixty-day "cooling-off period" before some strikes could begin. If the Republican party had accepted Keynesianism, the Democratic party could reexamine its position on organized labor. Consequently, in 1959, the Landrum-Griffin Act, aimed at ridding organized labor of gangsterism, included provisions from Democrats John Kennedy of Massachusetts and John McClellan of Arkansas relating to union elections, pension trusts, and boycott-related strike activities.

The Cold War rivalry with the Soviet Union and the growth of the defense sector of the economy were accompanied by a garrison state mentality in the postwar period — something the country had never had before. Thus, in his Farewell Address of January 1961, it was no less a figure than President Eisenhower, the former five-star general, who warned against the dangers of the "military-industrial complex."

THE 1960s: THE NEW FRONTIER AND GREAT SOCIETY

The election of 1960 was waged more on foreign and defense issues, such as a supposed missile gap with the Soviet Union, than on domestic ones. Economics is always important in presidential elections, however, and the idea of getting the country moving again was a prominent theme. John Kennedy had been schooled in the activist governmental ideas of the late 1930s, but many liberal Democrats had regarded him with suspicion during the 1950s because of his lukewarm support of civil liberties.

Following Kennedy's narrow victory over Richard Nixon, there was a vigorous search for managerial talent in an effort to "hit the ground running." An impressive administration team was assembled, and a feeling of movement, of momentum, of somehow being under way, could be felt in Washington. Still, Arthur Schlesinger (1965, pp. 18, 160, 212) felt that Kennedy's New Frontier would be more like Progressivism than the New Deal, and he contrasted New Dealers, "chain talkers" and moralists, to the

New Frontiersmen, who were more rational, casual, laconic, and mistrustful of political evangelism.

Relations with business soured when the administration was trying to prevent steel price increases. On April 10, 1962, the president was angered when Roger Blough, chair of U.S. Steel, announced that he was raising prices by six dollars per ton. "My father always told me that all businessmen were sons-of-bitches," Kennedy said, "but I never believed it till now." The conflict polarized business executives and the Republicans in Congress against the administration. Some in business circles adopted the sobriquet of "Sons of Business" and wore label buttons with the inscription "I'm an SOB." When the administration persuaded three firms to hold the line on increases, however, the president won. In October 1962, the enactment of an investment tax credit and the decision to put the communications satellite system (ComSat) in private hands were attempts to placate the business community.

Kennedy had a difficult time effectuating his economic policies. Coming to office during a worsening recession, he considered increased spending and tax relief. An improving economy, however, combined with business opposition to a tax credit for modernization of plant and equipment, resulted in an administration defeat in Congress. Business preferred a liberalized depreciation allowance and got its way (Schlesinger, 1965, p. 631) Then, in addition to the trouble with the steel industry and the defeat of Kennedy's hopes for a countercyclical tax reduction, there were other setbacks in housing, medical care for the elderly, and education. Often domestic issues were forced to take a back seat because of international crises: the Bay of Pigs debacle in 1961 and the Cuban missile crisis a year later. Kennedy was not without legislative successes, however, including area redevelopment for depressed and rural regions of the country and the Trade Expansion Act of 1962, which institutionalized U.S. ability to conduct multilateral bargaining in future trade with the European Common Market.

All this activity screeched to a halt, along with the innocence of the nation itself, on a Friday noon in Dallas. The shots rang out, the sirens wailed, and the silence was eerie. After November 22, 1963, political murder never seemed to be distant during the turbulent 1960s: Malcolm X; Medgar Evers; Michael Schwerner, Andrew Goodman, and James Chaney; Martin Luther King, Jr; and Robert Kennedy as he was campaigning for the White House in 1968.

Lyndon Johnson came to the presidency with a number of advantages. His own interest in activist government was helped by Congress's willingness to memorialize Kennedy by enacting many of his stalled initiatives, and this momentum carried over to many of Johnson's own policy wishes. There was the Johnson style—"the treatment," as it was known at the personal level— that allowed him to extract a great deal from others. His congressional experience and his service as majority leader in the Senate from 1955 to 1961 gave Johnson intimate knowledge of how Congress operated and of the hopes and fears of most of its members. More than anything else, perhaps, was the landslide defeat of Barry Goldwater in 1964 that yielded the 89th Congress, a unique body with a strong majority of northern, urban, liberal Democrats.

Lyndon Johnson's Great Society was the paradigm of governmental activism. Civil rights, medical care for the aged, elementary and secondary education, urban mass transportation, a war against poverty, crime control, and environmental policies all indirectly affected the nation's economy. But there were direct impacts as well. The Tax Reduction Act of 1964, with the goal of stimulating purchasing power, reduced personal income tax rates from a range of 20 to 91 percent to a range of 14 to 70 percent. There were reductions in corporate tax rates as well. The Housing Act of 1965, just as the model statute of the 1930s, sought to stimulate construction as much as to provide shelter. The country entered another round of regulation during the 1960s, albeit regulation designed to provide physical safety and protection rather than to increase employment. Exemplary here were the National Traffic and Motor Vehicle Safety Act of 1966, the Clean Water Restoration Act of 1966, and even the 1970 Occupational Safety and Health Act (OSHA).

Two more developments were particularly important for the economy in the Johnson years. Under the notion of entitlement, the potential beneficiaries of any number of programs, whether they were individuals or local governments, were guaranteed governmental assistance if they met certain statutory criteria. This process caused budgetary outlays to grow independently of specific congressional or presidential intervention. Over time, these entitlements became automatic and "uncontrollable" in the absence of repealing legislation—legislation that was quite unlikely. By 1990, this uncontrollable portion of the federal budget reached nearly 70 percent of all domestic expenditures.

Another Johnson innovation was the unified budget. Designed to replace a number of separate budgets, the new process consolidated federally administered trust funds like those for Social Security, highways, and airport construction into a single budget. Although advocated as a more rational way of making budgetary policy, the unified budget made it easier to conceal the true magnitude of the federal deficit at a time when the costs of the Vietnam War were escalating.

In the end, it was the tragedy of Lyndon Johnson to be remembered more for his failed policy in Vietnam than for his domestic initiatives. The war generated bitterness at home and division within his own party. To compound the irony, Hubert Humphrey was confronted by angry crowds chanting "Dump the Hump" because of his unwillingness to distance himself from Johnson's foreign policy.

STAGFLATION AND THE TROUBLED 1970s

By 1970 it was becoming apparent that America's postwar economic hege-mony would not continue forever. Some of the signals came from abroad: Imports, especially automobiles and electronic consumer goods from Japan, were arriving in abundance. In 1971–1972, for the first time in the twentieth century, the United States recorded a deficit in its international accounts. Simultaneously, the services sector of the economy outstripped manufactur-ing in numbers of people employed, and the country became an importer of copper, lead, zinc, and manufactured products. Some saw the economic problems as the product of the Johnson-era "guns and butter" policy— fight-ing a costly war without drawing attention to it by raising taxes, while at the same time increasing governmental outlays for Great Society programs. President Nixon's response was a wage and price freeze in 1971 and impoundment, the refusal to spend money that had been appropriated by Congress. Impoundment became one of the causes for revising the federal budget process in 1974.

A chronic problem with energy costs, habitually called a "crisis," devel-oped throughout the decade. As early as 1947, the United States had been a net importer of petroleum, and by 1953 it imported 10 percent of its oil. Oil importation raised concerns for the profitability of American-centered oil producers, as well as for national security, and caused the Eisenhower administration to secure voluntary agreements to limit imports to 1954 lev-els, or 12 percent of U.S. production. This quota was mandatory between 1959 and 1973, when increasing prices and the demand for foreign oil caused Nixon to abolish the quota system. Then the 1973 Yom Kippur war yielded an Organization of Petroleum Exporting Countries (OPEC) boycott of the United States at a time when the country imported fully one-third of its petroleum needs. The effect of oil price increases on the costs of produc-tion and transportation were dramatic, and prices began to climb. First Richard Nixon, then Gerald Ford, created offices and agencies to manage energy supply and demand—the Federal Energy Office, Federal Energy Administration, and Energy Independence Authority. That became the era of "energy czars"—George Lincoln, James Akins, Charles DiBona, John Love, and William Simon in 1974 alone. In 1977, President Carter's National Energy Policy Act (NEPA) recast the focus toward reducing demand through conservation and alternative energy sources. Then, in December 1978, oilfield workers in Iran began a general strike that led to the abdica-tion of the Shah and to a chain of anti-American events that reverberate even today. Skyrocketing oil prices contributed even more to the inflationary spiral.

It was during the 1970s that one of the ancillary concepts of

Keynesianism was found to be flawed. If, as its critics maintained, Keynesianism was prone to inflation, at least there was an offsetting benefit—an inevitable decline in unemployment. Using a century of British data, A. W. Phillips (1957) had found that all things being equal, as inflation increased, unemployment invariably declined. During the 1970s, unfortunately, this Phillips curve broke down, leaving the worst of two conditions: both increasing inflation and rising unemployment — a condition popularly known as stagflation. Its persistence was an important contributor to the defeat of Jimmy Carter in 1980.

One of the most important developments of postwar economic policy has been the deregulation movement that emerged in the 1970s and that continues today. It began as a critique of the administrative process itself, and soon, terms like *policy whirlpool, cozy triangle,* and *subgovernment* were applied to hundreds of arrangements linking congressional subcommittees, regulatory agencies, and regulated industries and client firms, all of which profited in their own way at public expense. "Revolving doors" were discovered through which people entered government as professional staffers or appointed officials, then returned to the private sector with an insider's knowledge of how Washington works, only to appear again in an even higher governmental position. Although ethics regulations have sought to slow this rotation between the public and private sectors, they have exempted former members of Congress from such restrictions.

Coming on top of the reformist critiques of the regulatory process was the inflationary spiral of the 1970s. The inflationary pressures that caused the wage and price controls and the 1973 oil shortages focused attention on regulatory diseconomies, for example, the Interstate Commerce Commission (ICC) rules that forced truckers to follow circuitous routes to their destinations. The following year Gerald Ford ordered that Inflation Impact Statements (IISs) must accompany all new regulatory rules. By 1976, Economic Impact Statements (EISs) were ordered for all regulations emanating from agencies rooted in cabinet-level departments. Estimated to have an impact of more than $100 million in their first year, these EISs were cleared through the presidential Office of Management and Budget and a new Council on Wage and Price Stability.

Deregulation became a reality during the Carter years. In the airline industry, John Robson and Alfred Kahn at the Civil Aeronautics Board (CAB) used intrastate air competition in Texas, California, and Hawaii to argue that rates could be reduced and service provided to a wider range of people through deregulation. Liberals joined in their support as a result of the hearings on airlines held by a Judiciary Committee panel chaired by Senator Edward Kennedy in 1975. Interestingly, the only air carrier to favor deregulation was United Airlines, the strongest firm financially. The CAB under Kahn began to allow airlines to set rates competitively in 1976 and to make their own route decisions two years later. The Airline Deregulation Act of 1978 gave statutory authority to these changes, and the CAB itself was phased out over a seven-year period. It closed its doors on January 1, 1985. In trucking, forty-five-year-old regulations were set aside in the Motor Carrier Act of 1980. Once again, the belief from the New Deal era that circuitous routes would provide service to remote places and generate more jobs in the industry was abandoned when diesel fuel was in short supply. Similarly, railroad rates were marketized by the Staggers Rail Act of 1980, soon to be followed by the deregulation of banks in the Depository Institutions Deregulation and Control Act of 1980. It allowed commercial banks to raise interest on savings accounts and to pay interest on checking accounts and established uniform reserve requirements. But in perhaps the most costly act of all, it also opened a Pandora's box by permitting savings and loan institutions to compete in commercial real estate loans as well as traditional home mortgages. From that act there soon flowed a host of new problems.

Two things should be noted about the deregulation movement. First, it began during the administration of the most conservative of the Democratic presidential candidates who had entered the 1976 campaign, Jimmy Carter. Second, most of the firms within the industries being deregulated were not happy about it. In case after case, regulated firms warned of dire consequences if regulation were to upset the status quo—air carrier bankruptcies that would end with only one airline; low profits from trucking that would undercut maintenance, increase drivers' hours and diminish highway safety; and communities that might be denied air, truck, or bus service.

When asked recently whether he had any regrets about his long service in the Senate, Robert C. Byrd (D-WV) said that he had only two: his vote against the Civil Rights Act of 1964 and his vote for airline deregulation in 1978.

DISCUSSION QUESTIONS

1. Democrats often charge that Herbert Hoover did nothing to forestall the stock market crash or to ameliorate the hard times that followed it. What did Hoover do? Why didn't he do more?

2. Compare the impact of the Depression on American life with the impact of other periods of hard times, for example, 1819, 1837, and the panics of 1893 and 1907.

3. Republicans often say that what ended the Depression was not the New Deal but World War II. Why did it take so long to emerge from the Depression? What could the administration have done differently?

4. If the New Deal was so radical, why was the government during the 1930s so reluctant to apply Keynesian financial programs?

5. Remembering both World Wars I and II, why are Americans so willing to put up with governmental expansion during wartime and so anxious to get rid of it when peace returns?

6. Charles E. "Engine Charlie" Wilson, President Eisenhower's secretary of defense, once said, "What's good for General Motors is good for America." What did he mean?

7. What was the impact of the Kennedy administration on domestic economic policy?

8. During the 1960s the Johnson administration both fought a costly war overseas and pursued an expensive domestic program at home. Why did it follow a policy of *both* guns and butter?

9. How did the deregulation movement come about during the 1970s? How successful has it been?

10. Compare the importance of government in general and of the president in particular as economic factors before and after 1932. Why the difference?

REFERENCES

Bailey, Stephen K. 1950. *Congress Makes a Law: The Story Behind the Employment Act of 1946.* New York: Columbia University Press.

Barber, James D. 1985. *The Presidential Character: Predicting Performance in the White House,* 3rd ed. Englewood Cliffs, NJ: Prentice Hall.

Blaug, Mark. 1990. *John Maynard Keynes: Life, Ideas, Legacy.* New York: St. Martin's Press.

Brinkley, David. 1988. *Washington Goes to War: The Extraordinary Story of the Transformation of a City and a Nation.* New York: Knopf.

Brown, E. Cary. 1956, December. "Fiscal Policy in the Thirties: A Reappraisal." *American Economic Review,* 46, 857-879.

Dearing, Charles, Paul T. Homan, Lewis L. Lorcvin, and Leverette S. Lyon. 1934. *The ABC of the NRA*. Washington, D.C.: Brookings Institution.

Pearce, David W., ed. 1983 *The Dictionary of Modern Economics*. Cambridge, MA: MIT Press.

Phillips, A. W. 1957. November. "The Relation Between Unemployment and the Rate of Change of Money Wage Rates in the United Kingdom, 1861–1957." *Economica*, 25, 283-299.

Schattschneider, Elmer E. 1935, 1963. *Politics, Pressures, and the Tariff*, rev. ed. Hamden, CT: Archon Books.

Schlesinger, Arthur M., Jr. 1965. *A Thousand Days: John F. Kennedy in the White House*. Boston: Houghton Mifflin.

CHAPTER FIVE

REAGANOMICS AND THE BUSH SEQUEL

The era of Reaganomics blossomed in the months following the election of 1980 and continued to influence public policy through the Bush years. Although analysts disagree about whether Reaganomics was the result of a truly critical election, the Reagan-Bush years resulted in a number of major changes in the American economic system. A different outlook toward rewarding individual effort resulted in redefined notions about efficiency and compensation, which in turn yielded important changes in the revenue system and in the distribution of wealth in America. Industry was reorganized through mergers and buy-outs, and ironically, during the tenure of our most conservative president since Calvin Coolidge, budgetary deficits grew phenomenally. At the same time, many Americans fell through the social safety net as homelessness, drug abuse, crime, and an underclass emerged. Although the economic policies of the Bush administration after 1988 differed in some ways from those of the Reagan years, clearly they were an extension of the Reagan revolution.

This final historical chapter examines developments in political economy that have taken place during the last decade. Its focus on an even shorter time period brings the greatest degree of resolution to bear on contemporary issues. Because the election of Ronald Reagan was the central causal element in the changes of the past decade, we begin with it. Next, we identify the components of Reaganomics itself. Third, we examine the 1980s in the light of Reaganomics and the ability of the Democratic coalition to counteract it. Fourth, we examine the record of Reaganomics: Has it profoundly altered life in America, as its supporters and opponents have both hoped and feared? Or was it "a revolution that failed," as some former members of the administration have written? Finally, we explore the continuity and changes in economic policy under George Bush.

REAGAN-ERA ELECTIONS: ISSUES OR PERSONALITIES?

Many believe that the election of 1980 was a mandate for Reaganomics; but did Ronald Reagan win in 1980 or did Jimmy Carter lose? Two sets of factors, those having to do with issues and those associated with the candidates themselves, usually determine election outcomes.

Two issues loomed over the reelection hopes of Jimmy Carter. One was the depressed economy. Although the largest oil price shocks had come in 1973–1974, the issue surfaced again in 1977, when Carter used national television to assert that the energy crisis was "the moral equivalent of war." Energy price increases again in 1979 contributed even more to the stagflation brought on by high energy costs and falling employment levels. With inflation growing, Carter's appointment of Paul Volcker as chair of the Federal Reserve began a policy of tight money to control inflation, which had reached 12 percent as the election drew near.

The other issue was of "America held hostage." For 444 days after the fall of the Shah of Iran and the sack of the embassy in Teheran, American diplomats and Marine guards were paraded before chanting Iranians. It was a terrible spectacle for Carter because for all its military power, the United States seemed to be helpless.

Electoral decisions are driven by perceptions of character and competence. As the election drew near, a Center for Political Studies (CPS) survey found that Carter held advantages of from 5 to 20 percent over his challenger on "character issues"—honesty, lack of hunger for personal power, and morality. On perceptions of competence, however, between 16 and 40 percent of respondents found Reagan to be the stronger individual—more inspiring and more capable of providing strong leadership. If elections involving a sitting president are said to be the incumbent's to win or lose, the malaise in the land that was symbolized by "the incredible shrinking president" as caricatured by editorial cartoonists, ended in a Carter defeat rather than a Reagan victory.

To what extent was the election of 1980 a referendum on Reaganomics? Arguments that the voters' choice was based on specific economic policies seem overly demanding of public cognition. Many voters cannot recall the name of their own representative, although as Thomas Mann has shown, those most likely to vote usually can select the correct response from among a short list of names. How many can see behind the notion of tax rates to realize the importance of the taxable base on which that rate will be applied? It seems improbable that large numbers of voters can distinguish among the prescriptions of a monetarist like Milton Friedman, a supply-sider like Arthur Laffer, or a Keynesian like Paul Samuelson.

Whether they win by 5 percent or by 50, many winning politicians are quick to use the term *mandate*. Reagan probably was not elected because of careful consideration of the specifics of Reaganomics (Frankovic, 1981, p. 115). Once in office, however, his administration was relatively successful in putting in place a thoroughgoing blueprint for economic change. That these ideas gained wide acceptance was due to the vast storehouse of personal good will among the American people that Ronald Reagan was able to build during his eight years in office.

The Republican successes in 1984 and 1988 again involved perceptions of the candidates' competence, as well as the party that held the White House not making missteps that would result in its own defeat. These elections also involved Democratic issue placement and campaign ineptitude. In 1984, although Mondale held a surprising advantage on "warmth," the CPS survey shows that Reagan defeated him because of public perceptions of both competence and integrity. In 1988, both Vice-President Bush and Governor Dukakis began the campaign with low approval ratings. Negative campaigning, including the Willie Horton advertisement that played on racial themes while overtly attacking Dukakis as being soft on crime, contributed to perceptions that important issues were not being addressed by either side. Bush was able to bring momentum to his cause with televised spots emphasizing his competence and integrity, whereas the inept Dukakis camp was unable to overturn the governor's image as a member of the party of "tax and spend."

WHAT WAS REAGANOMICS?

Reaganomics was the most integrated set of ideas about public policy toward the economy since the New Deal. There was a better understanding in 1981 of what was to be attempted in the years ahead, a more consistent agenda, than had existed among the New Dealers who descended on Washington after 1932. In general, the new president's views were conservative, and his policies sought to change the nation by getting back to what was believed to have been the good old days. It was no coincidence that Reagan's favorite predecessor in the White House was Calvin Coolidge. But just what was Reaganomics? In the most general sense, it was a preference for the private over the public sector. It was a preference for economics over politics as a decision-making tool—or rather, for the marketplace in preference to democracy. Four of its key elements were set forth in *A Program for Economic Recovery*, sent to Congress by the new president on February 18, 1981. Others were more latent within administration policy as it evolved during two administrations.

First, because the centerpiece of Reaganomics was the conservative axiom that governmental programs are replete with waste and inefficiency, the goal was to decrease the rate of growth in federal spending. Unfortunately for this thinking, the budget is politically difficult to reduce. About 70 percent of it is held to be "uncontrollable," which really means only that most of the budget is particularly difficult to reduce because it consists of Social Security and related payments to individuals, interest on the federal debt, and obligations resulting from contractual agreements from previous years. Since the Reagan administration was committed to military rearmament, virtually all budgetary reductions would have had to come out of the $122 billion spent on domestic civilian programs—programs that constituted only one-eighth of the total budget and most of which had substantial clientele groups and congressional supporters of their own. Thus, cutting the budget was far easier to talk about in the abstract than to do where specific programs were concerned.

There were two important corollaries about changing the budget. One was to reduce overall spending for welfare. Americans are ambivalent about welfare spending. When the word *welfare* appears in questions, it draws negative responses; but when it is packaged as *relief*, the public is far more supportive. The idea of a "safety net" soon emerged to keep the "deserving poor" from a cruel fate.

The other corollary was the goal of dramatically increasing military spending. Fear of the Communist drive for world hegemony has been part of conservative doctrine since the October Revolution of 1917, let alone since the beginning of the Cold War; and the necessity for military might was seen as crucial to America's survival as a democratic nation. Given the dramatic events of *glasnost* and *perestroika*, the fall of the Berlin wall, and related events of the end of the Cold War, it must be remembered that as recently as 1984 the president was referring to the USSR as an "evil empire." The desirability of a military increase was also driven by the image of how much American power had eroded during the Carter years and how that image took on the appearance of reality during the Iranian hostage crisis. So, first, if military line items were to be increased, then of necessity it would be domestic expenditures that must be sacrificed.

The second identifying feature of Reaganomics was supply-side tax policy, which consisted of a number of proposals for reducing taxes on both personal incomes and on the earnings of corporations. Ronald Reagan once mused about his days in Hollywood and how he made no more than two movies each year because the increased income from added work would be eaten up in taxes. He found a kindred spirit in Donald Regan, soon to be his

Secretary of the Treasury, whose successes as a young securities broker had similarly been siphoned away by government. This idea that productivity would be reduced by high tax rates was ingrained from personal experience. Later, when the youthful USC economist Arthur Laffer restated the hypothesized relationship between higher tax rates and the higher revenues they would *fail* to reduce, Reagan could relate to the idea from personal experience. Although there might be disagreement about the location of the inflection point at which tax rates begin to yield total revenues and about the exact shape of the curve itself, the idea on which it was based was a principle that supported the Reagan tax cut of 1981 as well as the tax rate restructuring of the Tax Simplification Act of 1986. That there would be a balanced budget was not a principle of Reaganomics; but unfortunately the administration overestimated the stimulative effect that the tax rate reduction would have on federal revenues. This failure, combined with the intractability of many proposed domestic budget reductions and the increases in military expenditures, caused the deficit to rise significantly. Lowering the rates on the wealthy also contributed to an increased concentration of wealth. The Reagan tax plan also called for accelerating the depreciation of business investment in plant and equipment in order to create new jobs in the corporate sector.

The third component of Reaganomics, as set forth in the 1981 program, was to expedite the deregulation movement that had begun during the Ford administration but that had proceeded in earnest during the Carter years. However, because of the perception that the Reagan era heralded a major shift to the right, many came to believe that deregulation had begun only in 1981. The dissolution of the Civil Aeronautics Board on January 1, 1985, for example, occurred on the Reagan watch. But many people overlooked the fact that the events of that day had been set in motion by Alfred Kahn in 1977. Although the idea of deregulation continued to be popular throughout the 1980s, by the end of the decade demands for reregulation were perceptible in the airline and trucking industries, were noticeable in cable television, and were in full cry for the savings and loan industry.

Fourth, there was to be a commitment to restoring a stable currency and healthy financial market through the adoption of a new monetary policy. The concept of "monetarism" emerged during the 1980s not so much as an integral part of Reaganomics but as a policy that was correlated with it in time. The monetarist ideas of Milton Friedman, Nobel Prize-winning economist from the University of Chicago, had a particular appeal to conservatives. Under Keynesianism, governmental intervention to lower or raise taxes was needed to stabilize the business cycle, and bureaucracies were needed to oversee spending programs if the government was to participate on the expenditure side of the Keynesian prescription as well. It was the monetarist thesis that careful, measured growth in the money supply would alleviate the gyrations of the business cycle and enable the heavy hand of governmental intervention to be reduced. It was the continued presence of Paul Volcker as chair of the Federal Reserve system, however, more than any conscious decision to implement the ideas of Friedman, that brought monetarist policies to the Reagan White House.

Reaganomics evolved into more than these four principles. Among its ancillaries was the principle of *devolution*—a term borrowed from British politics that meant returning the financial responsibility for a number of federal programs to the states. Again, this principle was grounded in conservative views of American politics—that federalism is an important concept in the American system, that the position of the states has eroded as the power of the national government has grown, that government is best when it is closest to the people, and that programmatic decisions are better made at the state level than imposed from Washington. Most important, devolution meant that the federal budget could be reduced by placing responsibility in the hands of the states.

Devolution had problems of its own, some of which were inherent in the concept of federalism. States vary widely in the needs of their citizens and in their ability to meet the costs of providing services for them. Although measures of "tax effort" often praise poorer states for making stronger efforts to tap into the revenue sources that they have, it is clear that many states simply lack the wherewithal to cope with problems of social need. Many states also lack professional staffs with the training and sophistication to provide levels of service equal to those supplied by a federal level of organization. If welfare recipients are also citizens and are entitled to equal protection under the law, then they are victimized by states that provide lower levels of service. For uniform support levels to occur across the nation, the members of all fifty state policy-making systems must have the fortitude to raise revenues to provide that support. This seems unlikely.

A sixth feature of Reaganomics was a reliance on the concept of efficiency in evaluating merger and takeover activity. Antitrust policy in America has traditionally focused on two rather different topics: the structure of corporate organization and the way in which business behaves. It is the first of these, the organization of business, that the efficiency concept addressed. If there is a monopoly when a single firm offers a product or service but competition might mean that twenty firms will supply it, it is important to ask about the point at which mergers among competing producers would constitute a monopoly. Antitrust sanctions have been applied sporadically since the passage of the Sherman Act in 1890; but during the 1980s, mergers between firms that consented to them and hostile takeovers of firms against their will were a major feature of business life. Against those who argue that business combinations and large size are worrisome for a number of reasons, it has long been argued that economies of scale contribute to increased efficiency of operations. The belief that inefficiency contributes to inflation and to the declining position of American products in the international marketplace led to the rise of the Chicago school of economists. This efficiency argument, and the economists who espoused it in the Antitrust Division of the U.S. Department of Justice, came to dominate merger policy during the Reagan administration.

Seventh, privatization was a prominent feature of Reaganomics. Privatization means converting as many governmental functions as possible into private enterprises. Many enterprises are public either because they are inextricably linked with the public health, welfare, and safety— because their return on investment is too low to attract private investors— or because mismanagement has caused them to fail. The largest privatization of the 1980s involved ConRail, the public corporation founded in 1976 out of the ruins of the bankrupt Penn Central Railroad—itself an amalgamation of many railroads that had been created under the oversight of bankruptcy courts some years earlier. Contrary to Reaganite theology, ConRail proved to be embarrassingly profitable. After an attempt to sell it to Norfolk Southern Railroad foundered on the shoals of antitrust considerations, ConRail was "taken private." Attempts to kill outright the last surviving rail passenger service, AmTrak, seemed to end in 1989.

Finally, Reaganomics included a "get tough" policy toward organized labor. The summer of 1981 saw a strike by the nation's Professional Air Traffic Controllers Organization (PATCO). Reagan followed through on his threat to fire those controllers, who were federal employees, if they failed to return to work. And on the regulatory front, the president's appointees to the National Labor Relations Board (NLRB) moved that commission closer to the position of management.

REAGANOMICS IN ACTION: THE 1980s

The first months of the Reagan administration were packed with activity. Although the Iranian hostage crisis dissolved on inauguration day, the economic crisis did not. Then, only two months into the term, there was an assassination attempt that only narrowly failed. Where political economy was concerned, however, a Reagan dynamo soon took hold.

Nothing better typified Reagan's program, as well as his successes, than the field of public spending. Jimmy Carter had left behind a budgetary proposal for fiscal year (FY) 1982 of $739.3 billion. It quickly went under the knife. A first round of budget cuts began on February 18, and when work was finalized on August 13, the administration had recorded an impressive victory. Some $35.2 billion had been removed from various programs, ranging from AmTrak and the arts to public broadcasting and the National Zoo. There were reductions in consumer protection, education, housing, student loans, unemployment benefits, and trade adjustment assistance. The controversial Comprehensive Employment and Training Act (CETA) program was ended altogether. Reagan was aided by a Capitol Hill liaison team, headed by Max Friedersdorf, that stood in bold contrast to Carter's harried staff, and by a capable strategy devised by the Office of Management and Budget (OMB) Director David Stockman. By consolidating all of the budget cuts into a single major bill, the Gramm-Latta Reconciliation Resolution, the administration was able to prevent individual attacks on specific cuts that might have been mounted by interest groups. It was easier for the administration to defend a single whole than a diverse series of individual parts. Congress gave the president most of the reductions he had requested as well as increases in military spending because of his personal efforts, the superior political strategy of his lieutenants, and the honeymoon effect that is important to all new presidents.

Parallel developments took place on the revenue side of the budget. The Kemp-Roth proposal for stimulating the economy by reducing personal and business taxes by 10 percent each year for three years had been a prominent part of the Reagan program during the election campaign. By midsummer 1981, it had grown into a five-year, $749 billion tax reduction package, with Democrats seeking additional reductions to curry support with their own interest groups. When the bill passed on July 29, forty-eight Democrats defected to the Reagan plan; Representative James Jeffords (R-VT) was the sole Republican to side with the Democratic majority in the House. In the area of defense, in contrast, the budget produced an $18 billion *increase* over the proposals that Carter had left behind.

By September of that first year, however, the high-water mark of Reaganomics had been reached. In winning on the first round of cuts, in his victory on taxation, and in increasing defense appropriations, Reagan had exhausted his congressional coalition of traditional Republicans, supply-side Republicans, and conservative Southern Boll Weevil Democrats. Now a second round of budget cuts fell short, and only $4 billion more in savings were achieved. Some of the Republican moderates in Congress had to protect their own pet projects; others were growing concerned over a deficit of $100 billion that was growing in their very midst. Institutional costs within Congress were mounting as well. The congressional budget process, a reform of 1974 that seldom worked as well as had once been hoped, was now in a shambles because of Stockman's tactics. The Reaganites also had no qualms about bruising congressional egos. By the end of the 1981 session, the Democratic outlook was summarized by the Chief Deputy Whip Bill Alexander (D-AR), who said that it was fortunate that Reagan had won or the Democrats could have been blamed for the ensuing deficits (*Congressional Quarterly Almanac*, 37, 1981, p. 16). By year's end, the 97th Congress had given the president most of what he had sought.

The administration had a more difficult time after the first year. Continuing bad economic news demonstrated to the satisfaction of the critics of supply-side economics that its theories were not ending the recession.

Although interest rates and inflation were declining, the unemployment level of 10.8 percent was more than it had been at any time since World War II. High interest rates supported by the Federal Reserve, with the prime rate at 16 percent at midyear, were strengthening the dollar internationally, which in turn caused a record high trade deficit. Now the president and Congress really began to knock heads. Reagan had vetoed only two bills in his first year, but he rejected thirteen more in 1982. Congress successfully challenged two of the five bills that it sought to override, one of which was an appropriation bill for nearly $1 billion. This "budget buster," as the president called it, restored some of the cuts in social programs from the year before. There was also a $98 million increase in taxes; but to ease the embarrassment of those who had supported a tax reduction twelve months before, the measure was called a "revenue enhancement" that would close loopholes and promote taxpayer compliance. In the end, the Reagan recession of 1982 was a contributing factor in Republican losses of twenty-eight seats in the House elections, but it was the beginning of a historic period of growth in the national economy. Even with the reassertion of congressional prerogatives in 1982, Reagan had dominated the 97th Congress with the abandon of a bronco buster out of the Old West.

Reaganomics lost momentum in 1983. Unlike the first two years, the president did not seek sweeping changes during the 98th Congress. To be sure, important Social Security reform was attained in a compromise solution arranged by "two Irish pols"—Reagan and Speaker "Tip" O'Neill— by adopting recommendations put forward by a National Commission on Social Security Reform. The remedy included increasing the retirement age to sixty-seven by the year 2027, increasing payroll deductions by both employers and wage earners, and taxing the benefits of higher-income recipients. And it was true also that even as the first streaks of prosperity began to dawn, traditional Senate Republicans like Robert Dole of Kansas, chair of the Finance Committee, and Pete V. Domenici of New Mexico, chair of the Budget Committee, sought to fashion a package of spending cuts and tax increases that would lower the deficit by $150 billion—to a shortfall of only $50 billion. Within the White House itself, Martin Feldstein, chairman of the president's Council of Economic Advisers, drew criticism from the supply siders by calling for tax increases.

Now Reagan's attention began to turn to other issues. One of them was foreign affairs—Central America, the shooting down of a Korean airliner in September 1983, and the bombing of the Marine barracks in Lebanon six weeks later. Social issues were another distraction from an economic focus. The president failed to attain congressional support for antiabortion and school prayer constitutional amendments or of tax credits for parochial school tuition or for urban enterprise zones that would have created jobs in depressed areas.

The second administration was quite different from the 1981 beginning, with Congress now recapturing the initiative from the White House. The president, despite his impressive victory over Mondale, now was a lame duck, unable to succeed himself in office. This always is a setback in presidential power. There were significant changes in the White House team, too, as James Baker and Donald Regan exchanged their positions at the top of the Treasury Department and the White House office staff. The timing of the change, coming after the new Congress had already assembled, was awkward, and as the new Chief of Staff, Regan did nothing to overturn his reputation of being difficult to work with. By year's end David Stockman was gone at OMB, having been replaced by James C. Miller III. Equally important was the change in Republican Senate leadership, where Robert Dole was a more disputatious majority leader than Howard Baker (R-TN) had been before him. Although Dole was with the administration on foreign and defense matters, he parted from it economically. His first priority was action on deficit reduction, whereas Reagan maintained that tax reform was his highest goal. And as Norman Ornstein (1985) observed, the administration had exhausted all of its new ideas; the only new ideas left were those from Congress. (*Congressional Quarterly Almanac*, p. 10). By 1987, domestic conflicts involving the failed Supreme Court nominations of Bork and Ginsberg, the ethical problems of former counsel to the president Michael Deaver, and the scandal at the National Security Council over Iran-Contra all combined to divert attention from economic matters.

Nevertheless, important economic policy was still being made during the second term. One important innovation emanated from the Senate and was aimed at the public debt—the Balanced Budget and Emergency Deficit Control Act of 1985, better known as Gramm-Rudman-Hollings (PL 99-177). Signed on December 12, 1985, it called for a steady reduction in the deficit from not more than $171.9 billion in FY 1986; through $144 billion, $108 billion, $72 billion, and $36 billion in the next four fiscal years; and finally to a goal of no deficit at all by 1991. If the projected deficit failed to reach these targets in any year, automatic spending cuts in military and domestic programs alike would be implemented with equal percentage cuts on an across-the-board basis—or across-the-board except for about half the budget that was given over to entitlement programs like Aid to Families with Dependent Children (AFDC), veterans' pensions, food stamps, and Medicaid. The idea was to make draconian reductions that would be offensive to liberals and conservatives alike, and this provision would make Congress more responsible in dealing with the debt. Unfortunately, the law proved to be problematic. First, a complicated enforcement mechanism for making the cuts automatically had transformed a legislative branch official, the Comptroller General, into a key administrative agent for implementing them. This arrangement was invalidated by the Supreme Court as a violation of the principle of separation of powers. Thus, a "less automatic" procedure was put in place after 1987. It called for the OMB and the Congressional Budget Office to prepare the numbers and for the president to issue any orders for spending cuts. Second, the allowable debt ceilings in Gramm-Rudman-Hollings were raised, so that the discipline that would have been imposed by the feared cuts was never felt.

The other major innovation was the Tax Reform Act of 1986 (PL 99-514). The law was the result of public cynicism—the belief that somehow the rich were beneficiaries of tax loopholes—and of extensive congressional action. The reform movement had begun with Democrats like Senator Bill Bradley of New Jersey and Representative Richard Gephardt of Missouri in 1982; but two years later the President cited a promise of making the taxing process fairer and called for a revenue neutral revision that would eliminate favored treatment for "special interests." The elimination of special advantages for individuals and businesses would be counterbalanced by across-the-board rate reductions—down from fourteen brackets, ranging from 11 to 50 percent, to only two rates of 15 and 28 percent plus 34 percent for corporations. The personal exemption was virtually doubled, to $2,000. Many of the loopholes that were closed, however, had sheltered items that taxpayers who were very middle class indeed had enjoyed, including the tax-exempt status of unemployment compensation and scholarship money. Passage of the bill was hailed as a triumph for House Ways and Means Chair Dan Rostenkowski (D-IL), who was able to defeat repeated attempts by lobby groups to retain advantages for themselves. With the final bill totaling more than 1,100 pages, however, there was doubt about how much "simplification" it had attained.

THE EFFECTS OF REAGANOMICS

Recent presidencies and their policies are always difficult to assess dispassionately, but three perspectives can be identified concerning Reaganomics. One school is commendatory. Reaganomics has been hailed by the right because it reversed Wagner's law, the idea that the public sector will grow inexorably, at least where the number of federal employees was concerned. At the same time, devolution had the effect of increasing the numbers of state and local governmental workers, with a resulting net gain in the total number of those in the public sector. On another front, the financial community has lauded Reaganomics for the unprecedented string of 92 months of economic expansion and prosperity through July, 1990. Typical of this view is the editorial position of the *Wall Street Journal* (1990), which maintained that it was the supply-side tax rate reductions that stimulated productivity and generated this strength.

There is also positive evidence of upward mobility from a Treasury Department panel study of those who filed tax returns over the years 1979 through 1988. By dividing into quintiles some 14,351 taxpayers, the Treasury's Office of Tax Analysis found that only 14.2 percent of those who were in the lowest one-fifth at the beginning of the time period were still languishing there at the end. Nearly a fourth of them had worked their way up to the fourth, third and second quintiles, respectively, and 14.7 percent, most of them young, had reached the top 20 percent by 1988. In general, there was more mobility upward than downward, although nearly 60 percent of those in the top one-fifth in 1979 remained there a decade later. According to Representative Richard Armey (R–TX), the analysis showed considerable mobility in economic status and revealed the flaw of class-based rhetoric in American politics. However, upward mobility may have been overstated because of the absence of data from the very poor, who may file no tax returns, and the 1979–1988 summary really tells little because there are no similar analyses from other periods with which it can be compared.

There is also a neutral position toward Reaganomics. Some proponents of its ideas lament that its policies were never allowed truly to take effect. To the extent that Reaganomics was implemented, it occurred primarily during the first administration because of the system of checks and balances—and especially because of the honeymoon effect. Presidents really have only their first term (because of the Twenty-second Amendment), or only their first two years (when the coattail effect influences representatives who were elected with them) or even their first six months in office before congressional opposition and criticism in the press begin to mount. Internecine conflicts broke out within the administration and closed the door on new thinking and led, in the views of Paul Craig Roberts (1984), William Niskanen (1988), and Peggy Noonan (1990), to a "revolution that failed."

Finally, there are the critics of Reaganomics, most of whom are on the left. They believe, first, that support for many useful programs was reduced to the degree that they were made ineffective. Research on energy independence was slashed by Reagan, for example, and represented an opportunity cost during the Iraqi crisis of 1990. Second, the growth of the nation's indebtedness looms larger each year. Ironically, it was during the administration of this conservative president that the government was most willing to buy on credit. Given their own history of deficit spending, the jeremiads by Democrats about the size of the debt could be ridiculed as disingenuous. Given their opposition to governmental spending, the creation of huge annual-interest obligations by Republicans could be a tactic for disarming social expenditures for years to come. Third, some liberals point to the financial rubble left behind by the hostile takeover mania of the 1980s. Countless careers were harmed and families disrupted as a result of takeover battles, with the least injured being those high-level executives who enjoyed "golden parachutes." Companies that were restructured with junk bonds were left to face debts they could not repay. Fourth, the deregulatory movement allowed a financial disaster to occur in the savings and loan industry.

Federal bailouts of those who lost money will result in a redistribution of wealth from the northeast to Texas and the Southwest. Fifth, as Republican strategist Kevin Phillips (1990) observes, there is a new gap between the rich and the poor that was exacerbated by the changes in the rates of personal taxation and the reduction of social spending. Finally, there was a challenge to the notion that government service is an honorable calling. John F. Kennedy inspired many idealistic young people to enter government in the 1960s, but Reagan-era insistence that government is equated with waste, fraud, and abuse may have deterred many of the best of a college generation from public service.

Was Reaganomics revolutionary? The answer is yes if we focus on its goals. There was synoptic change in reducing governmental spending while simultaneously reducing taxes, as well as in elevating the role of monetary policy. However, the response is no if actual performance is the test, as it should be. Its implementation through budget reductions was modest and incremental. Deregulation was not significantly greater than under Carter, although the limitation on what government might do because of budgetary restrictions was real.

BUSHONOMICS

George Bush came to the Oval Office after eight years as vice-president. Although he had branded supply-side tax policy as "voodoo economics" during the 1980 primary elections, his acceptance of conservative economic and social doctrines after receiving a place on the ticket reminded some of the conversion of faith that St. Paul had undergone on the road to Damascus. To others, it did not. During his term as vice-president, Bush had developed further his foreign policy specialty. Then, in 1988, after a hateful campaign that centered more on nationalistic symbols, racial tensions, and the fear of crime than on economic issues, Bush handily defeated Michael Dukakis.

Although some saw Bush's vision of "a kinder, gentler America" as a gratuitous slap at Reaganomics, there were few changes in economic policy from the Reagan years. Changes at the Department of Justice did signal a tougher policy against mergers, but the central tenets of the rest of Reaganomics remained in place: capital gains tax reductions, no tax increases, continuation of free trade, privatization, and reductions in social service spending. Because of this continuity in administration policy and the change of leadership in both houses of Congress, the first year of the Bush administration was a honeymoon period. The emphasis was on foreign policy. These were the months when the former USSR dissolved, Panama was invaded, and the democracy movement failed tragically in China. Soon, too, came the electoral defeat of the Sandinistas in Nicaragua and the freeing of Nelson Mandela.

If the first year had been calm, Congress and the president went to the mat in year two. The main event was the FY 1991 budget. In May, while the House and Senate were unable to concur on the First Budget Resolution, which was part of the annual budget process, economic forecasters were predicting a falling economy and, as a consequence, a burgeoning budget deficit. As Treasury receipts threatened to fall, the president took the unprecedented step of calling for a "budget summit" between Congress and the White House. As spring gave way to summer, the administration team and twenty-one members of the House and Senate became hopelessly stalled. Then, on June 26, a major breakthrough occurred. Bush offered to consider selected tax increases in order to get the talks moving again. Negotiations resumed at Andrews Air Force Base across the Potomac from Washington, with the discussions eventually being limited to only a core of eight insiders — five from Congress (Senate Majority Leader George Mitchell and Minority Leader Bob Dole, House Speaker Tom Foley, and House Majority and Minority Leaders Richard Gephardt and Bob Michel) and three representing the president (OMB Director Richard Darman, White House Staff Chief John Sununu, and Treasury Secretary Nicholas Brady). When put to a vote in the House, the outcome was an embarrassment to the formal congressional leadership. Democratic liberals objected to program reductions, Republican conservatives complained that the pledge of "no new taxes" had been broken, and both opposed the way that a few insiders had overridden the normal procedures of the budget process. The vote was 179 for to 254 against.

After a series of late-night congressional sessions in late October and early November, an agreement emerged that was a net loss for the administration. Bush had offered to talk about tax increases in June on the condition that capital gains taxes would be reduced to offset them. Six months later, however, only the tax increases remained. In the end, top tax rates were raised from 28 to 31 percent for the wealthiest taxpayers—the same people who were to have their ability to use itemized deductions phased downward as well. There was also an increase from 21 to 24 percent in the alternative minimum tax, which is paid only by certain wealthy taxpayers. Still, half the new revenue was to come from excise taxes: five cents on each gallon of gasoline; new taxes on beer, wine, and liquor; and a tax on "luxury" purchases of expensive automobiles and yachts. The boat taxes in particular became objects of derision. The wealthy simply bought used yachts, and the people who built expensive watercraft lost their jobs. Although the president claimed that 70 percent of the deficit reduction package came from spending cuts and only 28 percent from "tax changes," the memory of the tax increases was carried into the 1992 Republican National Convention by economic conservatives.

The following year, 1991, harbored a remarkable turnabout in presidential popularity. The 100-hour destruction of the Iraqi military machine that was Operation Desert Storm left Bush with the highest presidential approval rating in history, but the recession that had prompted him to convene the economic summit the year before soon had countervailing effects. According to the National Bureau of Economic Research (NBER), the recession began officially in July 1990; and as grim economic news arrived throughout 1991 and 1992, Bush slid steadily in the polls. Only scant months after some had wondered whether any Democrat at all would be willing to run in 1992, the question had become whether Bush could close the 20 percent gap between himself and the Clinton-Gore ticket by November. He couldn't.

WHAT HISTORY TEACHES US

This group of three chapters has attempted to provide a historical context in which governmental institutions and issues of specific public policy can be viewed. It has identified several sweeping themes and singled out people and policies in the belief that both are important for our understanding.

Three general lessons emerge from this historical narrative. From the longest view, the three centuries through 1932, it should be apparent that the concerns and social patterns of a generation are usually forgotten as new habits cover them over. Just as archaeologists excavating a tell make important new finds by digging 10 feet deeper, so too do surprises await the archeologist of public policy. In the dynamic and ever youthful United States, less thought seems to be given to recalling the struggles and victories of the past than to devising new mechanisms to cope with the future.

In the intermediate span of time, the period from the Great Depression to the dawn of Reaganomics, it is clear that ideas can move from one political party to the other. Keynesianism, once anathema to them, has been embraced by Republicans. The idea of government purposefully stimulating the economy to get it moving again was abhorred by Herbert Hoover, who seldom referred to it as anything but "Marxist-Keynesianism." However, both Reaganomics and Bushonomics promoted intervention that stimulates production through such devices as capital gains tax reductions. The national debt, which was a fearsome thing to the GOP during Eisenhower's tenure, is of little concern to many economic conservatives today, whereas Democrats decry it because interest payments eat into the money that could otherwise be spent for social programs. Free-trade views that appealed to Democrats in 1934 are now criticized for promoting unfair competition and the export of American jobs. Was Emerson right about the lack of consistency when he identified it as "the hobgoblin of little minds," or is it that the interests of the two parties have changed significantly over the years?

Finally, as this chapter has shown, people are important in public policy. Without the particular skills of Ronald Reagan, the economic ideas of his era surely would NOT have gained their day in the Statutes-at-Large or the Code of Federal Regulations. The skills of the White House chief of staff have a major impact. The men and women who represent the president on Capitol Hill, Reagan's Friedersdorf in contrast with Carter's Frank Moore, can make or break a president's professional reputation.

QUESTIONS

1. Did Ronald Reagan win the presidential election of 1980, or did Jimmy Carter lose it? What difference would it make for American politics?

2. What were the sources of the ideas central to Reaganomics? Were these ideas new in American political history?

3. Why was President Reagan successful in dealing with Congress at the beginning of his first term? Why did this success decline across time?

4. If Reaganomics had not occurred, what would life be like today?

5. Since Reaganomics did occur, how long-lasting has it proven to be?

6. What does "conservative" mean? Was Reaganomics a conservative movement?

7. In what ways have the economic programs of the Bush administration been different from those of Reagan?

8. How far back do we have to go before "current events" become "history"?

REFERENCES

Anderson, Martin. 1988. *Revolution.* New York: Harcourt Brace Jovanovich.

Barone, Michael. 1990. *Our Country: The Shaping of America From Roosevelt to Reagan.* New York: Macmillan/Free Press.

Burnham, Walter Dean.(1970) *Critical Elections: Mainsprings of American Politics.* New York: Norton.

"Editorial." 1990, August 16. *Wall Street Journal,* p. A12.

Frankovic, Kathleen A. 1981. "Public Opinion Trends." In Gerald Pomper, ed. *The Election of 1980: Reports and Interpretations.* Chatham, NJ: Chatham House, pp.97–118.

"Legislative Summary: 97th Took Bold Steps to Reduce the Federal Role." 1981. *Congressional Quarterly Almanac,* 37, p. 16.

"Legislative Summary: On Balance, A Year of Taking the Initiative." 1985. *Congressional Quarterly Almanac,* 41, p. 10.

Miller, Arthur H. 1986. "Realigning Forces in the United States Elections of 1984," *Electoral Studies,* 5 (Number 1), 3–18.

Niskanen, William A. 1988. *Reaganomics: An Insider's Account of the Politics and the People.* New York: Oxford University Press.

Noonan, Peggy. 1990. *What I Saw at the Revolution: A Political Life in the Reagan Era.* New York: Random House.

Phillips, Kevin. 1990. *The Politics of Rich and Poor: Wealth and the American Electorate in the Reagan Aftermath.* New York: Random House.

Regan, Donald T. 1988. *For the Record: From Wall Street to Washington.* New York: Harcourt Brace Jovanovich.

Roberts, Paul Craig. 1984. *The Supply-Side Revolution: An Insider's Account of Policymaking in Washington.* Cambridge, MA: Harvard University Press.

Stockman, David A. 1986. *The Triumph of Politics: Why the Reagan Revolution Failed.* New York: Harper & Row.

PART THREE

THE POLICY-MAKING PROCESS:POLITICS, INSTITUTIONS, AND FUNCTIONS

Political economy consists of the reciprocal relationships between economic enterprise and the political process. It is a contest between two ways of decision making: an individualistic process in which decisional units are monetary values, and a collective approach in which the votes of all participants are equally weighted. Each decisional process is championed by its own advocates—the former by a host of market-based economists and conservative activists, and the latter by a perhaps smaller clutch of democratic theorists and liberals.

Part Three examines the governmental and political components of political economy in three ways. Chapter Six begins with the notion of the policy life cycle, then focuses on the roles of pressure groups and of political parties in that policy process. Does it really matter to the economy whether the Democrats or the Republicans control the White House? If so, to whom does it make a difference? All this action occurs in the realm of popular politics—the world of policy entrepreneurs, lobbyists of all shades, and (since the 1970s) high-stakes campaign finance and PAC money. Since economics is important in election outcomes, we will isolate the impact of economic variables as they affect individual voting decisions as well as the effect that elections have on postelection economic performance.

Chapter Seven examines the institutional structures and functions of the three great branches of government as they affect economic policy-making, beginning with Congress. That institution has undergone a number of important changes since World War II that are significant for economic policy-making. We then focus on the presidency and the executive branch, from which most of the impetus for policy leadership now comes. Although the courts remain important in many ways, since 1937 their significance in economic decision making is much less than before. Finally, we consider the evaluation of policies.

Chapter Eight explores relationships between the government and the economy in a different way. At issue here are the several functions that government performs. First, it provides myriad supports that few people think about but that become apparent upon reflection. Second, to some extent, it also acts as an entrepreneur in its own right by providing services that the private sector is unable to supply or by offering products that stimulate competition in the marketplace. Third, the government also manages the economy through the ups and downs of the business cycle, as we shall see in Part Four of this book. But particularly important, and the topic of much of this section, is the extent to which the government regulates conditions in the marketplace—advertising, product safety, and the maintenance of competition.

CHAPTER SIX

THE POLICY LIFE CYCLE
AND POPULAR POLITICS

The idea of the policy life cycle provides a useful way to approach the topic of political economy. The life of a particular policy or program is seen as analogous to that of an organism: a conception; a gestation, an actual birth which usually takes the form of statutory enactment (though it may be a judicial decree or treaty or even a regulation); growth and maturity; and eventually old age and decline. Most programs can be distinguished from organisms in one important way, however, and that is in the absence of death. Indeed, most programs seem to be immortal. The early stages of the policy life cycle are preinstitutional, in that they have not yet arrived at the doorstep of any legislature, administrator, or court. Bringing public problems to the institutions of government, and even having them accepted as legitimate concerns of government, falls within the purview of public opinion and the media. Pressure groups and political parties deserve special attention. Finally, since elections determine the sorts of people who get into public life, this chapter will conclude by examining those aspects of the electoral process that bear on economic policy.

THE POLICY LIFE CYCLE

The term *public policy* refers to broad issue areas—agriculture, economics, environment, foreign affairs, governmental operations, labor, and others. Just how many distinct policy areas there are depends on how specific we want to be and which sources we consult. Economic policy might stand alone, for example, or it might be subdivided into categories like fiscal policy, monetary policy, antitrust, financial institutions, taxation, and the like. But what about an area like foreign trade? Should it be part of economic policy or foreign affairs? If the trade involves agricultural products, should it be seen as a farm issue? Regardless of just how many general policy areas there might be, within each of them there are dozens of specific *programs* that are intended to achieve a particular purpose. Given the nature of the pluralist policy-making process, programs themselves are often purposefully vague and sometimes contain even mutually exclusive goals.

Several conceptual frameworks have been developed to help us understand public policies. Theodore Lowi (1964) once argued that there are three fundamentally different types of policies: distributive, redistributive, and regulatory. James Q. Wilson (1980) later expanded on this typology on the basis of who and how many people pay for programs and benefit from them. His categories of majoritarian, entrepreneurial, client, and interest-group policies are intriguing ways to think about the effects of programs.

Particularly useful is the policy life cycle idea. Due to the work of Charles O. Jones (1977) and others, it envisions programs as moving through a number of stages: from an initial perception that some sort of problem exists, through defining what the problem really is, organizing to bring attention and demands to bear on it, and formulating some policy for attacking it. A number of additional steps follow later in this series (see Figure 6–1). Some would say that the analogy to the human life cycle breaks down in the final stage. People do have finite life spans, but programs and policies seem to be immortal. Still, the Civil Aeronautics Board (CAB) is one prominent example of agency mortality (1938–1985), and there are calls to end another New Deal agency, the Rural Electrification Administration. Instead of winding up operations altogether, the more usual conclusion of a bureaucracy is to reorganize it into a new department.

PROBLEM PERCEPTION

The first crucial stage in the policy life cycle is agreeing that a problem falls within the legitimate purview of government. Accepting responsibility for

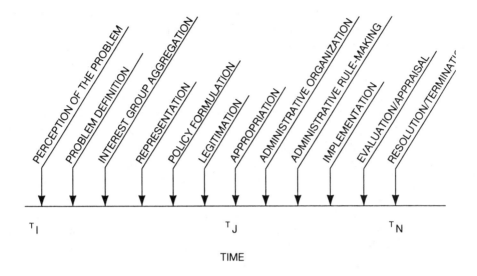

TIME

Figure 6-1. Adopted from Charles O. Jones, An Introduction to the Study of Public Policy, 2nd ed., (Belmont, CA: Duxbury, 1977), pp. 10-13.

the management of the business cycle is one typical example. Recognizing that the economy was in a downturn, even in the absence of systematic indicators, was not difficult; but deciding that the government had a positive role to play in responding to it was long troublesome. Given the teachings of Adam Smith about the harmful effects of mercantilist intervention in the economy, as well as the lack of a constitutional basis for intervention, little action was taken during the Panic of 1837. Still, Martin Van Buren became the first president to be defeated for economic reasons when he ran for reelection three years later. Nearly a century later, although a number of limited steps were attempted by Herbert Hoover, acceptance of an interventionist government still had not penetrated the higher circles of government. It was up to Franklin Roosevelt to legitimize the role of bringing government to the problem and then up to the passage of the Employment Act of 1946 to provide a bipartisan confirmation of that new function.

As in medicine, so too in economic policy: Defining the causes of the problem is usually more difficult than simply perceiving it. Is a downturn simply a "normal cyclical thing" that "every economist knows will happen," as former OMB Director James C. Mitchell III has said, or is a protracted recession due to some other cause? Are the root causes fundamental structural changes in the economy such as the reduction in high-paying manufacturing jobs and the proliferation in part-time minimum-wage jobs without retirement benefits or medical coverage? Is the diminution of a demand for goods a greater causal factor than the lack of rewards for producers? Or is a downturn the result of some foreign-induced problem, such as increased raw-materials costs? Is it a downturn in purchases by our trading partners, throwing Americans out of work? Is it tied to weather cycles that drive the agricultural sector, as many nineteenth-century economists once thought?

The ability to perceive problems adequately is another facet of the policy life cycle. The usefulness of economic indicators is a case in point. Market economists like Alan Greenspan tend to rely on measures of economic performance; businesspeople and bankers who are more politically attuned—people like Bush's Treasury Secretary Nicholas Brady—are more likely to supplement these data with opinion polls that gauge the public mood.

One of the recent developments in problem perception is the enhanced role of television. Offices at both ends of Pennsylvania Avenue often have at least five television sets on at once, and each is tuned to a different network: ABC, NBC, CBS, PBS, and CNN. It has been argued that the White House failed to perceive the seriousness of the situation in Florida that was caused by Hurricane Andrew in 1992 because the networks focused on the future path of the storm as it headed toward Louisiana rather than on the devastation left behind in Dade County. One or two days of response time were lost as a result.

PRESSURE GROUPS AND THE POLITICAL PROCESS

According to the majoritarian view of politics, public policy changes when, somehow, "voices are raised" in opposition to the status quo. The passive voice is appropriate here because it helps to avoid the question of just whose voices these are and how they happen to be audible. Perhaps they belong to elected representatives and are raised because of what these politicians heard while running for office or from their constituents in isolated, unorchestrated communications. Or maybe they emanate from a concerned civil service, the bureaucracy, which in doing its job has discovered new needs or ways to improve on old services.

A more realistic depiction of politics is the pluralist conceptualization that relies on group organization. As Alexis de Tocqueville pointed out even in 1835, Americans have a penchant for organizing groups of all sorts. There are religious groups, groups for sports and entertainment, groups for the environment, and neighborhood improvement groups. And especially there are groups concerned with business and economic life: labor unions, business corporations, and trade associations made up of businesses.

The legitimacy of pressure-group politics is a concern for democratic theory in the United States. Certain political institutions, certainly Congress and the executive establishment, are axiomatic to the political process. Since the earliest days, and certainly since *Marbury* v. *Madison* in 1803, the notion that the federal judiciary is a legitimate player in the policy-making process has been accepted. And as unseemly as political parties appeared to be at the onset, they too have been an integral part of American democracy for generations. What has never been accepted is that Americans, in myriad organizations and acting under the aegis of the "petition" clause of the First Amendment, are also legitimately a part of the political process. Instead, calling them "selfish interests," it is usual to brand private interests as self-serving.

What is disturbing to many about interest-group politics is the uneven access that some groups clearly enjoy. For example, to the extent that successful lobbying groups represent the less successful in the marketplace, government can serve as an alternative to the market in allocating values. Some critics of pluralism are concerned because the access of the powerful to the political process has been enhanced by a number of developments. Political action committees with their campaign monies, Washington law firms with special access through prior government service and old-boy networks, and groups whose initial purpose is in fact the pursuit of political power have proliferated to the point where big-league pressure groups can dominate the decision-making process. To the extent that the rich and the wellborn dominate the corridors of power, government is merely an extension of the private sector. Part of the struggle between conservatives and liberals, between Republicans and Democrats, and between rich and poor is the determination of which sorts of interests will dominate in the governmental process.

Functionally, pressure groups are ubiquitous. Either they discover problems or they are receptive to those who do. They represent those who suffer from the problem and educate that part of the public that will be relevant to dealing with it. One part of the group process that has become critical in this era of interest-group politics is building coalitions with other organizations with similar attitudes. Being able to amass information cogently and often to employ representatives with access to key decision makers (perhaps by hiring Washington law firms like Hill and Knowlton) have become the sine qua non for success. Finally, if the intervention is successful and a new programmatic course is established, monitoring it as it unfolds provides a rationale for reopening the battle in the future.

Pressure groups come in all sizes and shapes, but the majority are fundamentally economic. Taken together, individual corporations, trade associations whose members are corporations, important business-pressure groups, and organized labor unions (local unions, individual industry unions, and important unions like the AFL-CIO and Teamsters) make up about 60 percent of all of the groups registered to lobby Congress.

In politics now, as never before, money talks. It has always been the mother's milk of politics, but now with the importance of media-influenced public opinion, money buys focus groups, opinion polls, campaign consultants, and access to victorious candidates. What it buys beyond this stage is variable and questionable, but if it gets an organization to this point, that may be enough. In matters of economic policy, American politics is a beehive of interest-group activity.

POLITICAL PARTIES

Political parties are ubiquitous throughout the policy process. Parties are organizations that serve as intermediaries between the public and its government by linking the government with the governed (and vice versa). They can be envisioned as organized groups of the electorate, but they are equally important as vehicles that facilitate communication among officeholders in various parts of the government. Political parties recruit, nominate, and elect individuals to public office; develop policies that reflect the interests of their followers; and are the "firms" of the political process whose products can be purchased again at election time or rejected out of hand after a poor performance. As with Congress, Americans have a love-hate relationship with parties. But because of their ancient age and the process of political socialization, they are, unlike pressure groups, an accepted part of the political process.

The number of parties and the nature of their members should depend on the distribution of public opinion. In the unidimensional world that Anthony Downs (1957) posited, where opinion is distributed in a bell-shaped curve, one would expect to find two parties, each seeking to attract the support of all those in the middle of the distribution—from somewhere well to the right (or left), all the way to the median, and then just a bit past the center. Because far more of the electorate is near the median, more attention is given to attracting them than to retaining the tiny numbers found in the tail of the distribution. We would also expect a two-party system if there were a bimodal distribution of opinion, but one with far less similarity in the views of the two parties. Tri- and other multimodal opinion distributions also can be envisioned, each attracting its own party following.

Determining the number of parties on the basis of the number of clusters along a single dimension oversimplifies the matter because the world of politics is multidimensional. In addition to an economic dimension (or closely correlated clusters of economic issues) it is easy to recognize a second issue cluster based on national security and a third on moral values ("family issues," sexual preferences, and perhaps reproductive rights). If each of these dimensions were multimodal, there would be a multiplicity of parties—something not difficult to envision in the socially heterogeneous America of today.

Given the opportunities for multipartyism, why does the United States have a two-party system? All sorts of reasons have been suggested: People are naturally either liberal or conservative (they are not); it has always been this way (it has not), or the duopoly of Democrats and Republicans have all sorts of ways to ward off new parties (they do). Accounting for the persistence of only two parties is one of the staple activities of political science. The most plausible explanation has been offered by Douglas Rae (1971), who credits the effect of electoral law: the plurality winner, single-member district (SMD) system. The plurality winner is simply the person with the most votes. Clearly, in a two-person contest, the winner will obtain a majority of the votes cast. But in a three-way race (and there are many of them) or in an election with even more candidates, the winner may receive far less than 50 percent of the votes. The SMD is simply the situation in which only one person wins. It contrasts with the at-large elections that are typical of many city councils. There, it may be that the top eight vote-getters, out of perhaps sixteen candidates, are elected. With a single technical exception for Louisiana, all of those elected to Congress, in both the House and Senate, are elected from SMD, plurality-vote districts. Because the Electoral College awards states on an all-or-nothing basis, the same is true in presidential elections.

The result of this electoral system is a "seats/votes relationship" which is expressed as the "cube rule" or "Matthew effect" (Rae, 1971). A dramatic penalty is paid by any party when the percentage of votes that it receives sinks much below 50 percent. The party with 45 percent of the vote should win only 35 percent of the seats; 40 percent of the votes yields only 26 percent of the seats. Of course, the converse is also true, and as a party climbs upward from 50 percent its proportion of the seats in a legislature or votes in the Electoral College begins to soar. As a result, canny politicians connect themselves with the largest possible coalitions, the result being two-party politics. There are problems with this explanation, not least of which are the periods of multipartyism in American history. But in general, when added to the likelihood that Democratic and Republican leaders act to maintain their duopoly in a number of ways, the electoral law explanation makes sense.

However many distinctive dimensions of party conflict there may be and whatever the causes of two-partyism we might discover, the duopoly of the Democratic and Republican parties is one of the major facts of American political life. And it is here that we return to the insight of Anthony Downs (1957), for in vying for victory, the significant conflicts are at the middle of a continuum or in the center of a multidimensional hyperspace. Radical notions, and even many ideas that are not so radical, may have been discerned by the media or put forward by interest groups, but they may have great difficulty getting on the agenda. The result is a party system in which there is little difference between candidates. Here is an explanation of why there is consensus on all of the fundamental principles of how the American economy is organized.

But are the two parties really as similar as Downs's (1957) analysis suggests? Just the opposite, says Edward Tufte (1978). The Democrats and Republicans display all of the differences of classic parties of the left and the right. His analysis of platforms compels the conclusion that Democrats are in favor of larger government, a redistribution of income away from the wealthy, and a greater willingness to tolerate inflation in favor of unemployment. For Republicans, just the reverse is true. At least among its activists and spokespersons, the GOP prefers market-based action rather than government, a reward system that concentrates income among the wealthy in the belief that this class is the generator of prosperity, and a greater fear of inflation than of unemployment.

Can one judge the parties on the basis of what their platforms say they will do at election time or on the basis of the statements of their candidates who are jousting for the voters in the middle? Tufte's (1978) contention about party differences is validated in the demographics of the two parties. The sorts of people who are Democrats tend to have lower incomes, to have a lower occupational status, and to be more likely to suffer from the actuality of unemployment than the threat inflation poses to investments that they do not have. Thus, the Democratic party is more attuned to the problems that stem from unemployment and favors programs of increased governmental spending to fix them. Republicans tend to enjoy higher income, middle- and upper-middle-class status, and the benefits that come from invested wealth. As D. Roderick Kiewiet (1984, p. 79) points out, inflation and unemployment are very different in the sorts of costs they entail and in terms of who bears their costs; and the two parties are aware of those differences.

ECONOMIC INFLUENCES ON VOTERS' CHOICE

Voting behavior, as examined from the perspective of political economy, has two facets. The first is the question of whether or not the individual voter will *participate* in an election or referendum. This perspective on participation has been set forth cogently by David B. Johnson (1991), who has concluded that people decide to vote not because they believe that they themselves will determine the winner—that their particular vote will be the tiebreaker—but to avoid social pressure from peers, family, and even themselves. Following Johnson's analysis, someone with an income in the $50,000 to $100,000 range, who is one of 100,000 voters, might anticipate a benefit from voting of only a few cents. That person's costs of participation, however, if two hours are needed to gather information and actually to vote, if his or her time is worth $10 per hour, would be $20. With that sort of benefit-cost ratio, voting is irrational from a purely economic perspective.

Although complaints about low voter turnout are commonplace, they may not be completely warranted. Turnout is greatest in November presidential elections—between 51 and 60 percent since 1960—and it ranges downward for off-year and local elections. These are not enviable performances, but comparisons with other countries must be made with care. American turnout percentages are calculated on best estimates of who is eligible to vote—on estimates of the numbers of citizens who are eighteen and over. Estimates for most other countries are based on those who have been identified to vote by the state, and not everyone is always included. The turnout among registered Americans usually places the United States in about the middle of democratic nations. The United States also has more elections—primaries, general elections, federal elections, state and county offices, and nonpartisan municipal elections, plus the odd local tax levy—than any other democracy. But particularly important, the United States lacks both the compulsion and degree of party conflict that typify other democracies. It has been estimated that fines and intense party competition can each contribute about 8 percent to voter turnout.

Partisanship is the realm of voter choice once the decision has been made to participate. Many models of voter choice have been developed by political scientists. Work in the 1940s focused on the importance of information during campaigns. *The American Voter*, an important study of a generation ago, developed the "funnel of causality" idea—the notion that vote choice is the final link in a chain that begins with an individual's socioeconomic and family background, moves through party affiliation, and reaches its penultimate stage in the perception of candidates and campaign events (Campbell, Converse, Miller, and Stokes, 1976, pp. 24–32). More recent explanations have borrowed from research in market segmentation.

Within the last decade vote choice has often been seen to be a result of two sets of factors: *issues* and *candidates*. According to a view put forward by Downs (1957), voters locate both candidates and themselves on relevant issue continua and vote for the person to whom they are closest on the most salient dimensions. This idea of *issue proximity* has been superseded by estimates of *performance* by candidates on these issues. If it is performance rather than proximity that counts in the mind of the voter, perceived incompetence makes the reelection of incumbents difficult; but incumbents who do meet the competence test will be difficult to unseat. As we have seen earlier, voters' perceptions both of candidates' *character* or integrity and of their *competence* are often of greater importance than issues, especially since the media underreport most issues.

Other factors help to explain Republican success in presidential elections and the divided government of Republican presidents and Democratic Congresses. One is the politics of *race*, which has changed importantly since the Civil Rights Act of 1964 and the Voting Rights Act of 1965. Although a majority of blacks left the party of Lincoln in the 1930s and two-thirds of them were Democrats in the 1950s, fully nine black voters out of ten supported Democratic candidates for the presidency in the 1980s. This apparent Democratic advantage was more than offset by the loss of a majority of white Southerners, who now vote Republican for president, and means that Democrats had an exceedingly difficult time in carrying the region that was once their bastion of support. Democrats also have lost their advantage in the mountain states of the West. Because of these regional shifts and ethnic changes, Democrats tended to nominate candidates who were more liberal than before—something that further exacerbated their problem in winning the White House. Although Bill Clinton was able to overcome those tendencies in 1992, only time will tell whether a new pattern has been established.

Every politician believes that the state of the economy affects what voters do when they go to the polls. Generations of Americans have said that they vote their pocketbooks, and recent rhetoric asserts that "the three leading issues are jobs, jobs, and jobs." Polling data also show that in many presidential election years, Americans refer more to their economic hopes and fears than they do to concerns about any other single policy area. Although this belief in the importance of the economy is not directly challenged by empirical political science, it is questioned on the ground that it lacks precision. Research has sought to sharpen the relationship between voting and economic conditions by discovering just which specific types of economic problems are most important, under what conditions, and in what order of importance. Although good studies abound, their findings have been found to differ by the particular election year under scrutiny, the type of office being contested (presidential, senatorial, or congressional), the level of government (federal, state, or local), and whether it is a candidate-centered election or one involving referenda and millage levies. Thus, a finding that might be valid for presidential elections when the economy was doing well (e.g., 1964) may be quite different for an off-year congressional election when the economy has turned sour (as in 1982).

Kiewiet (1984) has summarized the literature on the effect of the economy on voters' choice and expanded on it through his own work. His analysis of polling data from the thirteen national elections from 1956 to 1980 can be envisioned in a tree diagram consisting of four dichotomous choices.

First, there is the question of which frame of reference the voters are using. Are they drawing on their own personal economic experiences, or are they choosing on the basis of their assessment of the needs of the nation at large? Second, which economic issues are the voters focusing on? Although there is a wide range of possible concerns, such as growth or taxes or regulation, Kiewiet places special attention on two problems—inflation and unemployment. The impact of these two issues is not reciprocal, for each affects different sorts of people and with different results. Unemployment is direct and personal; inflation's effects are diffuse and are felt more by owners of capital than by daily wage earners. Third, does the voting decision involve a choice for president or for a member of Congress? Finally, does the decision appear to focus especially on the performance of the party that holds the White House—is the choice incumbency-oriented—or is it a more policy-oriented choice from between competing courses of action?

Two other possible dichotomies are latent within Kiewiet's (1984) discussion, although they are not addressed directly. One is the partisan dichotomy between Democrats and Republicans, which is not stressed because it is contained within the concept of presidential party incumbency. Restated, *incumbency* is taken to mean all candidates who belong to whichever party holds the White House at the time of the election. The distinction between retrospective and prospective voting, of whether votes are cast because of past actions or in the hopes of future possibilities, also is addressed only in passing.

Several findings leap out at us. One is that whereas we might expect personal experiences to be more influential than diffuse perceptions of some national need, it is clear that large numbers of people really do decide on the basis of what they believe is in the best interests of the country at large. Although some analysts have decried low levels of public knowledgeability in other areas, Kiewiet (1984) concludes that poll respondents are aware of economic events. For example, he says, "The percentage of respondents in each survey who believed that either inflation or unemployment were the most serious problem facing the country closely paralleled the years' objective inflation and unemployment rates" (p. 116). Again, polling data show that perceptions of how families have fared economically show less annual variation than do perceptions of how well the economy at large has been performing.

Another important finding concerns the impact of unemployment. According to Kiewiet, when it occurs to the head of a household, its impact is immediate and more dramatic and personal than inflation, the general condition of the economy, or anything else. Since relatively few heads of household actually do lose their jobs, however, the effect of unemployment is so widely diffused throughout the population that its actual effect on votes cast is quite small. Also, there is a rapid decay in the effect of unemployment, in that the unemployment of a head of household seems to be largely discounted after a year or so. As Kiewiet (1984) writes, "People tend to discount past experiences with unemployment fairly quickly" (p. 51).

A third finding concerns the voters' posture toward incumbency. Probably because presidents are held responsible for economic performance, the electorate is more likely to judge the incumbent presidential party more harshly because of poor economic performance. As we recall, however, individual representatives are more likely to be evaluated favorably because of casework, positive perceptions of them personally, or the absence of a strong challenger. Thus, there is attenuation in the weight of economic factors in congressional elections.

Finally, there is asymmetry in the electoral effects of unemployment and inflation. Democrats benefit more electorally from voters' unrest when unemployment increases than Republicans tend to gain from the electoral protests of those who object to increasing inflation.

Kiewiet also found that some economic effects were noticeably absent. When asked about the problems that most bothered them, many poll respondents answered in only broadly economic terms. With the exception of issues that were distinctively associated with government—high taxes or too much regulation—many voters seemed to feel that their economic circumstances were of their own doing, for good or ill. This "ethic of self-reliance" (Sniderman and Brody, 1977; quoted in Kiewiet, 1984, p. 23.) reduces the economy's impact in the voting booth. Again, although inflation and taxes were blamed on the government, neither party was seen as consistently more at fault than the other during the years surveyed. It was also true that findings concerning economic motives were always weaker for congressional elections than for presidential ones. And finally, because few if any questions have been asked about inflation over the years, its effect on voters' choice is not as well understood as is the apparently greater influence of unemployment.

It remains to be seen whether these findings are replicable for more recent elections. In one way they are not: Inflation was found to have increased consistently across the fifteen years, but one of the features of Reaganomics, particularly during the Bush years, has been the taming of the inflationary trend and the emergence of new concerns about growth and unemployment. Still, most if not all of the assertions strike a responsive chord with most electoral observers today.

HOW ELECTORAL OUTCOMES AFFECT THE ECONOMY

Anyone who has witnessed the quadrennial bloodletting of American presidential campaigns can only conclude that elections are very important to the future quality of the economy. "Elect me," say candidates from both parties, "and prosperity will continue (or return); elect them, and disaster is (or soon will be) guaranteed." But then, as we listen to what is said on the street, it really makes no difference who is in office because the results will be the same; that is, elections and parties make no difference at all.

The argument for "no difference" arises from several premises. First, there is Downs's (1957) notion, based on electoral strategy, that the two parties differ little on fundamentals. Both accept the principles of market-based capitalism, and both are competing for votes from among those in the center of the distribution of public opinion. Second, there are so many other ways, apart from elections and parties, to influence public policy in America. This thinking emanates from the group theory of politics, which sees government as little more than a referee among competing pressure groups. And third, there is the radical or Marxian belief that the American political economy is constituted in such a way that what passes for democratic politics is irrelevant to the economic issues of life, for the decisions of government are actually made on Wall Street or in the board rooms of the Fortune 500 companies.

Fortunately, whether or not parties make a difference is an empirical question, subject to testable analysis. Since 1900, the Dow Jones Industrial Average has increased 28 percent, on the average, during the four years after Democrats have won the White House and 31 percent after a Republican victory. A different time frame, however, can give different results. Looking at the first year after a presidential election beginning with 1932, a Democratic victory has been better for the Dow. In fact, there probably is no significant difference between the effects of the parties on the stock market.

The one certainty for electoral outcomes is that victory by the incumbent means that few policy changes can be expected. On a sector-by-sector basis, however, differences probably are important. For example, for investments in the 1990s, Health Maintenance Organizations (HMOs) (which figure more prominently in Democrats' health plans) should do better than other health-care issues since Clinton plans to place caps on total health-care spending. Infrastructure stocks also should do better under Democrats than under Republicans. If the GOP had won, its promises of tax cuts would have benefited stocks over bonds, and lower inflation rates would help both stocks and bonds.

Tufte's (1978) area of interest was whether parties made a difference in employment and inflation. Several analyses do show differences between the parties on unemployment because placing a Democrat in the White House has resulted in lower unemployment rates (Hibbs, 1977; Kiewiet, 1984, p. 14; Sundquist, 1969). During periods of higher unemployment, voters have chosen Democratic congressional candidates and shunned Republicans when the GOP has held the presidency (Kiewiet, 1984, p. 14).

When inflation is the measure, Kiewiet (1984) found that from Eisenhower through Carter, the one discernible trend was an upward slope in inflation, which he felt was more likely to be the result of external dynamics than which party had control. He found it likely that Republicans would be, ceteris paribus, in favor of lower inflation. Since the 1980s, however, the record should show that under the GOP, inflation probably has been lower. Democrats yield about 2 percent more inflation, and a Republican administration results in less inflation but an increase in unemployment.

DISCUSSION QUESTIONS

1. Why is the way in which problems are perceived so important in the policy process?

2. What are the oldest continuing programs you can think of—programs that seem to be immortal?

3. What sorts of indicators can be used to assess how the voters are likely to react to economic conditions?

4. Can you think of any situations in which public opinion has been bimodal? Trimodal? How do party politicians react to them?

5. From an ethical, normative perspective, what do you think of a pressure-group system based on self-interest?

REFERENCES

Campbell, Angus, Phillip E. Converse, Warren E. Miller, and Donald E. Stokes. 1960, 1976. *The American Voter*, rev. ed. Chicago: University of Chicago Press

Downs, Anthony. 1957. *An Economic Theory of Democracy*. New York: Harper and Row.

Hibbs, Douglas A. 1977, December. "Political Parties and Macroeconomic Policy." *American Political Science Review*, 71, 1467–1487.

Johnson, David B. 1991. *Public Choice: An Introduction to the New Political Economy*. Mountain View, CA: Mayfield Publishing.

Jones, Charles O.(1977). *An Introduction to the Study of Public Policy*, 2nd ed. Belmont, CA: Duxbury.

Kiewiet, D. Roderick. 1984. *Macroeconomics and Micropolitics: The Electoral Effects of Economic Issues.* Chicago: University of Chicago Press.

Lowi, Theodore J. 1964, July. "American Business, Public Policy, Case Studies, and Political Theory," *World Politics*, 16, 677-715.

Lowi, Theodore J. 1979. *The End of Liberalism: The Second Republic of the United States*, 2nd ed. New York: Norton.

Manley, John F. 1983, June "Neo-Pluralism: A Class Analysis of Pluralism, I and Pluralism II." *American Political Science Review*, 77, 368-383.

Rae, Douglas W. 1971. *The Political Consequences of Electoral Laws*, rev. ed. New Haven, CT: Yale University Press.

Sniderman, Paul M., and Richard A. Brody. 1977, August. "Coping: The Ethic of Self-Reliance," *American Journal of Political Science*, 21, 501-521.

Sundquist, James L. 1969. *Politics and Policy: The Eisenhower, Kennedy, and Johnson Years.* Washington, DC: Brookings Institution.

Tufte, Edward R. 1978. *Political Control of the Economy.* Princeton, NJ: Princeton University Press.

Wilson, James Q., ed. 1980. *The Politics of Regulation.* New York: Basic Books.

CHAPTER SEVEN

THE THREE GREAT BRANCHES

The later stages of the policy life cycle fall largely under the jurisdiction of the formal institutions of government. After interest aggregation, the representation of views and the development of programmatic responses usually occur in the legislative arena; and so, too, do the complexities of legitimation, which occur through the dance of legislation. Statutory authorization requires money with which to achieve its goals, and examples abound of programs that, once authorized, have languished from lack of appropriations. The ways in which administrative arrangements are structured and policies are implemented are as important as the legislative process itself for the success of any programmatic goal. And in the United States, always a litigious society but never more so than now, nothing of importance goes far without incurring some sort of legal challenge. Adjudication has become part of the implementation phase. Program appraisal, beginning with benefit-cost analysis during the Kennedy administration and continuing through zero-based budgeting and "sunset" provisions, remains important today. Under Reaganomics, however, the belief spread that little that government does is ever cost effective. Even many liberals concurred, especially when they contemplated the effects of regulation. The evaluation process is as highly charged politically as any other facet of the policy process.

This chapter explores selected aspects of the three great branches of government as they relate to political economy. The guiding principle of American government is a preference for liberty over efficiency. Except for the exigencies of war and depression, there has been more of a concern with what government might do *to* people than of what it would do *for* them. The result is a diffusion of governmental power through the separation of powers and federalism. This distinction among legislative, executive, and judicial authorities further complicates the way policy is formulated and effectuated.

CONGRESS

Congress is paradoxical in American politics. On the one hand, legislatures are the central institution of democracy. At the time of the Revolution, opposition to British rule began in the colonial legislatures and was spearheaded by the Continental Congress. Later, to the framers of the Constitution, it was the House of Representatives, not the executive mansion, that was "the people's house." In nineteenth-century Europe, when democracy caught fire, it was the legislature that grew as the bulwark against monarchical tyranny. Today's irony, on the other hand, is that more people see Congress as the source of the problem with government than as the foundation for popular control. Conservative critics see Congress as a spendthrift and an unwanted meddler in the marketplace. Liberals, in contrast, criticize congressional parsimony in social programs or view Congress as controlled by big-business interests that are unconcerned with the problems of the average American.

Congress's role in the political economy has changed over time. The Constitution specifically assigned "all legislative powers" to it, specifically the powers to tax, spend, and borrow, to regulate commerce, to establish laws on bankruptcy, to coin money and regulate its value, and to foster creativity through patent laws and copyright protection. The requirement of a decennial census soon became a basis for economic self-study and ultimately developed into the valuable vehicle that it is for sales and marketing. Because of the *necessary and proper* clause of the Constitution, Congress was able to base a protective import tariff on the taxing power, create a national bank, and develop a system of roads and canals in the name of providing postal service. After the Civil War and especially during the 1930s, the *commerce clause* (Article I, Section 8, Clause 3) gave the national government the upper hand over the states in instituting economic regulation.

Its authority in economic policy-making can be seen in the functions that Congress performs. Under the lawmaking, or *legislative function*, the Senate and House of Representatives have an important role in policy-making on all kinds of topics—antitrust, regulation, money and banking, and all the rest. Because the framers of the Constitution envisioned Congress as a check on administrative tyranny, the *oversight function* has great potential utility. We see it when the chair of the Federal Reserve system, for example, appears twice yearly before the banking committees of the House and Senate. Hearings on appointments to regulatory bodies and other agencies, part of advise and consent or *executive* function, allow Congress to give cues about expected future behavior once the appointment is approved. The *casework function*, in which the member of Congress responds to dozens of constituent problems each week, provides avenues for help in dealing with the government and also helps members to become aware of programmatic or administrative shortcomings.

The place of Congress as a policy innovator has eroded over time. According to Whiggish notions of early America, the legislature had the primary duty of setting policy, whereas the executive was relegated to an administrative role. During the twentieth century, under the activist leadership of Theodore Roosevelt and Woodrow Wilson and culminating under Franklin Roosevelt, the expectation for innovation passed to the White House—an expectation that is ingrained now among both congressional Democrats and Republicans. In issue after issue, whether coping with the budget, dealing with recession, or reconsidering regulation, people as diverse as Senate Minority Leader Robert Dole (R–KS) and Speaker Thomas Foley (D–WA) conceive of Congress as a reactive body that must always await presidential initiative.

In evaluating Congress and its members it is important to understand that, as Richard Fenno (1975) has pointed out, Americans seem to love their representative but hate Congress because they use two different standards of judgment. As an institution, Congress is denigrated because of its reputed inability to legislate with dispatch or act with fiscal prudence—two often incompatible goals. When the focus is on policy-making, the public usually dislikes the slowness and compromising that it sees. Individual members of Congress, however, do quite well in bringing federal dollars back to the district and staying in touch with constituents. For the new breed of representative, each aided by an eighteen-member personal staff, access to air travel, television coverage, and abundant opportunities for claiming credit, favorable publicity is a constant goal. Thus, the reelection rates of individual members are about 98 percent, although the approval ratings of Congress as a whole are low.

Congress has always been an institution in change and has existed in three major organizational patterns since World War II. The first pattern, sometimes called the "textbook" Congress or the conservative coalition era, existed from the late 1940s until the early 1970s. It was made possible by the partisan configuration of the country at that time, with three one-party regions (the Republican Midwest and New England and the solid Democratic South) and a narrow Democratic majority in both chambers. When these factors were combined with the importance given to seniority, it

meant that committees in both chambers were chaired by elderly conservatives from south of the Mason-Dixon line whose districts contained few of
the tensions of twentieth-century life. This was the time of malapportionment, with House districts ranging from fewer than 150,000 people in the
smallest (and invariably rural) cases to 900,000 or more in places like mid-
town Manhattan or Detroit. This was the heyday of the conservative coalition
between Republicans and southern Democrats that had begun about 1937,
and the larger numbers of Republicans meant that whenever the coalition
came into play it usually won. And this was also the time when the "Old
Bulls" who chaired the standing committees could dominate them, bottling
up progressive legislation that never saw the light of day. Professional staffs
were small, partly because they increase knowledge, knowledge is power, and
the committee chairs were not about to share their power with anyone.
Policy leadership during this textbook period came from the executive
branch; but if an issue could attract the support of the leadership—at any
time a shifting group of about forty, which would include relevant committee chairs—congressional action could be guaranteed. Still, with norms of
behavior that discouraged junior members from meaningful participation, service in Congress could be suffocating.

Outcries by liberals in the mid-1960s ushered in a period of reform
called a "power earthquake" by Hedrick Smith (1988, p.20). The causes
included a "new breed" of member who was policy-oriented, had little previous party service or loyalty, and was drawn to public life by the turmoil of the
1960s—Vietnam War protests, environmentalism, and the civil rights and
women's movements. Changes in the rules of the House Democratic Caucus
began with a committee headed by Julia Butler Hansen (D–WA), and by
1975 they had culminated in the virtual end of secret "executive session"
committee meetings. Three senior members were turned out from their
committee chairs. There were changes in methods of budgeting, and the
apprenticeship norm that muffled young members had fallen away. But the
most important changes were the "subcommittee bill of rights." All committees were now required to have subcommittees, subcommittee jurisdiction
would be established by a vote of the full committee's members, subcommittee chairs would be elected by each panel, no one could chair more than a
single subcommittee, and professional staff members could be hired by both
party delegations on each subcommittee. Although these reforms were
hailed as democratization, power soon became diffused on Capitol Hill. It
seemed that everyone in a third term was a chair of something and enjoyed
significant staff support and control over some important piece of public
policy. In the words of Christopher Matthews (1960), a Democratic media
consultant, they were "all pumps, all guns." With the diffusion of power it
became nearly impossible for even as skillful a politician as Speaker "Tip"
O'Neill to lead the House.

By the late 1980s it was apparent that a return of discipline was needed to counterattack the Reagan administration. The result was the postreform period, which characterizes the House today. Signs of a tighter Congress abound: fewer bills (though longer ones) being sponsored by individual members and important legislation being bundled into "mega-bills," with single up-or-down votes on an entire package that allow members to avoid blame for any individual components, arguing that the benefits of the whole outweigh the costs of any single part. There are more noncontroversial commemorative resolutions for which members can claim credit. A newly empowered speakership also appeared with the brief tenure of Jim Wright (D–TX), although problems with the House's own "bank," with its post office, and with a series of ethics problems were a major embarrassment to Speaker Foley, whose own forte had been said to be his skill as a political manager. Just how distinguishable the postreform period will be from the period that preceded it is still to be seen.

These events leave us with a Congress that displays several characteristics that condition its role in policy-making. Some of these characteristics are organizational: the committee structure, the importance of professional staff, the new breed of member, and decentralization. Others, as we will see, are endemic in the way that Congress and its members behave.

The dominant organizational feature of American legislatures is the standing committee. Although no committee of Congress is without some sort of impact on the economy, some stand out above the crowd. The House Committee on Ways and Means and the Senate Finance Committee are at the forefront of fiscal policy, taxation, Social Security, and foreign trade. The appropriations committees of each chamber are responsible for apportioning money for specific programs, and the House and Senate budget committees created in 1974 are important for coordinating an overall plan of the federal budget. Occasionally, as in the summer of 1990, they break down and outside forces intervene in the budgetary process. Other committees rank just below these in importance. The Senate's Committee on Banking, Housing, and Urban Affairs (BH and UA), together with its House counterpart (Banking, Finance, & Urban Affairs) is important in monetary policy and in oversight of the Federal Reserve. The special role of the commerce clause during the New Deal thrust the Commerce Committee of the House into battle during the 1930s, and it was in the commerce committees of the House and Senate that the deregulation battles of the 1970s occurred. Other committees are important for specific sectors of the economy (agriculture, defense, labor, and transportation), for commerce (international trade and small business), and for particular regions of the country (the West and coastal areas).

The subcommittees of Congress have become even more important in policy formulation than the full committees. With the subcommittee bill of rights, the number of hearings held at the subcommittee level nearly tripled between 1955 and 1975, increasing from one in four to nearly three in four.

Bills are "marked up," or amended, in subcommittee, and full committees often do little more than pass bills along to the Rules Committee or to the full House. Coalitions are built at the subcommittee level, where bill managers emerge to play key roles on the House floor.

A distinctive feature that began a quarter of a century ago was the new type of member who was attracted to congressional life—the"new breed" of representative. These people had come of age politically during the turmoil of the 1960s. They were not beholden to party organization; were involved in the antiwar, antiracist, and antisexist protests of the time; had immediate policy goals; and were intrigued by the possibilities that television offered to the political process. They were important in the rules reforms of 1973 and 1975, and by the 1990s they had made their way to the center of power not only in the House but in the Senate as well. It is hard to overestimate how these politicians used staffs and other resources to make themselves electorally impregnable. It is also difficult to see how they and their successors can be easily guided by any group of congressional leaders, no matter how skillful.

The growth in professional staffs has also been striking. Numerical growth alone is impressive, as professional staffs have risen from a few dozen in 1900 to 6,000 in the mid-1960s to about 25,000 people today. They are divided among the personal staffs of members; committee staffs; staffs of the party leaders; and auxiliary agencies like the Congressional Budget Office, Congressional Research Service, General Accounting Office, Office of Technology Assessment, and even the Copyright Royalty Office. An expansion of staff can be justified by any organization, anytime, by using the argument that it will increase responsiveness. More capable staffs allow committees and members to multiply their individual efforts, and skilled analysts can supply more expertise than can the elected members themselves. The complexity of a modern economy contains intellectual nooks and crannies that the keenest of individuals will miss, and staff aides can become teachers to Congress. Critics on the right, however, like Richard Malbin (1980), counter that staff growth has been more pathological than palliative. Large staffs promote turf wars among those for whom they work and yield needless legislation. Simultaneously, individual staffers swell with hubris and wield authority that only elected members should have.

A final structural feature of congressional politics is its *regional* dimension. The self-selection of members to committees means that some of them are especially important to specific parts of the country, especially for products or industries that are associated with individual regions.

In addition to the structural attributes of Congress, there are behavioral ones as well—patterns in the way Congress does business that affect the policy-making process. *Incrementalism* is a characteristic of pluralism that results in policy-making by a series of small adjustments rather than through major, synoptic changes. It can be seen in substantive areas like antitrust, labor policy, and the environment, but it is especially recognizable in the budget and appropriations process that recurs annually. Still, Congress does infrequently become a caldron of activity. A clear example was the 63rd Congress (1913–1914) which yielded the Federal Reserve system, the Federal Trade Commission, the Clayton Act, and other progressive legislation. To a greater degree there was the 89th Congress (1965–1966) which enacted most of the Great Society programs of Lyndon Johnson. And the leading case is the 73rd Congress (1933–1934) which produced the First Hundred Days legislation of the New Deal. Other Congresses occupy a slightly lower level of activity— the 51st Congress, which passed the Sherman Act in 1890, and the Republican revisions to the New Deal by the 80th Congress (1947–1948). These periods of congressional activism were brought about by deviating elections, such as that of 1912; realigning elections, such as the one in 1932; or simply by a landslide for or against a particular party, such as that against Goldwater in 1964.

Subcommittee government and the policy entrepreneurship of individual members are associated with a second feature of congressional behavior —*subgovernments*. Subcommittees, the executive branch agencies with which they interact, and the interest groups of the private sector that constitute their clients are "iron triangles," "cozy triangles," "policy whirlpools," or other venue where, many assert, policy is really made.

A third behavioral characteristic of congressional life is *vote trading*, or logrolling. Legislatures are social institutions where members seek to gain an advantage for causes they strongly support by backing the programs of others. It is a normal response—I'll vote for your provision on labor regulation if you will support mine on small business. When this trading occurs, bills can have unclear and even contradictory provisions.

The lack of clarity or the internal contradictions of legislation based on vote trading have important policy considerations. Fuzziness in statutory language or internal contradictions give administrators and judges as much authority to act as they are willing to take. The Sherman Act, for example, was interpreted as authorizing the government to act more vigorously against labor organizations than against business monopolies in the restraint of trade.

The growth of subcommittee government, the rise of professional staffs, regionalism, and the entrepreneurial tendencies of the modern representative, all interact to yield the decentralization of Congress. When combined with behavioral characteristics like incrementalism, subgovernments, and logrolling, it is no wonder that Congress, in its dance of legislation, is not particularly quick on its 1,070 feet.

THE INSTITUTIONALIZED PRESIDENCY

Presidents and presidencies are invariably drawn into economic issues. As candidates, presidents promise to get America moving again, to put a chicken in every pot, or to guarantee a full dinner pail. During the 1992 campaign, George Bush discerned soon after the Republican National Convention that "family values" were far less important than economic proposals, and with a new White House staff under former Secretary of State James A. Baker, changed his messages accordingly. Economic news is monitored closely in the White House because presidents are more punished by downturns than rewarded by upticks. And because Americans vote their pocketbooks, it is axiomatic that the incumbent party in the White House will be retained by prosperity (as was Bush in 1988) but defeated by poor economic performance (as were Carter in 1980, Hoover in 1932, and Bush in 1992). The effect that the economy has on presidents is a function of four items: (1) their personal interests and capacities, (2) the circumstances of their time in office, (3) the abilities of their economic aides, and (4) their ability to work with Congress.

Consider the president's professional interests in the economy. Although most presidents are interested in economic policy, they differ in their commitment to detail or in the time that they can commit to it at the personal level, as Lance LeLoup (1986) has pointed out. The federal budget provides a major vehicle for intervention in the economy, and Harry Truman said that it should be required reading for all Americans. Truman himself was as good as his word, and only he and Gerald Ford truly poured over each of the budgets that were formulated during their terms of office, perhaps, LeLoup suggests, because of their previous personal experiences in Congress. Kennedy and Nixon expressed concern with budgetary construction as well, but after the first budgetary iteration their personal involvement waned; budgets had not been the forte of either president when he served in Congress. Ronald Reagan gave few directives to his subordinates. Those recruited to the administration seemed to understand intuitively his policy orientation and to act accordingly, at least before 1985. There is no better testament to George Bush's emphasis on foreign affairs than his delegation of the crucial 1990 budget process to Darman, Brady, and Sununu while he concentrated on relations with the Soviet Union and on the Persian Gulf.

The conditions that confront presidents may not be of their own making but can rise up to confound or delight them. In a market-based system like that of the United States, unlike the managed economies of Europe, the economy is less easily controlled by government in the short run. Some presidents, like Coolidge, led charmed lives in that the bad economic news arrived after they had stepped down. When the economy failed to rebound after the recession of 1990, it was said that Bush was lucky during his first year and a half of office, and that his luck had run out.

It is the organizational help available that identifies the modern, institutionalized presidency. At the apex of the executive branch of government are several organizations that since 1939 have made up the Executive Office. All exert some influence on economic policy-making, but four are particularly important—the Office of Management and Budget, the Council of Economic Advisers, the Office of the U.S. Trade Representative, and the personal counsel available in the White House. Although none of these organizations directly administers any program that affects economic life, each exerts power indirectly by influencing the presidential direction of departmental bureaus and independent agencies or by reviewing regulatory agency decisions.

The Office of Management and Budget (OMB) is the strongest vehicle of presidential leadership in the arena of economic policy because of its power over the preparation and administration of the federal budget. Money is power, and governmental agencies controlled their own destinies until World War I because they drafted and sent to Congress their own budgetary requests independent of presidential control. Then, in 1921, the Bureau of the Budget (BOB) was created to centralize the budget-making process. By the mid-1930s, Franklin Roosevelt added "central clearance" to the agency's responsibilities, which meant that any bill for substantive legislation originating in the executive branch had to be routed through the BOB and circulated among those departments that might be affected by it. Authority for controlling rates of expenditure by agencies and a name change to the Office of Management and Budget were added in 1970.

The selection of a director for the OMB is the president's most important economic appointment. Directors were regarded as so integral a part of the presidency that they were exempted from senatorial advise and consent until 1974, when the many disagreements between Nixon and Congress, including actions by OMB Director Roy Ash, ended that arrangement. A number of directors have been especially close to the president they serve; even after his departure from the Carter administration, former Director Bert Lance tried to convince the president not to appoint Paul Volcker as chair of the Federal Reserve. One who was not especially close was David Stockman, a young congressman from Michigan who was brought into the Reagan administration because of his keen interest in reducing expenditures. Stockman was prominent in Reaganomics until he was quoted as harboring extreme doubts about it in an article by William Greider (1981). Although he was supposedly absolved by President Reagan after having been "taken to the woodshed," Stockman was unable to regain his early status and was not retained for the second term. During the Bush administration, Richard Darman was at the forefront of the president's economic policies.

The Council of Economic Advisers (CEA) was created by the Employment Act of 1946, which added the role of manager of the economy to the list of presidential jobs. The chair is always the most visible member of the three-person council since its inception. A survey of the 48 advisers who had served through 1991 shows that while both parties tend to draw their advisers from academia, Democratic presidents also draw from labor, and Republicans are more likely to tap those from major corporations and banking. The council carries a certain immunity from accusations of partisanship because it is charged with representing the state of the art in economic knowledge. For this reason, it was the CEA chair in 1990, albeit often with the support of the White House chief of staff, who articulated the Bush administration's criticism of the tight money policy of the Federal Reserve. Arguably, the CEA's indicators gave better early warning of an economic downturn than did the readings of the Federal Reserve's own economists.

The Office of U.S. Trade Representative is an outgrowth of increases in world trade after World War II. After enactment of the Reciprocal Trade Agreements Act of 1934, the Department of State was empowered to negotiate bilaterally with other nations for trade concessions. Although protectionist sentiments critical of the department's bargaining sagacity surfaced in Congress every few years when the program was reauthorized, a commitment to freer trade guided American foreign economic policy into the postwar years. The Trade Expansion Act of 1962, which was the first major legislative victory of the Kennedy administration, relocated the bargaining agency within the Executive Office, and empowered an ambassadorial-rank special representative to negotiate multilaterally with the European Common Market. Eight rounds of trade negotiations, each taking place over several years, had occurred through 1990. Although world tariff levels once were the major obstacles to trade, their reduction has resulted in an array of more subtle trade barriers. When Elizabeth Dole resigned as secretary of labor in 1990, the U.S. Trade Representative, Carla Hills, became the highest-ranking woman in the Bush administration.

The Executive Office itself is an important source of guidance for presidents, who have always had a personal secretary and a small staff of intimate advisers. Meriwether Lewis, the explorer, served in this capacity for Thomas Jefferson, just as "Colonel" Edward House did for Wilson a century later and as Raymond Moley did for Franklin Roosevelt. But it was not until 1939, pursuant to the recommendation of a blue ribbon commission on public administration, that an actual White House office was created. Designed to be the president's personal counselors on the fullest range of issues, they can themselves become important policy-makers. John Sununu, White House chief of staff for Bush and a former governor of New Hampshire, emerged in 1990 as one of the most significant economic decision makers in Washington because of his control over access to the Oval Office.

DEPARTMENTS AND ADMINISTRATIVE AGENCIES

The fourteen cabinet-level departments encompass a wide array of economic activity. Cabinet status really denotes two things: (1) a collection of agencies concerned with a particular function or policy area and (2) policies that by their nature are more susceptible to presidential and partisan direction. In contrast with European-style parliamentary systems, the cabinet has no basis in either the Constitution or in statute law. Presidents do work closely with individual secretaries, and the cabinet does meet collectively periodically; but it has no collective governing role, as it does in parliamentary systems. The bureau is the building block of departments, and the proportion of departmental activity that is primarily regulatory, as opposed to administrative, shows considerable range.

As with congressional committees, it is also impossible to find any cabinet department that is devoid of economic impact. Five of them play especially important roles, however, although the Departments of Education and State may be the most limited in their effect.

The "independence" of each of the sixty independent establishments and government corporations derives from the fact that they are organized outside of the fourteen cabinet-level departments. Some of them, like the Federal Reserve system, are relatively autonomous from White House influence. The Central Intelligence Agency (CIA) and the Environmental Protection Agency (EPA), however, are as closely directed by the president as any of the cabinet departments. In each case, an institutional history informs the way that the organization reacts to presidential directions.

Independent agencies, which exercise a combination of legislative, executive, and judicial functions, are at variance with the principle of separation of powers. Independent Regulatory Commissions (IRCs) may exercise the legislative function only in a narrow sense, for they are empowered to issue rules only within an area of authority specifically delegated to them by Congress. They can be headed by a single administrator or by a plural board or commission that ranges from two members to eleven; and they can be divided into those that are primarily administrative in nature or those that have some degree of regulatory authority.

The EPA is the only single-headed regulatory agency, which calls attention to the centrality of the independent board or commission in American regulatory policy. The Interstate Commerce Commission (ICC) has been the model for more than a dozen of regulatory authorities. Some of them, like the Federal Reserve, Federal Trade Commission (FTC), and Securities and Exchange Commission (SEC), continue today in basically their original forms. Others, like the Federal Water Commission of 1920 and Federal Radio Commission of 1927, were replaced by the Federal Power Commission and the Federal Communications Commission (FCC), respectively. In all of the years since 1887, the only example of an IRC that has truly disappeared is the Civil Aeronautics Board.

There are several lessons about the ability of presidents to influence the economy either positively or negatively. First, they vary widely in their interests and probably, too, in their talents. Most are attracted to other realms of policy. Second, economic policy is effectuated more by the institutionalized presi*dency* than by any personal presi*dent.* Third, institutionalized presidencies are often factionalized. Internecine warfare characterized Reagan's second administration, whereas there was far more homogeneity in the Nixon White House. It is a common mistake to assume that presidencies, or any organization, are a cohesive band of friends dutifully engaged in a common cause. The Reagan White House was characterized by infighting and warring factions. Leaks to the press were carefully planned for personal advantage. Although there were friendships (e.g., Baker, Darman, Stockman, and Craig Fuller), the White House was fraught with warring personalities. It was a place for forming alliances, not for forming friendships (Noonan, 1990). Fourth, presidents lack the ability to control those who work for them in the great bureaucracy beyond the White House, whether within the executive branch directly or within the structure of independent regulatory commissions. Domestic economic policy is often superseded by international crisis. Finally, although the executive branch is stronger in foreign policy, it deals from a much weaker position in the realm of economic policy.

DIVIDED GOVERNMENT

One of the distinctive features of post-World War II American politics is divided government—that clumsy condition in which a Republican president confronts a Democratic Congress. This situation is not unprecedented, for in the Congresses elected between 1860 and 1944 (37th through 79th), there were a Democratic House of Representatives and a Republican president in one-fourth of all Republican presidential terms, that is, for fourteen years out of fifty-six. And during the thirty-two years that the Democrats held the White House there were Republican House majorities for four years— the last two years of the Cleveland and Wilson administrations. Conversely, in thirty-four out of the forty-three Congresses, the party of the president and the House were the same. Since the end of Eisenhower's first two years, however, no Republican president has enjoyed a Republican House, although Reagan did have a GOP-controlled Senate from 1981 through 1987. Thus for six years of Eisenhower, eight years of Nixon-Ford, eight years of Reagan, and four years of Bush, the House (and usually the Senate) was in Democratic hands. Neither the Kennedy-Johnson nor the Carter administrations confronted Republican Congresses.

The fact of divided government begs two questions: Why do we have it, and what are its consequences? Two reasons for divided government that

Republicans often propose are the gerrymandering hypothesis (that Democrats in statehouses draw district boundaries to harm GOP chances) and the advantage of congressional incumbency (that Democrats controlled the House just as professional staffs became such a factor in enhancing reelection). Democrats, for their part, focus their views on their party's inability to regain the White House. They argue either that their party has nominated candidates who have been inept at campaigning or that antiblack sentiment in the wake of the Civil Rights Act of 1964 and the Voting Rights Act of 1965 has kept their candidates from competing effectively in the South.

A different response is that the "type D" voter did it! Envision a voter, perhaps a Democrat, who votes for Democrats for both president and Congress. Or imagine a Republican voter who chooses the GOP candidates for both Congress and president. Neither of them is responsible for divided government, for an electorate made up of people like them would yield executive and legislative branches of government in the same partisan hands. Nor is the person who votes Republican for Congress and Democrat for president responsible for divided government, simply because there have been no such conjunctures since Harry Truman and the 80th Congress nearly fifty years ago. Instead, it is the type D voter—the person who votes Democrat for Congress and Republican for president—who is responsible. There are two kinds of these voters (see Figure 7-1).

One sort are Democrats who vote Republican for president because they do not approve of their party's own candidates. Republicans defeated McGovern, Carter, Mondale, and Dukakis because their candidates were perceived as stronger on national defense or because the Democrats were painted as overly receptive to the liberal claims of minorities and women. The second sort of type D voter is the Republican who crosses over, perhaps only once in any election, to vote for a Democrat for Congress, perhaps because of the casework function. National election surveys suggest that perhaps 10 percent of Republican voters have had some sort of positive experience with their representative in responding to a constituent concern, perhaps a business problem or assistance with a tardy pension check. Alternatively, the incumbent Democrat may be favored because the Republican candidate is distressingly weak. The incumbency advantage can be so great that it dissuades strong Republican challengers.

What are the consequences of divided government? To someone familiar with parliamentary government it seems clear: There is an inability to govern, a "deadlock of democracy" that goes beyond interbranch rivalry alone. The failure of the legislative assembly, whether of the British, Israeli, or other form, to support the decisions of the executive cabinet in a parliamentary system results in resignations of the government, and thus either in new elections or in the appointment of a new government that will have the confidence of the legislature. In the United States, divided government

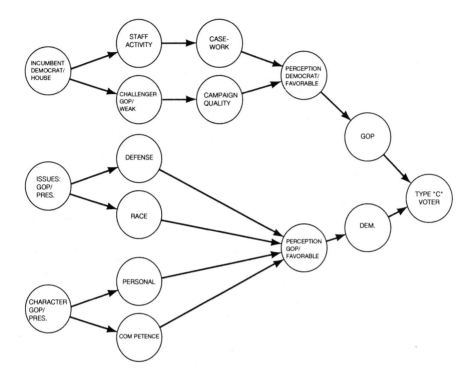

Figure 7-1.

results in finger pointing and name-calling between Republicans in the White House and Democrats in Congress. Nevertheless, to the extent that government appears conflictive and uncoordinated, it all plays into the minimalist preferences that the American political culture prefers.

THE COURTS

In no other country are the courts stronger politically than in the United States. At various times the U.S. Supreme Court has been a very important authority in determining economic policy—labor, antitrust, regulation, taxation, and even monetary policy. This was the case especially between 1882 and 1937.

Judicial power emanates from three functions that courts perform. First, they *settle disputes.* Economic life spawns countless conflicts: product liability suits between consumers and suppliers, contract cases over failure to fulfill obligations, civil actions under antitrust law, criminal cases like insider trading—the list is long.

American courts are particularly strong because of their power of *judicial review*—the ability of a court to invalidate a statute or governmental action because it is not in accordance with the Constitution. But of over 140 federal statutes found unconstitutional, it was not until the era of the Civil War that decisions involving economic power began to appear. In some cases, the Supreme Court upheld federal action—legitimizing Congress's power to tax state bank notes out of existence (*Veazie Bank* v. *Fenno*, 1869) or the right of the federal government to issue paper currency (*Second Legal Tender* cases, 1871). In others, federal action was struck down. And although the Supreme Court drew fire for finding unconstitutional federal regulatory activity on many occasions, the greatest storm of protest probably arose when thirteen pieces of New Deal legislation were ruled unconstitutional between 1935 and 1937. In the wake of that controversy, Roosevelt's threat to enlarge the Court and pack it with friendlier justices, and the rapid turnover in the Court's membership, the federal judiciary has never since used judicial review to overturn federal economic regulation. But even though economic issues have been moved aside by issues like civil rights, they remain important. Justice John Paul Stevens was elevated to the Court partly because of his recognized expertise in antitrust law.

Justice Oliver Wendell Holmes, Jr., once said that the Republic would not fall if the Supreme Court lost its ability to overturn federal legislation, but it would surely fail if it lost its ability to review the work of state legislative institutions. It is at the state level that the Court has long exercised its greatest economic power. As early as 1796 it invalidated a Virginia statute canceling debts owed to English merchants as a violation of a federal treaty (*Ware* v. *Hylton*). During the years between roughly 1877 and 1890, the Court changed from permissiveness toward state regulatory activity in *Munn* v. *Illinois* to a position that seemed to make regulation nearly impossible by either the states or the federal government. The Court developed whole areas of law involving contractual obligations, interstate commerce, banking, taxation, property rights, labor-management relations, and economic regulation by overturning *state* statutes, not federal ones.

The third judicial function, *interpreting statute law*, offers the greatest opportunity for intervention in economic life today. Statutes are often worded imprecisely because of the compromises needed to enact them in a pluralistic Congress or because events continue to evolve after the laws have been passed. Thus, despite the congressional intent not to equate labor organizations with business monopolies in defining restraint of trade, the Sherman Antitrust Act was used against striking workers in 1894, five years before it was successfully used against a business combination. Legislation has come to include sections that specify definitions, exceptions, provisos, and saving clauses in order to minimize judicial creativity. Still it is ultimately left to judges to define such things as the meaning of *market* in monopoly cases.

The adjudicatory structure of the federal government has three major components. At the core are the regular, constitutional courts organized pursuant to Article III of the Constitution. The 91 U.S. district courts are trial courts, or courts of original jurisdiction, complete with a judge, 12-person jury (often waived in complicated business cases), and witnesses called by the plaintiff or respondent (or prosecution and defense in criminal law cases). From two to twenty-seven judges are assigned to each district court. Above this level are thirteen U.S. courts of appeals—eleven appeals districts, an appeals court for the District of Columbia, and since 1982 a U.S. Court of Appeals for the Federal Circuit. There are 168 appellate judges. And atop it all is the Supreme Court.

A separate set of special, legislative courts has been created by Congress over the years pursuant to some very specific legislative functions. The taxation and tariff-raising function, for example, can produce such unique specialized questions that specialized tax courts and customs courts were created. Settling the obligations of the government gave rise to the Court of Claims. There is also a Court of Military Appeals associated with the Uniform Code of Military Justice. There is a separate route for appeals from each of these courts.

Another vital part of the adjudicative process is the extensive system of administrative law judges, or ALJs. Nearly 1,200 judges, once called hearing examiners, are scattered throughout the federal government, although about 750 are assigned to the Social Security administration alone. Recruited and overseen by the Office of Personnel Management, they preside over cases just below the board level in agencies like the FTC.

A number of characteristics distinguish judicial decision making. First, courts must wait for cases to be brought to them because adjudication is *reactive*. The judiciary can act only after a plaintiff or prosecutor has first filed a motion. Adjudication is *adversarial*, which means that unlike legislators who might select from a continuum of possible remedies, courts are restricted to *dichotomous choice*—to find for the prosecution or for the defense. (Settlements often do include compromises between the litigants.) A striking feature of judicial involvement with the economy can be its *conservatism*. This aspect has been significant in labor cases when those from upper socioeconomic levels sat on the bench. The principle of *stare decisis*, or of precedent, minimizes decision making by judicial whim. In the absence of statutory redirection, however, it leads to a resistance to change. As the American economy developed, those with the ear of the courts could suppress emerging economic interests, as seen in the use of hoary conspiracy doctrines against organized labor for more than a century, the application of substantive due process of law after ratification of the Fourteenth Amendment, and the adherence to simplistic notions of separation of powers during the 1930s.

The importance of reactivity, dichotomous choice, conservatism, and stare decisis all suggest that it should take longer to alter public policy through judicial rather than legislative or presidential action. But does it? The Supreme Court completely reversed itself on state regulatory power between the *Munn* case in 1877 and the *San Mateo* rate case of 1882, as well as on the unconstitutionality of the income tax between 1870 and 1894. The speed with which it moved compares favorably with the many years that were required by Congress to recognize market problems in the 1880s but not to provide a creditable response until the Clayton and FTC acts in 1914.

Although judicial activity after 1937 shifted away from conflicts over regulation, actions in civil rights and environmental law have allowed it to continue to exert an economic impact. Judges have been criticized as being unconcerned with the costs that flow from their decisions. During the Ford administration, attempts were begun to estimate the costs of proposed administrative regulations. The exponential nature of cost curves associated with reducing pollution or accommodating the handicapped have been cited as particular ways in which the federal judiciary intrudes in the daily life of American business.

The judiciary, despite its considerable authority, remains the weakest of the three great branches in economic matters. Weak, however, does not mean powerless. Unsustained by other political institutions, it cannot win against public opinion in the long run, as demonstrated in 1937. At the same time, the opposition that the courts mounted to organized labor, economic regulation, and antitrust law was long successful because the judicial branch enjoyed the support of public authorities, both major political parties, and typically the clergy and the press.

SYNTHESIS

Involvement of the three branches of government in the several types of economic policy varies. A simplified view of the separation of powers would expect the legislature to be the sole policymaker, the executive branch to have control over policy application, and the judiciary to be limited to settling factual or legal disputes that might arise. In fact, all three branches are involved in each governmental function. Congress has always dabbled in administrative minutiae through its oversight function, but the growth of the legislative veto after 1930 and White House complaints about congressional efforts to micromanage programs suggest that legislative activities often extend into the administrative process. And if policy-making ever was the exclusive purview of Congress, the presidency has long since evolved a policy-setting role of its own, especially since 1946. The federal judiciary, although less involved in economic policy-making than it was before 1937, remains an occasional and important economic decision maker.

DISCUSSION QUESTIONS

1. Why do Americans love their representatives but hate Congress? How does this love-hate relationship affect economic policy?

2. What does it mean to say that Congress is caught between centralizing and decentralizing forces?

3. Why are there so many committees and subcommittees in Congress? How do they affect the policy-making process?

4. The level of presidential attention to economic issues varies considerably within a single administration. Why?

5. How uniform, or homogeneous, is the economic advice that presidents receive from their advisers? Is this uniformity helpful or harmful to the president?

6. What were the framers' expectations about the role courts would play in the new nation? About how courts would influence economic policy?

7. How is judicial decision making different from the habits that guide the legislative process?

REFERENCES

Abraham, Henry J. 1986. *The Judicial Process,* 5th ed.; New York: Oxford University Press.

Fenno, Richard F., Jr. 1975. "If, as Ralph Nader Says, Congress Is the Broken Branch, How Come We Love Our Congressmen So Much?" In Norman J. Ornstein, ed. *Congress in Change: Evolution and Reform.* New York: Praeger.

Greider, William. 1981, December. "The Education of David Stockman" *The Atlantic,* 248, 27–54.

LeLoup, Lance T. 1986. *Budgetary Politics,* 3rd ed.; Brunswick, OH: King's Court Communications.

Malbin, Michael J. 1980. *Unelected Representatives: Congressional Staff and the Future of Representative Government.* New York: Basic Books.

Matthews, Donald R. 1960. *U.S. Senators and their World.* New York: Vintage Books.

Noonan, Peggy. 1990. *What I Saw at the Revolution: A Political Life in the Reagan Era.* New York: Random House.

Smith, Hedrick. 1988. *The Power Game: How Washington Works.* New York: Random House.

CHAPTER EIGHT

GOVERNMENTAL FUNCTIONS: SUPPORTIVE, REGULATORY, MANAGERIAL, AND ENTREPRENEURIAL

Thirty years ago, when political science was in the throes of the behavioral movement, a number of writers wanted to identify the core functions that government performs. Gabriel Almond (1960), writing as a structural-functionalist, isolated three output functions (rule making, rule application, and rule adjudication) and four input functions (political socialization, interest articulation, interest aggregation, and political communication). At about the same time, Theodore Lowi (1964) wrote that three functions subsumed all governmental policy, and his triumvirate of distributive, redistributive, and regulatory functions has proven to be valuable. James Q. Wilson (1980, pp. 367–372) has based his functional paradigm on how many people (or how few) actually bear the costs of public programs and how many benefit from them. His categories are distributive, entrepreneurial, client, and interest-group policies. Others, too, have written about the essence of governmental activity, but when it comes to economic policy, perhaps there are four special functions. This chapter considers three of them: supportive, entrepreneurial, and regulatory activities. A fourth function, managing the economy, is the common theme of the two chapters that follow.

THE SUPPORTIVE FUNCTION

One of Adam Smith's lessons was that economies do best when unfettered by government. Similarly, James Madison's political legacy includes the insight that the essence of constitutionalism is not a government's ability to control the governed but rather a government's obligation to control itself. Thus, a system known for limiting itself and for ensuring civil liberties contributes to a well-being and fosters a freedom of movement and communication that are crucial for markets. The constitutional guarantee for property rights is obviously important for a capitalist economy. A disturbing consequence of the war on drugs is the federal power to seize the property of suspected drug dealers when there is probable cause to believe that it is associated with an illicit transaction. Drug agents make mistakes, however. The property owner may never be charged with a crime; but his only recourse in redeeming the goods is through a civil action, where the burden of proving one's innocence falls on the person whose goods were confiscated.

The government acts positively to assist private action. Woven into the constitutional fabric is Smith's notion of fostering creativity, and 97,000 patents and 64,000 trademarks were issued in 1990. The value of maintaining public order, enforcing contractual obligations, and providing a stable medium of exchange becomes readily apparent to anyone who contemplates the sorry conditions in the former Soviet Union or the utter anarchy in what was once Yugoslavia. The inestimable value of all this activity is usually forgotten by those who denigrate the public sector.

The federal government offers a plethora of specific, targeted supportive programs. Some are directed at two traditional soft spots in the economy, farming and maritime shipping. The U.S. Department of Agriculture's (USDA) Farmers Home Administration provides low-cost loans for farm operations and rural housing. Money is available for the development of businesses in rural areas and cities of fewer than 50,000 people. Price support programs by the USDA for a wide range of commodities, a legacy of the New Deal, guarantee farmers a minimum price for their produce. The Maritime Administration of the Department of Transportation arranges subsidies to overcome the cost differential between goods carried in American ships and in foreign carriers. It also subsidizes construction in U.S. shipyards. Many supportive programs that originated during the Great Society are aimed at serving disadvantaged people—particularly ethnic minorities and women—rather than industrial sectors. Under the 1965 Economic Development Act, for example, loan guarantees are designed to help firms raise funds to expand their operations in depressed inner cities. Other supportive programs are attuned to expanding certain types of preferred activity. Exporting is targeted by programs from the Commerce Department and the Small Business Administration. The National Aeronautics and Space Administration (NASA) has long advertised the spinoffs to industry from the high-technology research that it sponsors. The Small Business Administration exists in the realization that it has been the small firm that has created jobs during the last decade, at a time when employment at Fortune 500 firms has shrunk by 800,000 jobs.

THE ENTREPRENEURIAL FUNCTION

Entrepreneurs are risk-takers—individuals whose fortitude and willingness to bet on their ideas, sometimes with second mortgages on their homes as collateral, are the driving force behind a private enterprise economy. By extension, the entrepreneurial function of government consists of competing in the market, just as would any private firm. Since public ownership or control of the means of production and distribution is Joseph Schumpeter's classic definition of socialism, however, and since socialism is negatively charged in the American political culture, there is an ideological bias against public enterprise in the United States. But opposition to the government's presence in the private sector comes from a more practical reason than mere ideology. No one in business welcomes competition from a government agency which is able to compete because it is supported by one's own tax dollars.

When it does exist, governmental entrepreneurship in the United States is justified on four grounds. First, there may be essential services that the private sector cannot supply because the start-up costs are too great or the potential market is so diffuse that revenues cannot recover capital costs. The construction of hydroelectric dams early in this century illustrates the former problem, and creating the Rural Electrification Administration (REA) to deliver electric power to remote farms typifies the latter.

Second, the government often acts as a business in cases of natural monopoly, for example, its ownership of public utilities. East of the Mississippi, the government usually regulates only investor-owned utilities through a public utilities commission. In the West, however, and especially where the vestiges of populism and progressivism linger on, there is a greater likelihood of public ownership. The extreme case is in Nebraska, otherwise a conservative area. In the home state of William Jennings Bryan, the 1896 populist Democratic presidential nominee, and also of U.S. Senator George Norris (the father of the Tennessee Valley Authority), all electricity is generated by publicly owned utility companies. When asked if this isn't socialistic, most Nebraskans will answer no. Their electric rates are cheaper, they say; and anything that's cheaper is better; and anything that's better can't possibly be socialist!

A third reason for governmental ownership is to offer an alternative source of supply in a market without workable competition. Municipally owned gasoline stations, offering gasoline at a fair value, can reduce the higher prices charged by oligopoly or monopoly pricing in the local market. Similarly, the rates charged by community-owned public utilities can serve as a yardstick by which to gauge the prices of private utilities. Grain elevators in North Dakota have been state owned to prevent price gouging by private owners.

A fourth reason for government ownership is to control the sale of potentially harmful products, particularly liquor. Many of the states that exercise state liquor monopolies are along the Canadian border, where the practice dates from the end of Prohibition. Such stores are reliable sources of revenue and patronage-based employment, and they probably suffer far fewer robberies than do private liquor stores.

This entrepreneurial function has been more evident at the state level than nationally, but the Consolidated Rail Corporation (ConRail) between 1973 and 1985 and AmTrak since 1970 are useful examples of direct federal action in business. Both are for-profit corporations rather than governmental agencies. ConRail was created by the Regional Rail Reorganization Act out of the bankrupt ruins of the PennCentral and other railroads. When, after astute management, this public enterprise began to be profitable in the early 1980s, the privatization component of Reaganomics argued for its sale. After an attempt to offer it to Norfolk Southern was foiled on grounds that monopoly problems would ensue in several Great Lakes states, ConRail was allowed to exist as a purely private corporation, as it is now. AmTrak, which provides most of the noncommuter rail passenger service in the United States, remains as a reasonably successful enterprise operating in a difficult market area.

THE REGULATORY FUNCTION

Regulation is difficult to define. As an *activity*, it is any attempt by the government to bring about changed behavior by transferring some degree of private-sector discretion to public control. In the way that it is *administered*, it can be self-executory (when regulations rely on private initiative for their application) or bureaucratic (when a governmental agency is used to apply them). *Legalistically*, it is as any process governed by the regulatory provisions of the Administrative Procedures Act of 1946 and its amendments. As an effect, regulation involves the application of sanctions to discourage undesirable conduct.

Students of public administration often distinguish between two varieties of regulation. One is *economic*, or "traditional," regulation which intervenes in the private sector on an industry-by-industry basis and sets rates that can be charged by firms, outlaws predatory competition, or divides markets that will be served by competing firms. The other is *protective*, or "new," regulation, which often cuts across industries and is especially concerned with public health and safety and with the environment. There are many examples of new-style regulation that date from the 1900s, however. During the deregulation movement of the past two decades, it has been primarily traditional, economic regulation that has been the target of reformers, although protective regulation has suffered from reduced appropriations.

Regulatory activity varies widely in its intensity. At the high end of the scale are functions that truly allocate values authoritatively. Regulators can establish rates that firms charge for services, decide whether a nuclear plant will operate, or set the monetary policy of the country. At the other end are the more limited activities—merely granting operating certificates to those who meet the most minimal of standards, announcing advisory standards to industry, or passing along information to consumers.

Because of the problems in defining regulation, it is difficult to know just how many regulatory agencies there are. The General Accounting Office (GAO), an arm of Congress, reported in 1978 that there were 116 federal regulatory agencies: (1) those that were predominately regulatory; (2) those that were regulatory but with important program responsibilities, (3) those with only a small proportion of employees in regulatory functions, and (4) those that were only investigatory or that had some power to establish standards. In its survey of federal regulations, *Congressional Quarterly* identified 107—thirteen "major" regulatory agencies (3 of which are located within cabinet-level departments) and 94 lesser ones. The Center for Study of American Business, in contrast, has identified only 54 federal regulatory agencies.

REASONS FOR REGULATING

If there are a hundred regulatory agencies, there are far more reasons for regulating. Many of them emanate from perceived deficiencies in the marketplace, that is, from more purely economic considerations.

> **(1.) Too little competition.** According to economic theory, excess demand for any product or process will stimulate new competitors to enter the marketplace. Occasionally there are barriers to market entry, such as the need for vast amounts of capital or expertise, that can result in a single supplier. Monopoly can also result from predatory practices that make it impossible for competitors to enter the marketplace—something that the FTC was created to oversee. Antimonopoly policy can be seen as regulation and is practiced either by breaking up the monopolist firm or, in the case of a public utility or "natural monopoly," intensively regulating it.

(2.) Too much competition. One of the complaints of the Great Depression was that too many firms were competing for customers' dollars in transportation, mining, oil production, and even in retail trade and other services. The National Recovery Act's (NRA) code authorities sought to remedy this cutthroat competition by waiving the antitrust laws to allow competitors to agree not to sell their products at a price below a certain level, but these were found unconstitutional in the *Schechter* case (1935). The problems of excessive competition are left to managers and investors in the private sector today, except in agriculture, where governmental programs seek to raise farmers' selling prices by lowering their production.

(3.) False advertising and misleading information. Market decisions hinge on information concerning what is being bought and sold. *Fin de siècle* newspaper advertisements touted cures for everything from hair loss to cancer, but all too often the "cure" was only a concoction of crude oil and alcohol. Misleading claims for manufactured products can gain the attention of the FTC, and misrepresentation in the securities market falls under the purview of the SEC.

(4.) Externalities. Market transactions between a buyer and seller may fail to reflect the important interests of third parties. For example, in environmental policy the price of electric power fails to reflect the environmental costs of air pollution or acid rain. The expression "the tragedy of the commons" was popularized by Garrett Hardin (1968), who used it to illustrate the net loss to society from farmers' attempts to profit by overgrazing their sheep on the village green (or commons), thereby ruining it for all.

(5.) Market instability. Market instability is endemic in the petroleum and coal industries and is a reason for the regulatory activity of the Federal Power Commission. Occasionally instability extends to the entire economy in a recession, and taking the volatility out of the nation's money supply was why the Federal Reserve system was created in 1913.

(6.) Unserved private needs. The unavailability of transportation services—of trucks, buses, and airlines—to out-of-the-way communities is one of the reasons for regulation during the 1930s. In return for receiving the lucrative certificates of public convenience and necessity that allowed them to serve major population centers, the ICC required truckers to provide services to small towns, too. This was a trade-off, or a system of cross-subsidization. In housing, the lack of mortgage money prompted the government to structure a system of federally chartered savings and loan associations (S & Ls) that were allowed to pay higher rates of interest on deposits to attract money that could be loaned out to promote home ownership. These S&Ls were not allowed to make loans in the business sector, however, and that more technical field was left to commercial banks until the 1980s.

Although marketplace deficiencies afford quite a litany for governmental intervention, there are other reasons for regulating that go beyond the market itself.

(1.) Infant industry. Problems from a lack of capitalization or expertise may impede the desirable development of new industry. The infant industry argument is more common where government functions in a supportive capacity, such as tariff protection, than in a regulatory one. The regulation of the airline industry in the 1930s was grounded on the need to foster orderly growth in that new transportation sector.

(2.) Macroeconomic policy goals. Although "traditional" economic regulation was usually industry-specific, the Federal Reserve system was created in 1913 because of the need to regulate the supply of money across the whole economy. The occasional use of wage and price controls is regulatory, and some people think of the built-in stabilizers of the income tax as a type of regulation.

(3.) Reallocating scarce resources. In a sense, all regulation is brought on by the need to allocate scarce resources, but occasionally there are particular shortages that demand governmental intervention, for example, the rationing of gasoline in wartime or during the petroleum crises of the 1970s. Rent control of apartments occurs in places like New York City or Boston, where housing is in short supply.

(4.) Physical safety. A good deal of regulation is to ensure the public's physical safety. The Food and Drug Act of 1906 was aimed at all sorts of materials that found their way into our food and drink, and in the 1930s the Federal Aviation Administration (FAA) began to regulate the maintenance and safety of commercial aircraft. But it was in the 1960s and 1970s that the corpus of "new" social regulation was aimed at automobiles, consumer products, children's toys, and the industrial workplace.

(5.) National security. Foreign trade restrictions on an extensive list of embargoed products are administered by the Department of Commerce. These were first directed at Soviet-bloc nations in the Cold War era, and they include prohibitions on the export of computer components, oil field drilling equipment, and strategic materials. The regulation of nuclear power in the 1950s was justified on the basis of national security, as well as for infant industry and physical safety reasons.

(6.) Protecting essential services. Few commodities are more essential to Americans than oil and food. The regulation of petroleum imports and prices during the 1950s was based on maintaining the domestic producing capacity. Agricultural support programs designed to ensure the continuation of the family farm also fall under this category. The problems with American farms might also be seen as the consequences of too much competition, market instability, unequal bargaining power between producers and processors, and even national security.

(7.) Crisis conditions. The perception of a crisis is a global, nonspecific cause of regulation, but it is a necessary condition for the enactment of regulatory policy. The national emergency of the 1930s pointed to the widespread crisis that gave rise to so much regulation in so many areas. Rachel Carson's *Silent Spring* imparted a sense of environmental crisis in the 1960s; and a sudden rise in traffic fatalities was a factor in bringing about federal auto safety regulations. The energy crisis yielded a plethora of regulations at all levels of government during the 1970s.

(8.) Unequal bargaining power. Regulation can be imposed to redress an imbalance in bargaining power among contending parties. The government entered into labor-management relations because the legal environment before 1935 favored owners, who were also perceived to have had a monopoly of physical force since the very beginning of labor organizations. Workmen's compensation programs arose at the state level because the costs of litigation and the fellow-servant doctrine often prevented injured employees or their survivors from winning suits against mill owners in the civil courts. The Equal Employment Opportunity Commission intervenes in cases of discrimination against employees on the basis of race, gender, and age.

THE WAVES OF REGULATION

If regulation means any attempt by government to effect changed behavior, it is as old as the country itself and includes the colonial-era Navigation Acts, the protective tariff laws of the 1790s, and the Jeffersonian-era Nonimportation Act of 1807. If we think of regulation as involving administrators with rule-making power conveyed by statute, the best example of it before the Civil War was the control exercised by the Second Bank of the United States, a quasi-public institution. But as a practical matter, regulation is a phenomenon of the industrial age. The use of a collegial body to make administrative decisions at the national level first occurred with the Tariff Commission, a nine-person board created in 1882 to make recommendations for import duties. A three-person Civil Service Commission was created under the Pendleton Act the following year to administer the new, limited, merit-based civil service law.

The first wave of economic regulatory activity was brought about by the abuses of monopoly. The Grangers, a farmers' organization founded in 1867 and augmented by small-town merchants and businesspeople was successful in getting the state of Illinois to create a railroad and warehouse commission to fix maximum rates in 1871. Other midwestern states soon followed suit. At first, the Court sustained these Granger laws in *Munn* v. *Illinois* (1877) as a legitimate use of the police power in businesses affected by a public interest. The laissez-faire counterattack was under way, however, and Roscoe Conkling convinced a conservative Court majority that the due process clause of the Fourteenth Amendment meant more than adherence to "procedural" fairness. It was also intended, according to this railroad attorney who had been on the committee that drafted the amendment, to extend the due process clause to corporations. The Court also gave a "substantive" meaning to due process as a defense of corporate property rights. It was argued, moreover, that state railroad regulations infringed into interstate commerce and thus were unconstitutional.

National remedies for industrial abuses were sought as early as 1874, when a bill introduced by Representative George McCrary (R–IA) called for a federal commission to fix maximum railroad rates. It passed the House of Representatives but failed in the Senate. The judicial rulings on state regulatory attempts, plus mounting public demand, produced an 1885 congressional committee chaired by Senator Shelby M. Cullom (R–IL). After hearings held in various locations in the country, Cullom recommended the creation of a federal commission to regulate interstate commerce. The resulting legislation passed the House by 219 votes to 41, and the Senate by 43 to 15, in 1887. At first the ICC was located within the Interior Department, but the possibility of unwanted presidential influence caused Congress in 1889, with the forthcoming inauguration of Republican Benjamin Harrison, to establish it as a stand-alone agency.

The ICC was empowered to require annual reports from railroads about their operations and finances, and it could require uniform accounting rules to allow comparability among firms in order to investigate railroad management. The ICC had the power to subpoena documents and witnesses and issue cease and desist orders; however, these could be appealed to a hostile federal judiciary, and the railroads appealed often. Although it could bring suits in federal courts, the ICC lacked the power to issue its own rulings. Within a few years the railroads were able to get around ICC demands, and its findings were blunted by the Supreme Court (*Maximum Freight Rate* case, 1897; *Alabama Midlands* case, 1897). By the end of the century the commission had become little more than a statistical collection agency. What resuscitated the ICC was the Hepburn Act of 1906, which gave it final rate-making powers, and the Mann-Elkins Act of 1910, which allowed it to suspend new rate proposals and set original ones. It was the latter act that gave the ICC the authority to set maximum railroad rates and placed the burden of proof in challenging them on the railroads themselves. The law also widened ICC jurisdiction to include railway express and sleeping car companies, oil pipelines, and ferryboats. Subsequently the Mann-Elkins Act of 1910 added telephone, telegraph, cable, and other communications companies to the ICC's jurisdiction.

A second wave of regulatory reform broke with the Progressive movement. The Theodore Roosevelt administration developed a reinvigorated antitrust policy, which President Taft pursued even more vigorously a few years later; but regulation moved in new directions as well. The Pure Food and Drug Act of 1906 and companion legislation for meat inspection drew the federal government into the arena of protective regulation for the first time. At the state level, progressivism generated a flood of legislation regulating wages and hours of employment, employment of women and children, workmen's compensation (Maryland, 1902), and minimum wages (Massachusetts, 1912, but overturned in *Adkins* v. *Children's Hospital*, 1923). The crest of the Progressive wave nationally, however, followed the election of Wilson in 1912. The Pujo Committee led to the creation of the Federal Reserve in 1913 and to the Clayton Act in 1914. The regulatory commission model was reprised with the birth of the Federal Trade Commission (FTC), a five-person body that was part of Wilson's antitrust program but that soon became an agency charged with a wide range of regulatory activities. It could investigate unfair business practices identified in the Clayton Act and issue cease and desist orders designed to combat them. Later, FTC attention was directed to false advertising claims and the mislabeling of products.

The 1920s were not devoid of regulatory initiative, and five agencies with regulatory authority were created between 1920 and 1931. First came the Water Commission, created in 1920 to oversee the emerging hydroelectric activity. This commission was followed by the Commodities Exchange Authority (1922), Customs Service (1927), and Federal Radio Commission (1927). The Federal Power Commission replaced the Water Commission in 1930, and the Food and Drug Administration appeared in 1931. But it was the failure of regulation in the securities industry that set the stage for the stock market crash in 1929, and the errors of monetary policy by the Federal Reserve that triggered it.

The third wave of regulatory activity arrived with the New Deal. With the country mired in the Depression, the administration was anything but homogeneous philosophically, and policies of often contradictory sorts were attempted simultaneously. The first Franklin Roosevelt administration contained many who believed that social structures had gone wrong and that regulatory discipline was needed, but greater emphasis later came to be placed on fiscal policy. Immediately following inauguration, the Treasury Department and the comptroller of the currency were given broad discretionary powers over the banking system by the Emergency Banking Relief Act. Agricultural regulation was instituted by the Agricultural Adjustment Act and vested within the Department of Agriculture. The IRC device was applied again with the creation of the SEC and FCC in 1934, the National Labor Relations Board (NLRB) in 1935, the U.S Maritime Commission in 1936, and the CAA in 1938. But most of the new regulatory authority was vested in dozens of agencies located within existing cabinet-level departments. The regulatory intrusions into everyday life caused by World War II ended with the cessation of hostilities.

Few new agencies were created between the New Deal and 1965, and it was not until the Johnson administration that the era of social regulation arrived. This fourth wave began in the environmental field, where Rachel Carson's (1962) book *Silent Spring* raised the specter of an environment devastated by the widespread use of pesticides. Carson's warning was echoed by the writings of Barry Commoner and others and by demands for more rigorous enforcement of existing regulations and the enactment of new legislation to enhance air and water quality. More immediate and physical dangers were presented by the automobile and by workplace safety. Automobile deaths per mile traveled increased suddenly during the 1960s, and Ralph Nader was at the forefront of those who blamed the increase on unsafe vehicles manufactured by Detroit—and particularly on an early entry into the compact car market, the Chevrolet Corvair. In *Unsafe at Any Speed*, Nader (1965) detailed not only the instability of the vehicle but also the threat from exhaust fumes while the car was idling in the driveway. Crude attempts by General Motors to discredit Nader drew congressional attention to the problem. In the atmosphere of expansive government that was the Great Society, Lyndon Johnson and congressional Democrats produced the National Highway Transportation Act. In all, automobile regulation began with safety regulation, then moved into fuel emission regulation, and finally to gasoline mileage requirements.

Safety on the job was also an objective of the spirit of the 1960s. Mining and manufacturing were joined by many other occupations that seemed fraught with accidents. Organized labor was blamed for having been more concerned with the wages and hours of employment than with safety on the job for the rank and file. Taking momentum from environmental and automotive politics, the Occupational Health and Safety Administration (OSHA) was created within the Department of Labor in 1969. By the reckoning of some, the pages of rules issued during the 1970s constituted an unprecedented level of regulation.

REGULATORY AGENCIES AND PROCEDURES

Under the Administrative Procedures Act of 1946, the regulatory process begins with a congressional statute charging an agency with new responsibility over an industry or perhaps with a perceived need for a new regulatory rule by the agency itself. Notice of public hearings is published in the *Federal Register*. The public, meaning as a practical matter firms, trade associations and public-interest groups, comment on the proposed rule and present information relevant to their point of view. The hearings are much like those held by legislative committees and usually result in revising or redrafting the proposal. One development in the Reagan administration was the empowerment of the OMB to review proposed rules. The rule is then published in the *Federal Register* with the notice that it is to take effect within a certain period—often sixty days—and ultimately takes its place in the *Code of Federal Regulations*. When used in specific applications, administrative rules can be challenged in federal court on grounds of vagueness, procedural unfairness, or extension beyond the agency's grant of power. Such *ultra vires* rules (literally, "beyond the power") will be null and void in the eyes of a court. New-style social regulatory agencies are more likely to issue rules, or to "legislate," than those that emphasize economic regulation.

The adjudicatory function is performed more by old-style, economic regulatory agencies. Adjudication concerns the settlement of factual disputes that arise under agency rules. It proceeds after someone is charged with a rule violation, when rates are established, or when licenses are granted to perform some public purpose. Notice of a violation or of relief from the rule is followed by an investigation by the agency staff. If the aggrieved party is unhappy with the staff recommendation, a trial may be held before an administrative law judge (ALJ). The rules governing submission of evidence are more lenient than in a regular judicial proceeding because those involved are experts within the policy area. The ALJ's final report decides the outcome, unless an appeal is made to the full commission—five members in the case of the FCC. Any subsequent appeal to the federal courts from an adverse decision by a regulatory commission is largely limited, under the Administrative Procedures Act, to procedural violations by the agency. Adjudicatory proceedings abound in the NLRB, for example, which decides hundreds of employee-union disputes each year.

Two major problems attract the attention of analysts today. The first is procedural delay. The length of time that some cases require can be vexing, even when they are disposed of in six to nine months—the average time span. The second problem concerns the quality of the commissioners themselves. Some critics fault congressional committees for their failure to be more diligent at the advise and consent stage. Others contend that the commissioners individually may be quite capable, but the collegial structure in which they work blunts their keenness. In other words, the whole is seen as being less than the sum of its parts.

ALTERNATIVES TO REGULATION

As governmental intervention became less popular under Reaganomics, a number of alternatives to regulation have been developed. One response has been simply to downsize the regulatory bureaucracy by appropriating less money for it but minimizing employees' hostility by decreasing the work force through attrition. This is only a difference in degree, however, and real reformers have sought more far-reaching changes. Some have touted privatized rule enforcement, under which an agency would continue to write regulatory rules but would rely on aggrieved parties to bring legal enforcement in court. This process raises the problem of the cost of litigation, which was a reason for creating public regulatory agencies in the first place. Still, 90 percent of all antitrust litigation begins in the private sector. Other alternatives to regulation include greater use of the law of liability; reliance on insurance; and the resolution of labor or consumer disputes through bargaining, particularly arbitration.

Other alternatives to bureaucratic regulation have come from market-oriented thinkers who have been concerned with controlling pollution, for example. Tax incentives can be given to those who take steps to abate wastes. The spirit of the Tax Reform Act of 1986 was to denigrate the pursuit of social policy goals through the federal tax system. California has considered removing the state sales tax from low-polluting new cars, with high-polluting vehicles paying up to $774. This sliding scale is designed to influence both consumers and manufacturers. Direct subsidy payments can be made to install pollution-control devices. Marketable permits can be bought or traded to allow the holder to emit a certain number of units of effluent. More and better information could be forthcoming about products, which would allow more informed choice. Consumer pressure can be brought to bear by disclosing the identity of polluters. Finally, education can better inform us of ways to minimize pollution.

THE EFFECTS OF DEREGULATION

The deregulation movement has continued to be important since the mid-1970s, but does it work? Assessments of the success of deregulation vary by industry. Deregulation in banking has meant the development of new products like interest-bearing checking accounts. But deregulation of S&Ls yielded dozens of institutions that loaned money on risky real estate ventures that went into default when real estate values declined in California and the Southwest. Because deposits of up to $100,000 each were insured by the Federal Savings and Loan Insurance Corporation (FSLIC), and the FSLIC derives its funds from the federal treasury, the cost to the taxpayer is at least $400 billion—something like $1,700 for every man, woman, and child in America.

The difficulty of assessing deregulation can be illustrated by the case of commercial airlines. There seems to be a consensus that it brought about immediate rate reductions and also that inflation-adjusted fares were about 20 percent lower in 1988 than just before deregulation. By 1988, however, when the merger movement waned and the cost-cutting that resulted from bigger planes and wage reductions had been realized, fares began to rise again.

Moreover, conclusions about airline deregulation differ widely for several reasons. First, because all airlines were deregulated at once, there is no control group that allows a comparison, and it is impossible to develop an acceptable quasi-experimental design. Second, the number of firms has changed as new entrants quickly entered the market after deregulation and offered bargain rates. Many of them have disappeared, and the industry is now more concentrated than it was before deregulation. Mergers and shutdowns left many cities with fewer major carriers, and a study by the General Accounting Office found that a flight from one of fifteen airports served by only one or two companies costs 27 percent more. Similarly, when supply is restricted at cramped airports like O'Hare, LaGuardia, or Washington National, fares are 7 percent higher.

Third, traffic patterns are different because of the hub-and-spoke networks that have appeared in the last decade, causing people to fly 5 to 30 percent farther than when there were direct city-to-city flights. Fourth, airline costs across time have been reduced because of wage cuts in the wake of mergers and takeovers of the 1980s (which would not have happened under regulation) and because of lower fuel costs and more fuel-efficient engines (which probably would have been introduced under the CAB).

Fifth, the conclusions of studies of deregulation's effects depend on the time periods involved. Because fuel costs had risen later in the 1970s, an analysis that includes numbers from early in the decade would show less dramatic changes under deregulation. Again, airline fares began to increase by the late 1980s, and with reductions in the numbers of firms (though not to reach their 1978 levels) any benefits of deregulation would be smaller. Sixth, there are disagreements on what measures of analysis should be used. Yield, or the price charged per passenger for each mile traveled, is an appealing measure of performance. The use of hub-and-spoke routes artificially improves this yield figure, however, because of the needless miles that are now flown.

Seventh, rate deregulation also affects differently varying types of travelers. The unrestricted coach fares used by business travelers apparently are higher than those for vacation travelers. Finally, few analyses include nonfinancial variables. The increase in numbers of seats per plane, the reduced crew size, the poorer quality of in-flight meals, and increased flight delays and bumping have lowered the ambiance of travel. There are those who fear that lower airline profitability is reducing the level of maintenance and that margins of safety are a matter of concern (Nomani, 1990).

The definitive measure of deregulation may be the simplest of all—an inventory of how the member firms have fared in the absence of CAB guidance. Of twenty-five interstate airlines in 1979, only nine were still in operation in 1992. Three of these, America West, TWA, and Continental, have been operating under the protection of bankruptcy laws. Thus, only six solvent carriers remained: American, Northwest, Delta, United, USAir, and Southwest. The final verdict on airline deregulation may be that the nation will be served by only one or two surviving carriers. One of them probably will be United, the one carrier that did not oppose deregulation in 1979.

SUMMARY: REGULATION AND ITS CAUSES

Regulation usually is the result of a universally held feeling of emergency. This consensus occurred during the 1930s, as Marver Bernstein (1955) found in a study of eight New Deal regulatory agencies, each of which was created without an overall plan or philosophy. Instead, they were specific responses to the ravages of the Great Depression. Crandall and his associates (1986) argue that a crisis atmosphere was generated over increasing automobile deaths during the 1960s. Related to a crisis is the long-harbored, pent-up demand for governmental intervention that is released when the partisan match between president and Congress allows the enactment of innovative legislation. The ICC and Federal Reserve were created in 1887 and 1913 in such an atmosphere.

It is important to remember that politics is people. Although some regulation is the result of massive support in public opinion, some is due to the leadership of particular individuals—political entrepreneurs—who discover an issue, "get out in front" with it, and bring it to fruition. The food and drug legislation of 1906 was the result of untiring efforts by Dr. Harvey Wiley. In our own time, it was first John Robson, then Alfred Kahn, who became identified with deregulation while serving as chairs of the CAB in 1975–1976 and in 1977–1978, respectively.

The fact that synoptic change comes in waves and moves across industries suggests that it is infectious. Derthick and Quirk (1985, pp. 53–56) point out that once the idea had caught on, all "right thinking people" inside the Beltway took up the cause as though there was no alternative, and deregulation became a "policy fashion." John Kingdon (1984) has contended that the success in airline deregulation gave impetus to reducing governmental intervention elsewhere as well.

There is a periodicity to governmental intervention in the economy. That is, there are times when government grows and the public sector enters the market economy through regulation. This is clearly what happened during the 1930s, and certainly it typified the Progressive era at the beginning of the century, the Kennedy-Johnson years, and even some of the momentum that carried over into the Nixon term. And there are other times, like the normalcy of Harding and Coolidge, the quiet years of the 1950s, and the reaction of the later 1970s and the Reagan-Bush era, when politics, government, and public administration are decried as illegitimate intervention into the free market.

DISCUSSION QUESTIONS

1. What does it mean to "regulate," and what are the purposes of regulation?

2. What are the several periods of regulation, and how distinct are the boundaries between them?

3. Distinguish between "procedural" and "substantive" due process of law.

4. Distinguish between "economic" and "protective" regulation.

5. What brought about economic deregulation during the 1970s? Why wasn't there more deregulation of "new," protective rules? Was deregulation a conservative movement?

6. Give an example of rule making, of administration, and of adjudication for an IRC of your choice. Can you do this for a second agency? A third?

7. Regulatory activity involves the creation and administration of whole hosts of "rules." Where are they found?

8. Agencies vary with regard to just how much regulating they actually do. Give an example of an agency that is fully regulatory. Give an example of one in which regulation is secondary. Give an example of an agency that really only advises and makes recommendations.

9. Some people believe that we need vigorous governmental intervention in the marketplace, whereas others eschew regulation. Why do people's views differ about regulation?

10. What have been the social forces that have brought about regulation in past eras? Are there any similarities?

11. How does regulation during wartime, or other times of crisis, differ from that which has developed during times of peace?

REFERENCES

Almond, Gabriel A. 1960. "Introduction: A Functional Approach to Comparative Politics." In Almond and James S. Coleman, eds. *The Politics of Developing Areas.* Princeton, NJ: Princeton University Press.

Bernstein, Marver H. 1955. *Regulating Business by Independent Commission.* Princeton, NJ.: Princeton University Press.

Carson, Rachel. 1962. *Silent Spring.* Boston: Houghton Mifflin.

Crandall, Robert W., Howard K. Gruenspecht, Theodore E. Keeler, and Lester Lave. 1986. *Regulating the Automobile.* Washington, D.C.: Brookings Institution.

Derthick, Martha, and Paul J. Quirk. 1985. *The Politics of Deregulation.* Washington, D.C.: Brookings Institution.

Hardin, Garrett. 1968, December. "The Tragedy of the Commons." *Science,* 162, 1243–1248.

Katzman, Robert. 1980. *Regulatory Bureaucracy: The Federal Trade Commission and Antitrust Policy.* Cambridge, MA: MIT Press.

Kingdon, John W. 1984. *Agendas, Alternatives, and Public Policies.* Boston: Little, Brown.

Kolko, Gabriel. 1965. *Railroads and Regulation.* Princeton, NJ: Princeton University Press.

Lowi, Theodore J. 1964, July. "American Business, Public Policy, Case Studies, and Political Theory," *World Politics,* 16, 677–715.

Nader, Ralph. 1965. *Unsafe At Any Speed: The Designed-In Dangers of the American Automobile.* New York: Grossman.

Nomani, Asra Q. 1990, April 19. "One Sure Result of Airline Deregulation: Controversy About Its Impact on Fares," *Wall Street Journal,* p. B1.

Stone, Alan. 1982. *Regulation and Its Alternatives.* Washington, D.C.: Congressional Quarterly Press.

Wilson, James Q., ed. 1980. *The Politics of Regulation.* New York: Basic Books.

PART FOUR

MANAGING THE ECONOMY

Business cycles are a characteristic of market economies. Adam Smith knew about them, and their work in equilibrium theory brought cycles to the attention of neo-classical economists as well. To Marshall, Pigou, and others, however, perturbations from equilibrium should always be temporary, with a prompt return to a new period of zero unemployment, a new balance between supply and demand, and the "clearing" of all markets. Even though panics occurred throughout history, their potential for bringing down regimes did not become apparent until our own century. The British general strikes of the 1920s, the Red scare, and American fears about organized labor, coming as they did on the heels of the Russian revolution, stimulated thinking about how to rescue capitalism from its achilles heel. The rudiments of how to do it were well known before 1936; but John Maynard Keynes provided a theoretical justification for it, and stimulated a body of research that became the orthodoxy of how to manage an economy through the ups and downs of the market system. Still, governmental intervention in the business cycle posed problems that were as much political as economic. It had to be accepted as legitimate in a market-based system, and there had to be discipline among the authorities to minimize inflation and control spending once prosperity returned.

Fiscal and monetary policy are complementary approaches for managing the business cycle. Increasing spending while decreasing taxes in hard times had been practiced before Keynes, including some modest attempts during the Hoover administration. But it was Keynes who made us feel more comfortable with incurring debt during recessions. Unhappily for fiscal policy, changes in taxing and spending require concerted action between the legislative and executive branches of government. Given divided government, the politics of credit claiming and finger pointing make this cooperation difficult to obtain. Fortunately, fiscally based counter cyclical policy can occur without direct governmental intervention because of "automatic stabilizers"— unemployment insurance and welfare that expand with hard times and contract with prosperity, relatively free from action by Congress or the president.

That the expansion or contraction of the money supply was associated with business activity was understood from the earliest days of the republic. But as Keynes again pointed out, making money and credit more readily available will not guarantee that people will rush to obtain them. More recently, the monetarist theories of Milton Friedman have gained acceptance among conservatives because they allow economic fine-tuning without creating large bureaucracies or the clumsy intervention of Congress or the president.

Whereas economic management is the organizing theme of the next two chapters, it also affords a vehicle for describing policies of taxation, expenditure, and debt, as well for examining the role of money, the operations of the Federal Reserve system, and the stakes involved in monetary politics.

CHAPTER NINE

MANAGING THE ECONOMY: FISCAL POLICY

Fiscal policy involves the use of the government's powers of taxing and spending to smooth out the highs and lows of the business cycle. This chapter begins by examining the notion of economic cycles, then describes the roles of taxation and of spending in trying to cope with them. Since deficits are inevitable with the increased expenditures and decreased revenues that occur during recessions, we conclude by looking at the issue of public debt. Through it all, we may see that there is as much politics as economics in trying to apply fiscal policy.

THE BUSINESS CYCLE

A particular feature of market-based, capitalist economies is the business cycle. One full cycle is the period of time required for an economy to pass through a complete rotation from "peak" performance; down to a bottom, or "trough;" and back to the next peak period. As measured by the National Bureau of Economic Research (NBER), there have been thirty–one cycles in the United States since 1854, or one about every four and one-half years (see Table 9–1).

TABLE 9-1 U.S. Business Cycles

BUSINESS CYCLE REFERENCE DATES		DURATION (IN MONTHS)	
		CONTRACTION	EXPANSION
TROUGH	PEAK	(trough from previous peak)	(trough to peak)
December 1854	June 1857	-	30
December 1858	October 1860	18	22
June 1861	April 1865	8	**46**
December 1867	June 1869	**32**	18
December 1870	October 1873	18	34
March 1879	March 1882	65	36
May 1885	March 1887	38	22
April 1886	July 1890	13	27
May 1891	January 1893	10	20
June 1894	December 1895	17	18
June 1897	June 1899	18	24
December 1900	September 1902	18	21
August 1904	May 1907	23	33
June 1908	January 1910	13	19
January 1912	January 1913	24	12
December 1914	August 1918	23	**44**
March 1919	January 1920	**7**	10
July 1921	May 1923	18	22
July 1924	October 1926	14	27
November 1927	August 1929	13	21
March 1933	May 1937	43	50
June 1938	February 1945	13	**80**
October 1945	November 1948	**8**	37
October 1949	July 1953	11	**45**
May 1954	August 1957	**10**	39
April 1958	April 1960	8	24
February 1961	December 1969	10	**106**
November 1970	November 1973	**11**	36
March 1975	January 1980	16	58
July 1980	July 1981	6	12
November 1982	July 1990	16	91
March 1991		8	--

Note: Numbers in bold face indicate periods of expansion or contraction that occurred during wartime.
Source: National Bureau of Economic Research, Cambridge MA.

Business cycles are not symmetrical. Periods of expansion have averaged about twice as long as those of contraction during the past 138 years. Furthermore, the periods of expansion themselves have become longer since the 1930s and the periods of decline have grown shorter. Since the New Deal expansion that began in March 1933, the eleven expansionary periods have averaged nearly 53 months in duration, whereas the contractions have averaged less than 12. Of course, these averages are greatly affected by the Reagan-Bush expansion from late 1982 through June 1990 and by the 106-month expansion during the 1960s, which is the longest recession-free period on record.

There is more than one way of looking at business cycles. The longest view is associated with the work of Nikolai Kondratieff (1925, 1944), a Russian economist, who perceived what he called "long waves," of forty to sixty years in duration, that affected economic life. Using data from France, Great Britain, Germany and the United States, he concluded that periods of expansion common to all of these countries had occurred from about 1790 to 1810–1817, 1844–1851 to 1870–1875, and 1890–1896 to about World War I. Later, the Englishman Joseph Kitchin used commodity prices, bank clearings and interest rates to argue that major trade cycles were actually aggregates of several minor cycles of about forty months in duration. It is this shorter "Kitchin cycle" that NBER data tend to reflect today. Then there was the view of Clement Juglar (1862), who found nine- to ten-year cycles in economic activity. In 1939, Joseph Schumpeter superimposed all three cycles on one another—Kondratieff's fifty-four-year average, Juglar's nine to ten years, and Kitchin's forty- month period—to produce his own three-cycle concept.

The work of Simon Kuznets (1930) on the concept of *growth cycles* is also important. Whereas Kondratieff, Kitchin, and others had examined fluctuations in absolute levels of business activity like prices and interest rates, Kuznets was interested in the *rates*, or percentages of growth. Even during periods of expansion, for example, growth rates can rise (e.g., growth at a robust 10 percent per year) or fall (e.g., an anemic 0.1 percent). By tracing deviations from trends, Kuznets was able to develop a more sensitive view of the economy and to reach somewhat different conclusions about business cycles. Focusing on building construction, population growth, and capital formation, he concluded that there had been peaks in the United States in 1873, 1892, and 1913 and troughs in 1878 and 1896. Analyses based on rates of change have become a cornerstone of today's concern with growth cycles.

If business cycles are a feature of market systems and if controlling the downside effects are a goal of public policy, developing measures of cyclical activity is essential. Adam Smith used a wide range of historical and commercial data in *Wealth of Nations*, and the decennial census became a device for gathering demographic data in America. Measures such as gross national product (GNP) are twentieth-century notions, however; and it wasn't until the 1940s that GNP became available more frequently than on an annual basis—a frequency that is crucial for any regime that wants to intervene in order to improve its economy. Today, literally hundreds of indicators are published monthly by the Council of Economic Advisers for the Joint Economic Committee of the U.S. Congress, the Bureau of Economic Analysis (BEA) of the U.S. Department of Commerce, and the NBER.

Business cycle indicators are usually categorized as leading, coincident, and lagging. Among the first, those that are associated with factory operations (e.g., new orders for products or changes in the number of people employed) have a lead time of six to twelve months. Governmental activities, such as tax law changes, tend to exert an impact over an even longer term. The shortest lead times, periods of one to six months, are associated with business inventories, which are difficult to measure. Although the average lead times for many of the individual indicators are reasonably well known (e.g., housing permits lead by thirteen months, average work week by eleven months, and new consumer orders by six months), their respective ranges have been found to vary considerably from one economic cycle to another. Nor does each of them reach its peaks or troughs at the same time. For this reason, each of the eleven leading, four coincident, and seven lagging indicators published monthly in the BEA's *Survey of Current Business* is a sophisticated composite of other primary measures.

Data-gathering problems abound with economic indicators. The figure for GNP varies according to whether it is measured from the income or the expenditure side of the national account. Unemployment can be measured through services provided by the Department of Labor, surveys of employers, or surveys of households, the percentage of those without jobs increasing with each indicator. When denominated in dollars or other value units, as opposed to physical units, there is the mathematical problem of establishing a base year: 1982–1984, 1967, or 1913.

An understanding of business cycles and their indicators is important for government if it is to guide economic policy. No two cycles are alike. Even if we think in terms of short-term, Kitchin cycles of three to five years, the countermeasures to be taken against recessions, panics, and depressions will never be precisely the same. To the extent that the government learns and acts incrementally, the decay in institutional knowledge will be greater as the increments between peaks increase. If we think in terms of Kondratieff's or Kuznets' cycles, environmental conditions will change even more. Indicators that may have served well in an earlier time may be useless today. For example, a number of changes in indexes were made after 1974 because that recession featured significant levels of inflation and a number of indexes that were sensitive to rising prices kept improving even though people were losing their jobs. Arguably, the indexes being used today may rely too heavily on measures associated with manufacturing at a time when 75 percent of all workers are in service occupations.

TAXATION

The subject of taxation can be massive, but it can all be summarized in the simple formula $T = B \times R$, where T is the amount of tax realized, B represents the tax base, and R stands for the rate or percentage of taxation. Let us consider these components separately.

Rates of taxation

The R of the equation represents the rate of taxation, or the percentage at which the tax is levied. There are three types of rates, and all of them are actually used. The simplest of them to envision is the proportional rate, in which the same percentage of tax is levied regardless of the value of the taxable base. The biblical tithe, or "tenth part," exemplifies this proportional tax rate, in that 10 percent is owed to the church by prince and pauper alike. A rate of, say, 2 percent per year that is levied on property, regardless of whether the property is valued at $20,000 dollars or $2 million, also typifies a proportional tax rate.

Progressive rates of taxation, the second type, are those in which the rate of tax rises as the value of the taxable base increases. They are justified by one of the central discoveries of neoclassical economics, the marginality principle. In this case, the declining marginal utility of money, or the idea that the last dollar earned by someone with a high income is not as vital as the last dollar earned by someone at the poverty level, is in point. Losing $100 would have little effect on a corporate vice president and her husband, but it probably would have serious consequences for the breadwinner of a low-income family of eight. To many people, the notion of progressive tax rates makes intuitive sense on grounds of equity; but to writers of the Chicago school like Blum and Kalven (1966) there can be no agreement about how rapidly the marginal utility of money declines—if, indeed, it really does diminish. There is also a different, supply-side argument against progressive tax rates that is based on the notion of efficiency, that is that high-income recipients will invest their gains and generate new jobs through investments in plant and equipment or home building. In both conservative scenarios, progressive rate structures represent uneconomic public policy. Historically, the United States has employed a great range in its nominal rates of taxation — from as low as a proportional 2 percent in 1893 to a progressive structure of 20 to 91 percent used from 1943 to 1964. The Tax Relief Act of 1986 created a two-tiered rate structure of 15 and 28 percent, since raised to a top of 33 percent.

Under regressive taxation, the third type of rate structure, the rate of tax declines as the tax base grows larger. Since no one argues that the marginal utility of money increases with larger incomes, it is difficult to praise regressive rates with any argument based on equity. Still, such a tax has been used. When the Social Security System was created in 1935, the tax that supported it was collected at a low percentage on only the first $3,500 earned, and all earnings above this level were exempt. The degree of regressivity has been reduced in seven major revisions over the years, but still the regressive basis of the Federal

Insurance Contribution Act (FICA) tax remains (Light, 1985, p. 37). In response to a question, President Franklin Roosevelt explained his rationale for using this approach at financing his great social innovation:

> I guess you're right on the economics, but those taxes were never a problem of economics. They are politics all the way through. We put those payroll contributions there so as to give the contributors a legal, moral, and political right to collect their pensions and their unemployment benefits. With those taxes in there, no damn politician can ever scrap my Social Security program. (Schlesinger, 1959, pp. 308–309.)

There is another aspect to the principle of regressivity as well—the effective regressivity that exists when one examines tax dollars paid as a percentage of wealth. Property taxes, for example, as well as sales taxes that include food items, have the effect of taxing away a higher proportion of wealth from low-income people than from the rich.

Actually, there has been a fourth rate of taxation. Called degressive, it has been the rate that Americans have actually paid when one adds the costs of all taxes at the national, state, and local levels combined and considers together their proportional, progressive, and regressive rate structures. Degressive rates resemble progressive ones by increasing as the taxable base grows. Eventually they reach an inflection point, however, beyond which they are negatively sloped in a way reminiscent of regressive rate structures. The unfairness of the higher-bracket rate decline became a major issue of tax fairness. Because U.S. tax administration relies on self-reporting, public questions about the inherent unfairness of the system threatened the integrity of the revenue process. Elimination of the loopholes available to upper-income taxpayers became an important feature of the Bradley-Gephart-Reagan tax reform law in 1985.

Tax base

As contentious as they are, tax rates alone are meaningless until applied against a taxable base, and it is in defining this base that the most serious tax politics is practiced (see Figure 9–1). Arguments over rate structures are visible; but defining what will be deducted, exempted, excluded, and otherwise untaxed is where the high-stakes game is played. As more than one lobbyist has said, "I don't care how high the rates are as long as I get to define the tax base my way."

The tax base is simply the thing being taxed. A tax base dating from biblical times is the capitation tax, or head tax, or poll tax. When "word went out from Caesar Augustus that all the world would be taxed," it was a poll tax that was being levied. But such a tax requires knowing the location of everyone if it is to be effective, and we know from the problems of administering the decennial Census just how difficult that job can be. Because it also strikes rich and poor

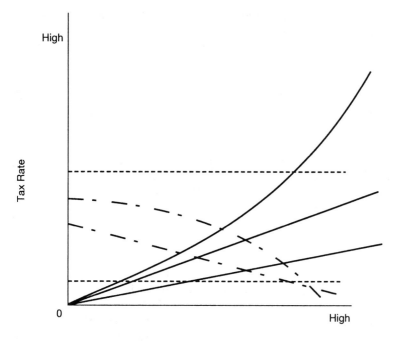

High

Tax Rate

0

High

Tax Base   (measured in monetary units)

Figure 9-1.

alike, the head tax fails to account for the ability to pay and seems to most people to be inherently unfair—or at least it did until the government of Margaret Thatcher levied one on Britons in 1990 and touched off a wave of riots in several British cities.

The earliest source of federal tax was the tariff on imported goods. It was a natural revenue tool because of the congressional power to regulate commerce with foreign nations. For a century and a half, tariff rates ranged from levels intended to generate revenue only to high levels designed to foster domestic industry. Abraham Lincoln won the presidency in 1860 in part because the high-tariff plank in the Republican platform helped him carry Pennsylvania. The high point of protectionism was reached with the Smoot-Hawley Tariff of 1930, a trade barrier that came to be blamed for initiating a world trade war that prolonged the Great Depression. The passage of the Reciprocal Trade Agreements Act in 1934 began a long decline in import duties that has culminated in the low rates of today. Bills for raising import taxes on such products as raw cotton and cotton cloth remain active in Congress, but today's trade barriers are more likely to take the form of import quotas or domestic content requirements than that of taxes.

Property, whether in real estate or in so-called intangible assets like shares of stock or jewelry, is widely used at the state and local level. Although there is some linkage between wealth and taxation, most critics argue that the ownership of property holds only a weak relationship with the ability to pay. Homestead exemptions for the elderly are one way to reduce these inequities, however. To the framers of the Constitution, both capitation and property taxes were "direct taxes" that would have to yield an equal amount of revenue from each state—a provision that they knew would make them unpalatable politically and would preserve them as sources of state revenue only. The national government has levied a property tax twice, first during the War of 1812 and again during the Civil War. The second experience was such an administrative nightmare that in 1870 the money was returned to the states from which it had come.

Excise and sales taxes are levies on products as they are purchased or consumed. Not to be confused with taxes on luxuries or "excesses," excises have traditionally been levied only by the federal government at some stage of the production process. They require a carefully organized agency of tax collectors for successful administration. It was an excise tax levied on distilled liquor that led to the Whiskey Rebellion of 1793 in the western regions of Pennsylvania and other states. Today, the federal government receives less than 2 percent of its revenues from excise taxes. Sales taxes have been used exclusively by state and local governments since World War II. They are collected at the time of sale by the merchant. A smaller tax-collection bureaucracy is needed as a result of using the seller as revenue agent. Both excise and sales taxes are regarded as regressive, although the exemption of groceries makes sales taxes somewhat less so. During times of war and also in 1990, the idea of a federal tax on luxury items has emerged. Democrats proposed a 10 percent tax on that portion of automobile prices above $25,000, on expensive yachts, and on expensive stereos and furs. Objections from sellers of the luxury items were based on the grounds that they would have to bear the incidence of the tax. Some of the taxes were avoided by selling stereo or personal computer components separately so that no one component crossed the relevant dollar threshold. In the case of yachts, however, the costs were borne by the skilled workers who were thrown out of work by lack of sales.

Some taxes are associated with the transfer of wealth between people. Estate taxes are levied on the property of a decedent before any assets are distributed to the heirs. Inheritance taxes, in contrast, are collected from the individual heirs after they have received their inheritances. Estate taxes are easier to administer by making the administrator of the estate liable for the payment of all taxes; it is easier to watch the whole than to monitor the distributed parts. From an equity perspective, however, the tax on distributed shares is fairer because it considers the circumstances of the individual heirs. Death taxes are usually supplemented by a gift tax to prevent death-bed donations to heirs that would avoid estate and inheritance taxes. Although there is a separate federal gift tax, gifts given less than three years before death are normally taxed at the higher estate tax rate.

By far the leading source of federal revenue today is the income tax (see Table 9–2). Although an income tax was considered during the War of 1812, it was not until the Civil War that financial need dictated a modest tax. In 1861, the rate was 3 percent on incomes above $800. Eventually the marginal rates rose to 15 percent on incomes over $10,000. The tax was found not to contravene the Constitution in *U.S.* v. *Springer* (1870). A generation later the Wilson-Gorman Tariff of 1894 included an income tax at rates of 2 and 4 percent, but in *Pollock* v. *Farmers Loan & Trust* (1895) it was found unconstitutional because it was held to be a "direct tax" contrary to Article I, Section 9, Clause 4. When Progressive reformers saw graduated tax rates as a vehicle for a modest redistribution of wealth, they revived the income tax through the Sixteenth Amendment in 1913. That amendment, which allows Congress to levy taxes on incomes from whatever source derived, was ratified just in time to allow an income tax for the support of World War I. The rates fell to low levels again during the 1920s and 1930s. World War II ushered in the modern era of the income tax, through the Current Tax Payment Act of 1942, by mandating payroll tax deductions. The simple device of deducting the federal tax before the employee receives compensation has long been blamed by conservatives for disguising the magnitude of the federal tax bite and for paving the way for "big government."

An examination of federal revenue sources makes apparent the increasing reliance on taxes associated with Social Security, in particular the contributions to FICA. Obvious also is the diminution in excise taxes across time, as well as the shrinking proportion of revenues derived from the corporate income tax. With the virtual disappearance of import tariff revenues, taxes levied directly on individuals, by whatever name they are called, have become the source of nearly all federal revenues.

TABLE 9–2

YEARS	TAX RATES
1861–64	3% on incomes above $800
1864–70	5 to 15% (top rate on incomes over $10,000)
1894	2% on incomes over $1,000
1916	2% to 15%
1919	4% to 12%, plus 1% to 65% surtax
1925	1 1/2-3-5% Mellon Tax Plan
1943–64	20% to 91%
1964–81	14 to 70%
1981–86	11 to 50% (15 brackets)
1986–90	15 and 28% (but 33% "bubble")
1990	15 and 31%

Regardless of whether it is a tax on incomes, estates, or property, the tax base must be expressible in monetary units. For property in the form of real estate, the tax base is the assessed valuation of a house and lot as determined by the county assessor. Sometimes there is only a weak association between the market price of real estate and its assessed value, but usually there is an appeals process for challenging the assessor's appraisal. Again, for import duties levied on a percentage (or ad valorem) basis, the tax base will be the tax levied on the (sometimes understated) wholesale value as shown on the cargo manifest. For income taxes, the tax base is net taxable income, or the gross income minus exemptions, minus exclusions for certain types of nontaxable income like life insurance, and minus income not taxed because it was spent in the course of making the money in the first place. Because of the difference between gross and taxable income, there is always a difference between the *nominal* rate of taxation (e.g., the 33 percent bracket) and the *effective* tax rate that the individual actually pays (e.g., 18.2 percent).

Purposes of taxation

Although we might think of the purpose of taxation as simply that of raising revenue, in fact taxes serve a wide range of social-planning functions as well. *Promoting private economic development,* a supportive function of government, is one of these. During the 2nd Congress, at the urging of Alexander Hamilton, higher protective rates were adopted to stimulate American manufacturing. For most of American history the party to the right of center—first the Federalists, then the Whigs, and after 1854 the Republicans—favored higher tariffs. Democrats, more responsive to the interests of consumers of the protected goods, usually championed the cause of a tariff for revenue only. Since 1934, our policy has steadily moved toward freer international trade, and the income tax has reduced the yield from tariffs to minuscule amounts. Today, tariffs are one part of a trade policy that is more concerned with promoting American exports, preventing unfair foreign trading practices such as dumping low-cost items in the United States, and protecting industrial jobs from competition by nations with low labor costs. But ironically, it is the GOP that promotes free trade and the Democrats that are more likely to retreat from it. This exchange of party positions reflects the changing interests of the groups that traditionally support each party.

Economic development is also promoted through the tax system today by lowering the taxes of firms that invest in newer, presumably more efficient machinery and, at the state and local level, by giving tax abatement to firms that agree to move into an area. Most tax-law revisions are made with a concern for their impact on stimulating or harming investment patterns. More favorable treatment for taxing capital gains is always accompanied by words from the right about its favorable impact on investment.

Sumptuary taxes, purportedly enacted to discourage unwise behavior, introduce issues of morality, life-style, and social class into the taxing process. When levied against products like tobacco, liquor, and beer, the consumption of which are relatively inelastic, moderate increases in price usually have little impact on sales. This inelasticity of demand makes tobacco and liquor popular subjects of taxation precisely because the revenue that they raise is predictable and stable. Since these taxes have little true sumptuary effect, they are popular politically because they play on American temperance and reformist traditions and also relate to concerns about health and accidents—lung cancer, heart disease, and drunk driving. The regressiveness of these taxes and the life-style issue surfaced a few years ago in Anheuser-Busch's advertisements to "Can the Beer Tax" in support of its opposition to higher taxes on the "workingman's" beverage. An honest approach, say opponents of sumptuary taxes, might be an informational campaign or strengthening laws against drunk driving. Using a taxing process that seems to approve of consumption is hypocritical.

Using the tax system to *redistribute wealth* became a goal of some reformers in the late nineteenth century. To shrink the immense fortunes of industrialists through taxes was the goal of Marxist advocates. But the notion that those who had not earned wealth themselves were not entitled to inherit it grew from the ideas of David Ricardo, was compatible with the American political culture, and even received support from industrialist Andrew Carnegie, the Scottish émigré who made a fortune in steel and had no heirs. The Progressives drew on the "unearned income" theme in advocating progressive rates of taxation for both income and inheritance taxes. When attention shifted to the place of consumer demand for the products of modern society, it became apparent to some that concentrations of wealth would drain away the purchasing power that was so necessary if there were to be people with the money to buy automobiles, washers and driers, and all of the other goods that modern life requires.

The function of taxation that survives as a Depression-era policy goal, however, is as a *countercyclical regulator of the economy*. Part of the Keynesian prescription for responding to recession was to leave more spending money in the taxpayer's pocket through tax reductions. Although an immediate cost to society would be deficit spending, it would be outweighed by the immediate benefit of contributing to aggregate demand—to purchases by consumers. Keynes, in other words, was a "demand-sider"; to him it was demand, not supply, that had to come first if the economy were to be righted. Although deficit spending had been used before, in wartime, the notion that peacetime conditions also could warrant it seemed revolutionary.

Keynesianism was more contentious politically than it was economically. Tax cuts during times of increased spending ran counter to Yankee frugality, especially during the 1930s. And if downside tax reductions were difficult, even more contentious will be the enactment of tax increases to repay the debt and quell inflationary pressures once prosperity returns. The steep tax increases enacted in 1943 to finance the war already were in place when the postwar boom began, and this fact negated a bloody legislative fight that would have been necessary if Keynes's full prescription were to be followed. The country came to grips with the national debt, not by paying it off but by outgrowing it.

For any countercyclical effect to be significant, there must be noticeable progressivity in the effective rate structure. This feature can be achieved either by employing a wide range in the nominal rates themselves (as in the years between 1943 and 1964) or by building a permeable tax base. When inflation becomes important, however, and as taxpayers are forced into higher-rate brackets without an accompanying increase in purchasing power, complaints about "bracket creep" can spawn cries for the reduction of rate progressivity. This is precisely what happened in the 1980s to bring down the rates and simultaneously to reduce the countercyclical effect of the federal income tax.

The most recent social policy goals harken back to the purpose of economic stimulation, but do so by standing Keynes on his head. Whereas Keynes was demand-oriented, the supply-side school and Arthur Laffer have contended that high taxes diminish industriousness (Tobin, 1988, p. 88). This was the point of agreement between Ronald Reagan and Donald Regan when they first met during the presidential campaign of 1980. Indeed, as the Laffer curve model also pointed out, reducing tax rates (especially on higher-income individuals) would increase individual initiative and actually result in increasing revenues to the Treasury. This was the thinking in 1980 that then-presidential candidate George Bush referred to at the time as "voodoo economics."

Tax politics and Adam Smith's canons of taxation

As with so many other subjects, Adam Smith had insightful ideas about taxation too. He offered five canons concerning the subject to guide the policymakers of his day: *adequacy*—sufficient revenue to meet governmental expenditures; *economy*—no harmful effects on productivity or health; *certainty*—minimal chances for citizens either to illegally evade their taxes or to legally avoid them; *ease of administration*—low cost to collect; and *equity*—fairness. These canons are useful for examining the leading issues of tax politics today.

The *adequacy* canon concerns how much revenue, or how little, should be raised. Here we encounter the American preference for less government rather than more. The Revolution-era rallying cry of "No taxation without representation" can be joined by the observation that Americans are not fond of taxation *with* representation either. In 1812, just after declaring war on Great Britain, Congress adjourned without making appropriations to fight it; and many in Congress in 1861 who were most anxious to fight the Confederacy were equally unwilling to raise the money to do so, probably because they were aware of the opposition that the tax increase would engender. Today it is accepted political wisdom that there will be no tax increases during election years, for fear that the electorate will vote the tax raisers out of office. For Reagan it was an axiom of his economic plan to reduce taxes, although he justified his position with the expectation not only of revenue increases because of the Laffer curve but of being able to reduce expenditures as well. Perhaps those around him did not foresee how difficult it would be to reduce spending or how easily the deficit could grow. Or perhaps they did recognize these things and shrewdly reasoned that a huge debt increase would serve to constrain further governmental activity.

Most recently, the violation of the adequacy canon is obvious in the annual deficits of $300 trillion—10 percent of the whole budget. The intractability of the problem was reinforced by Bush's 1988 command to "Read my lips—no new taxes." Because politicians believe that proposing to raise taxes is electoral suicide, they go to great lengths to avoid any association with tax increases, although some Democrats do toy with the notion of raising rates on the income earners at the highest levels. Regardless of political tactics, the deficits of the past decade directly contravene the canon of adequacy and reveal a profligacy hitherto unknown in American experience. Meanwhile, comparisons show that the United States has the lowest levels of taxation for any industrialized nation other than Japan, which lacks a costly defense sector.

The *economy* canon deserves attention too. The argument that marginally high rates depress activity by repressing individual initiative was central to the Laffer curve thesis and was important in the rate restructuring of 1986. Perhaps unexpectedly, it arose from populist quarters in opposition to the 1990 luxury tax provisions that ended, not with soaking the rich, but with leaving unemployed hundreds of working people who used to build luxury watercraft—while the wealthy simply bought used yachts instead.

Smith's canon of *certainty*, aside from the possibility of illegally evading the Internal Revenue Service (IRS), is associated with the incidence of taxation—with the question of who really pays the tax. "Don't tax you, don't tax me; tax that man behind the tree," as Senator Russell Long (D–LA), chair of the Senate Finance Committee, has said. The perception that others derive tax advantages that we do not drove the 1986 tax-revision law, although most of the "loopholes" that had existed benefited the middle class. Closing them meant raising taxes on middle-income taxpayers, whereas the bottom one-fifth and those at the top both received tax reductions. Reducing the top tax rates meant a windfall for those with family incomes above $150,000.

Easily the most contentious of Smith's canons concerns *equity*. Equity simply means fairness, and fairness in taxation means treating taxpayers in similar circumstances similarly. The problem is that no two taxpayers seem to be in just the same circumstances.

Words like *equity* and *fairness* convey great symbolic value in politics. Successful pressure groups always base their arguments for tax preferences for child-care expenses, capital gains, business expenses, double taxation of corporate earnings; and all the rest on the basis of equity and fairness. Helping people with special burdens is "the fair thing to do." But one person's notion of fairness is another's idea of a loophole.

Another equity issue concerns what James Q. Wilson (1980) calls client politics, which abounds in the area of taxation. Client politics is said to exist when a small number of people (the clients) benefit from the contributions made by the great majority. Variances from the tax norm, variously called tax advantages and loopholes, usually are the result of special pleading by interest groups, and of course they use words like *equity, efficiency,* and *reform* as they plead their case.

Equity is at issue, too, in the normally obscure procedures through which tax policy is created. Tax issues are complicated, and most bills are drafted away from the glare of publicity. Occasionally, as in 1985 and 1986, tax writing moves to center stage and becomes synoptic change. The lobbyists were said to lose out as the law was rewritten in what its advocates called the majority interest. At least, that was how it was interpreted at the time by Ways and Means Committee

Figure 9-2. Source: U.S. Executive Office of the President, Office of Management and Budget. 1990. *Historical Table: Budget of the United States Government, Fiscal Year 1990.* N.P.

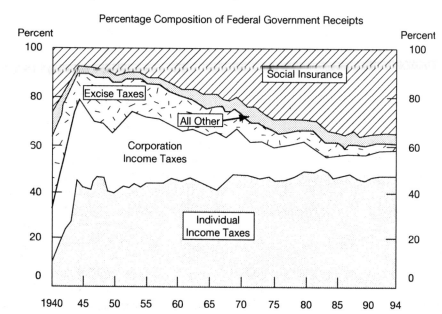

Percentage Composition of Federal Government Receipts

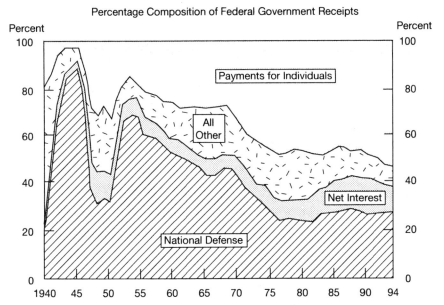

Figure 9-3 Source: U.S. Executive Office of the President, Office of Management and Budget. 1990.
Historical Table: Budget of the United States Government, Fiscal Year 1990: N.P.

Chair Daniel Rostenkowski (D–IL), Majority Whip Richard Gephardt (D–MO), Senator Bill Bradley (D–NJ), and Alan Murray of the *Wall Street Journal.*

EXPENDITURES

It is in the budgetary process that the battles over "who gets what, how, and with what effect" are fought out. Where managing the economy is concerned, adjusting expenditures to the needs of the business cycle is more easily said than done.

Budgetary rudiments

Before considering countercyclical spending, we need to examine some rudiments of the federal budget. Consider first the overall picture. Because of inflation, it is singularly uninformative to denominate revenues, expenditures, or deficits and debt in dollar amounts. All of them will show the characteristic exponential upsweep that many observers then describe as shooting or rocketing upward. Instead, we must regard each of these as proportions—as percentages of the GNP, gross domestic product (GDP), or some similar base. What we find is that since 1952, federal revenue as a percentage of the GNP has fluctuated within a rather narrow range—between about 17 and 20 percent. We see a more dramatic variation in the categories of expenditures, however. The range here is from about 17 percent of GNP to nearly 24 percent.

Second, consider how much discretion the budget allows for policy-makers. Because of spending for Social Security pensions (to which Americans have contributed at a regressive tax rate), entitlement programs, previously made contracts , and interest payments on the debt, nearly 70 percent of federal expenditures are uncontrollable because they are ear-marked for bills that must be paid. To be sure, the entire budget is "control-lable" under calamitous conditions; but as a practical matter only about 30 percent of the fiscal year budget comprises defense and civilian programs and foreign and domestic items, which are subject to annual negotiations between the president and Congress.

Third, consider the budget by function. This is not easy because ana-lysts differ about how to classify many outlays. Should a program that pays farmers for grain destined for Third World nations be classified as agricul-tural, international, or military in nature?

Countercyclical expenditures

Countercyclical spending can take two forms. Perhaps the more easily envisioned is direct expenditure by government to hire the unemployed. This function is problematic for many people because it is aligned with big government; but during the great duress of the Depression, necessity became the mother of the deed. The Roosevelt administration moved quick-ly to establish the Civilian Conservation Corps (CCC), Works Progress Administration (WPA), and Public Works Administration (PWA) to create jobs for needy Americans for whom no alternative employment was avail-able. The quality of the experiences varied, and it was easy to ridicule many of them. In some cases little was accomplished other than awarding a pay-check. But in others, such as the Federal Writers' Project, many lasting accomplishments were achieved. During the Great Society era, although gov-ernment employment was a feature, like the Job Corps, the goal was to teach marketable skills to the young and the poor and not to serve countercyclical purposes.

Given the absence of an economic emergency and the conservative tide in American opinion, countercyclical programs today are more likely to be channeled through the private sector than to involve direct public employment. Those who contend, with the Chicago school, that public sec-tor programs are inherently less efficient than market-based activity have held center stage. Thus, the flagship of countercyclical expenditure in 1991, the Transportation Development Act, was to make money available to the private sector, which in turn will stimulate private employment. The creation of the million construction jobs that it envisioned complemented the cur-rent fashion of rebuilding the nation's transportation infrastructure, but doing so through private enterprise.

Politics

One of the features of budget politics, whether in times of Reaganomics-related cutbacks, true fiscal stringency, or reducing expenditures with the return of prosperity, is the skill of administrators in maintaining their agency's share of the budget. A number of tactics that agency advocates use to outmaneuver a hostile OMB have been isolated by Lance LeLoup (1986). The strategy of *calling out the troops*, based on the notion of client politics, consists of drawing on an agency's beneficiaries to raise their voices in support. Since "all politics is local" and it is rare for representatives to turn a deaf ear to their constituents, it is important to have these "troops" voice their disapproval of underfunding to their local member of Congress. Often funds can be restored if the agency uses buzzwords that are the *current fashion*. For example, NASA was quick to move into energy research during the oil crises of the 1970s, and during the 1980s the operative words were *efficiency* and *competitiveness*.

In the *Washington Monument ploy*, an agency saves money by shutting down those programs that enjoy the most public support, such as elevator trips to the top of one of Washington's greatest tourist attractions. Public demand should bring about the reinstatement of the funds, and monies will not be subtracted from the less well-known programs that were deep in the background. In a section on *capture their imagination*, LeLoup (1986) emphasizes getting the various appropriations subcommittees to identify with an agency's sense of mission, and thus ensure a continued flow of funds. The technique of *obfuscate and inundate* relates to burying congressional or OMB staffs under vast quantities of data and testimony. *Getting a foot in the door* involves the realistic point that the hard part of the program is well under way. Why cut it off just when the benefits are about to materialize? Inherent in most of these tactics is *making an end run around OMB*, while at the same time LeLoup's final admonition is *to play fair*. Certain practices, like deliberately falsifying data, violate the norms of the budgetary process.

DEFICITS AND THE NATIONAL DEBT

The size of the national debt (the total amount owed by the government to its creditors) and the magnitude of each year's deficit (the excess of expenditures over revenue in any one fiscal year) are perennial issues of political economy. Just as with expenditures, however, it is important to avoid denominating the debt and the deficit in inflated dollars that show them rocketing upward. Instead it is wise to show them in constant terms as proportions either of the budget or of the GNP or else to put them on a human scale by expressing them in per capita terms.

In 1988, when per capita GNP was $19,783 and personal income was

$16,524 per person, federal taxes were $3,703 for each man, woman, and child in America. In the same year, federal expenditures were $4,301 per person. Thus there was a shortfall of $598 for every American. This shortfall, multiplied by a population of 246 million, accounted for the 1988 deficit of $147 billion. This amount, plus accumulated unpaid deficits from previous years, constitutes the national debt. For 1988 that debt was $2.601 trillion, or about $10,564 per person. The total national debt has fluctuated a great deal over time. The typical scenario was to increase borrowing during wartime (though not during the panics of the nineteenth century) and to repay the debt with the return of prosperity. Occasionally, an actual surplus was engendered—something that could cause its own share of bitterness and finger pointing. The national debt as a proportion of GNP was 16.2 percent in 1929, 53.6 percent in 1939, and 122.7 percent in 1945 because of wartime spending. After the war it steadily decreased: 96.3 percent in 1950, 57.4 percent in 1960, 38.6 percent in 1970, and 34.1 percent in 1980. This decline was reversed under Reaganomics, when it increased to 46.3 percent of GNP by 1985 and to 56.2 percent by 1988. By May 1993, the total debt per person had risen to $16,846, assuming a population of 255 million.

The great debt that loomed over the country at the end of World War II was not paid off through higher taxes, in the way that populistic presidential candidate Ross Perot would have the nation do today. Instead, the nation simply outgrew it during the boom years from 1945 to the end of the 1970s. Today, however, with the slower growth rate and a shrinking manufacturing base, there is a concern that outgrowing the present debt is no longer an option.

Reasons for Concern

The most immediate concern about the debt is the cost of carrying it. Because it is unthinkable that the United States would default on its debt, the payment of interest on it is truly mandatory—a portion of the uncontrollable part of the budget. These payments now account for 14 percent of the total budget and grow annually as long as the budget is out of balance. This sum not only dwarfs expenditures for antitrust enforcement, environment, education, and infrastructure reconstruction, but in fact is equal in size to all of the expenditures for controllable civilian programs!

A second concern is the impact of federal borrowing on the financial markets. When the government borrows it does so in many of the same markets where private corporations and individuals go to find money. As government competes for these scarce funds it drives up interest rates and shrinks the pool of money available to all. This result depresses lending within the private sector, which means that new machine tools will not be purchased, new houses will not be built, and new jobs will not be created. Although the most immediate impact is felt by interest-rate sensitive industries like automobiles and construction, eventually the costs are shifted to other fields as well.

Deferring the costs of current government to a later generation is another reason to worry about the debt. It seems inequitable that those who benefit directly from programs do not pay their costs but shift them to a younger age cohort through intergenerational transfers. And there are other causes for concern. An externally held debt, in which American promises to pay are concentrated among a few foreign investors, gives those creditors the power to cause financial mischief by dumping those securities on the market. Consider, too, that incurring debt in normal times suggests fiscal profligacy, which unsettles financial markets and exercises a depressing effect on the economy as a whole. Finally, not paying one's debts is at variance with the American ideal of Yankee thrift.

Politics

Perceptions of the debt itself and the identity of the perceivers have changed since 1945. The magnitude of the annual deficit was a constant source of complaint during the Truman and Kennedy-Johnson years, and even during the Eisenhower and Nixon administrations. Yet these deficits were far smaller than today's when measured as a percentage of the GNP or in terms of carrying charges. Ironically, those who traditionally were most alarmed over deficit finance were Republicans. Democrats, although they might have voiced their concerns, tended to be at peace with deficits that ran at 2 or 3 percent of GNP.

Figure 9-4 Jutila, Sakari, and Ooi Chai Tan. 1988. Macroeconomic Profile of the U.S. from 1950 to 1988. Toledo, Ohio: University of Toledo, Business Research Center, p. 22.

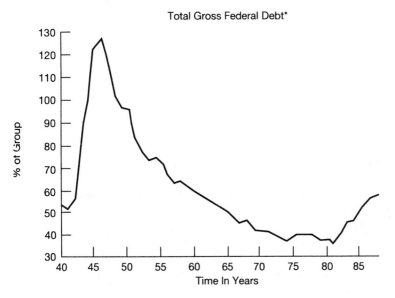

Total Gross Federal Debt*

The growth in indebtedness of the 1980s came when the White House was occupied by the most conservative president since Calvin Coolidge (see Figure 9–4). In considering this event, Andre and Franco Modigliani (1987) have rejected arguments that the public brought it on by demanding tax cuts or that democracies are inherently spendthrift regimes. Instead, they see the debt problem arising from three interrelated factors. The first was that President Reagan, or those in his administration who acted in his name, failed to recognize the magnitude of the gap between the 1981 tax reduction act and the simultaneous increase in military spending. The gap grew cumulatively across the decade and was exacerbated by the failure to seek new revenue sources in 1986 or at any other time.

Second, the administration failed to appreciate how difficult it is to reduce government programs. The tactics identified by LeLoup (1986) worked well within the executive branch, while program advocates in Congress, Republicans as well as Democrats, protected programs that were important to their constituents and to their committee jurisdictions. Although unsuccessful attempts to cut Social Security might exemplify these problems, there were hundreds of others. Finally, the Modiglianis contend that the Laffer curve was a delusion of ideology. People are often reluctant to cast aside their beliefs, and the notion that revenue gains would outstrip losses from tax cuts was a fundamental tenet of Reaganomics.

Another explanation for the growth in indebtedness during the 1980s is decidedly Machiavellian. Some argue that within the highest circles of the administration, it was believed that massive debt would be a preemptive strike against liberal, big-spending programs. With a mounting interest expense, how could even the most liberal of Democrats promote new initiatives? Arguably, if there was such a strategy, it was notably successful.

When viewed from the perspective of managing the economy, the striking thing about the increase in the national debt in the last decade is that it did not occur for countercyclical reasons nor even in the course of fighting a costly war. It came about during a period of prolonged prosperity (a prosperity that probably was induced by this massive injection of deficit spending) because of a failure of revenues to match expenditures in normal economic circumstances.

CONCLUSIONS

There are a number of factors to bear in mind about taxing, spending, and debt in order to understand fiscal policy. On the revenue side of the budget there is no such thing as a neutral tax. All tax bases and rate structures favor one group of taxpayers over another in some way. Some of them inspire ideological reactions from their supporters and opponents, and all have effects beyond the avowed one of raising funds for the federal treasury.

The expenditure side of the budget is even more disputatious. Although aggregate budgetary figures of $1.3 trillion make headlines, that total embraces a host of specific programs, each with its own subgovernment. The bureaucracy itself has a number of strategies of its own for defending its projects. Almost invariably, expenditures outweigh revenues, and usually the deficit will be far greater than had been foreseen. Debates over the size and importance of deficit spending and the debt were particularly intense during the 1980s.

Debates that center on fiscal policy also attest to some disagreements among the schools of economic thought. The classical economists had been appalled by the profligacy of governments in their day and taught the need for fiscal prudence and balanced budgets. Thus, there was disdain among orthodox economists when John Maynard Keynes called for deficits during downturns. Now, however, neoclassical post-Keynesians eschew activist policies because they see them as overly crude tools that are dependent on the intervention and coordination of too many decision makers.

The beauty of a monetarist approach to managing the economy is its reliance on a more careful manipulation of the money supply, and it is to this view of economic management that we now turn.

DISCUSSION QUESTIONS

1. Which of these is closer to the American dream: the "old republican" preference for general equality of conditions among citizens of the United States, or the "free enterprise" view that concentration of great wealth is a just reward for hard work?

2. Distinguish among proportional, progressive, regressive, and degressive rates of taxation. Which is most compatible with the Laffer curve?

3. Why is it important to distinguish between nominal and effective rates of taxation? Why are they different?

4. Why has there been such a shift in the revenue sources of the federal government during the last fifty years?

5. Which of Adam Smith's canons of taxation can be most profitably employed by a skilled lobbyist?

6. Who determines which portions of the national budget are controllable and which are not? Why does the *Wall Street Journal* usually print quotation marks around the word "uncontrollable" when it appears in one of its articles?

7. With regard to LeLoup's strategies for restoring cuts in agency budgets, can you think of any other ploys for safeguarding your budget?

8. What are opportunity costs, and how do they relate to interest payments on the federal debt?

9. Should we be concerned with the size of the national debt? What difference does it make to you as an individual?

REFERENCES

Blum, Walter J., and Harry Kalven, Jr. 1966. *The Uneasy Case for Progressive Taxation*, 2nd ed.; Chicago: University of Chicago Press.

Fenno, Richard F. 1966. *Power of the Purse: Appropriations Politics in Congress.* Boston: Little, Brown.

Juglar, Clement. 1862. *Des crises commerciales et de leur retour periodique en France, en Angleterre, et aux Etats-Unis.* Paris: Guillaumin.

Jutila, Sakari T., and Ooi Chai Tan. 1988. *Macroeconomic Profile of the U.S. Economy, 1950–1988.* Toledo, OH: University of Toledo Business Research Center.

Kondratieff, Nikolai. 1925, 1944. *The Long Waves in Economic Life.* New York: Foundation for the Study of Cycles.

Kuznets, Simon. 1930. *Secular Movements in Production and Prices: Their Nature and Their Bearing Upon Cyclical Fluctuation.* Boston: Houghton Mifflin.

LeLoup, Lance T. 1986. *Budgetary Politics*, 3d ed.; Brunswick, Ohio: King's Court Communications.

Light, Paul. 1985. *Artful Work: The Politics of Social Security Reform.* New York: Random House.

Modigliani, Andre, and Franco Modigliani. 1987. "The Growth of the Federal Deficit and the Role of Public Attitudes," *Public Opinion Quarterly*, 51 (1987), 459–480.

Schlesinger, Arthur M., Jr. 1959. *The Coming of the New Deal.* Vol. 2 of *The Age of Roosevelt.* Boston: Houghton Mifflin.

Schumpeter, Joseph. 1939. *Business Cycles: A Theoretical, Historical, and Statistical Analysis of the Capitalist Process.* New York: McGraw-Hill.

Tobin, James. 1988. "Reaganomics in Retrospect." In B.B. Kymlicka and Jean V. Matthews, eds. *The Reagan Revolution?* Chicago: Dorsey Press. Pp. 85–103.

Wildavsky, Aaron. 1992. *The New Politics of the Budgetary Process*, 2nd ed. New York: HarperCollins.

Wilson, James Q., ed. 1980. *The Politics of Regulation.* New York: Basic Books.

CHAPTER TEN

MONETARY POLICY

The value, availability, and stability of the money supply often have been controversial in American politics, and fluctuations in money have always been linked to economic performance. Establishing a medium of exchange was an objective of Alexander Hamilton during his term as secretary of the Treasury. Andrew Jackson's great battle with the Second Bank of the United States was with that institution's control over the money supply, and actions of the Federal Reserve system in failing to tighten the supply of credit deserve part of the blame for the Great Crash of 1929. Within recent decades, because it can function with minimal governmental intervention, a reliance on monetary policy has been advocated by conservatives as superior to fiscal policy for buffering the highs and lows of the business cycle.

To understand monetary policy and politics we begin by considering the nature of money—what it is, what it does for us, and what forms it takes. Because they are especially important in creating and circulating money, we then examine the role played by banks in creating the money supply. We next review the history of political controversies involving monetary policy and describe the creation of the Federal Reserve system and its operations. The chapter closes with a discussion of the dimensions of political conflict in monetary policy today.

THE NATURE OF MONEY

Money is important in all societies. Early man engaged in commerce by barter—a pig for a pair of boots or a barrel of wheat for a shirt. But barter is cumbersome, and just what an appropriate exchange rate ought to be between hogs and boots is subject to widely differing opinion. Thus, ancient governments sought to simplify commerce by supplying coins, usually stamped or cast from scarce metals—gold or silver or even copper or nickel. And if the intrinsic value of the coin was not sufficient, the portrait of a ruler or deity was often an official testimonial of its worth. The Athenian *tetradrachma* (ca. 550–480 B.C.), a silver coin bearing the head of Athena on its front and the figure of an owl on the back, was one of the most trusted currencies of the Greek world. Its use marked the spread of civilization from Asia Minor to Rome in pre-Christian times. A century later the Macedonian gold *stater*, bearing the head of Apollo, was issued during Philip II's rule. It became the most popular coin in Greece and was in use from southern Russia to Italy.

What is money, and what does it do? Money is most often thought of as currency—paper money in ones and tens and hundreds, or a handful of coins in our pocket or purse—and money allows us to buy things that we want. But there is far more to the definition and function of money than that, and we need to understand what money really is. In today's world we need a clearer definition of money, or of types of money and "near money." As described by the *Federal Reserve Bulletin*, (1993, p. A4) M1, the narrowest definition of money, consists of paper money and coins, or currency, and all deposits in banks and savings and loan institutions on which checks can be written. Coins constitute about 3 percent of M1, and paper Federal Reserve notes constitute about 25 percent. Checking deposits account for nearly three-fourths of this most basic money measure.

M2 expands the definition of money by including all of M1 plus the somewhat less liquid assets that we have in savings accounts, smaller time deposits, and short-term government securities that can be converted to currency or put into checking accounts without appreciable financial sacrifice to the holder. It is this M2 "monetary aggregate" that has become the definition that many influential policymakers recognize as the most important monetary target. M3 is an even more expansive definition. Included here is all of M2 as well as time deposits of more than $100,000. M3 is the measure of money that many economic forecasters find most useful in assessing future economic trends. For the week ending October 1, 1990, the nation's money supply was as follows:

Type	Amount (in $ Billions)			Cumulative Percent
M1 = $829.3				(20.3)
M2 = $829.3	+ $2,494.9 = $3,324.2			(81.3)
M3 = $829.3	+ $2,494.0 +	$763.5	= $4,087.7	(100.0)

Notice that a number of items are *not* included in the common definitions of money. Although Treasury bills and government bonds are widely traded, they are not sufficiently liquid to be regarded as money. Credit cards are also not defined as money but instead as a means for receiving a short-term loan from the bank or other institution that issues them.

Monetary politics begins with the belief that the quantity and quality of money are important in society but that coins and currency are only a small part of the country's total money supply. The Federal Reserve system uses three major instruments to expand and contract, as needed, the availability of M1, M2, and M3. Because of differing emphases, methodological orientations, and "feels" about economic direction, the system's seven governors, as well as the representatives of the regional banks that join them on the Federal Open Market Committee (FOMC), often adopt differing viewpoints on whether bank credit should be loosened or tightened.

The political stakes in monetary policy are associated with the three functions that money performs, with what money does for us. First, it is a *medium of exchange.* Coins, currency, and other forms of money are more portable and easier to handle than a young pig or a barrel of wheat. Second, money is a *standard* of value. It is far more convenient to state the exchange rate of commodities such as boots or shoes in only one denomination—shillings in colonial New York, for example—rather than in hogs, wheat, or hours of labor. Third, money is a *store* of value. It offers a convenient medium for storing assets across time because either precious metals or Federal Reserve notes should be less perishable in nature than pigs, wheat, or milk. Of course, the discovery of more silver or some other debasement of the currency can erode the value of our stores of money in ways that undercut this third function.

These three functional definitions of money yield a second facet of monetary politics: The particular definition one adopts can engender a preference for inflation, deflation, or stability. Buyers and developers, "plungers" and entrepreneurs, whether building settlements on the frontier or providing housing for the families of today, need ready access to money and credit for the things they want to do. Here the stress is on readily available money in the system—for enough of the medium of exchange. Paper currency was printed during the American Revolution to meet this need for a circulating medium, and the patriots' cause would have been lost without it. It is no accident that the geographic regions that experience the greatest growth, and industries like automobiles and construction that depend on borrowing, have a built-in preference for larger supplies of money and will accept moderate amounts of inflation. This feature also helps to explain the opposition of Andrew Jackson's western allies to the Second Bank of the United States and the coldness of the construction trades to the tight money policies of Paul Volcker during the 1980s. At the other end of the spectrum, those with savings already in hand are usually numbered among the economically conservative who have a vested interest in maintaining a hard, solid currency.

Here, the obvious emphasis is on the "store of value" aspect of money. If long-term deflation were to occur, their assets would grow even without being put to productive use. Finally, because price stability facilitates rational economic decision making across time and among products, the view of money as a constant store of value occupies an intermediate position in the balance between inflation and deflation, between "easy" money and "hard." Figure 10–1 displays the fluctuations in the general price level in the United States since 1800.

BANKS AND THE CREATION OF MONEY

Money can be created in various ways. One is by having the government stamp out gold or silver coins, then circulate them by paying its debts to contractors, soldiers, civil servants and others with this hard money. The government can stimulate the circulation of this coinage by requiring that taxpayers and any others who owe it money must pay their debts in specie, as the U.S. government did during the 1830s and 1840s. Of course, the government has the power to designate other scarce commodities as money and to require their use as the circulating medium. Some truly strange money has been created in this way in the past, including tobacco in early Virginia and playing cards in colonial Quebec.

The idea of creating banks as places for the safekeeping of money is ancient, and it is the sine qua non of commercial banking even today. There

Figure 10-1. Source: William Greider, *Secrets of the Temple: How the Federal Reserve Runs the Country.* (New York: Simon & Schuster, 1987), p. 720.

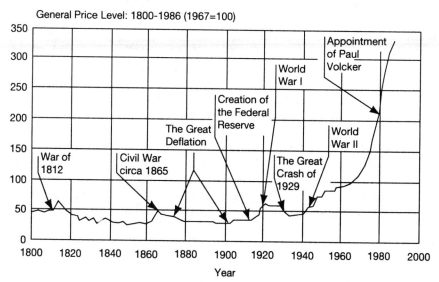

must be money in the vault before transactions can occur in the world of banking. Medieval goldsmiths (who by the nature of their business had strong vaults) were people to whom one could turn to keep safe a small bag of gold or a cache of silver coins. But a stash of gold sitting idly in a dark safe is such a waste. Probably in ancient Persia and Greece, and certainly by the thirteenth century in Genoa, Italy, commercial bankers began to lend out their gold stores to credit-worthy people in exchange for the return of the principle sum plus interest. A bank had to maintain a balance between loaning out enough of its funds to make money and retaining enough to meet the demands of depositors who might seek the return of their assets.

More usually, money has been created by commercial banks in one of two ways. Before 1913, a merchant might obtain a loan for $1,000 from a bank and receive it in "bank notes." These bank notes looked very much like today's currency but were printed by private firms (or by the United States or relevant state comptroller of the currency) and were signed by one or more officers of the issuing institution. The borrower would pay his or her debts with these bank notes, and those creditors in turn would conduct their own business with the same notes. It was understood that the final holder of the paper could redeem it for gold or silver at the issuing bank; and as long as all of the people who held a bank's notes did not appear at the bank's doors at the same time demanding payment in specie, the promise to pay in hard money was a good one, although occasionally runs on the bank did occur. As a general rule, the credit-worthiness of any individual bank was likely to be less the farther away it was located. Publications such as Thompson's Bank Note and Commercial Reporter appeared weekly to provide information about the diverse supply of notes in circulation before the Civil War.

A second method of money creation was for the bank simply to "debit" the borrower's checking account for the $1,000, thereby letting him or her write ordinary checks with this new money. But whichever method of money creation was used, the borrower would be expected to repay the debt on a regular basis—probably monthly. As that money flowed back into the bank it could be loaned to other borrowers in a similar process. The bank could lend as much money as seemed prudent, but it had to remember to hold back an appropriate "reserve" amount for those who might come in to redeem their holdings in bank notes or simply to remove the deposits they had placed there for safekeeping. But still the critical question was how large this reserve should be . By requiring a larger reserve to be maintained, the bank would be more limited in the funds that it might lend; conversely, requiring a smaller reserve would facilitate the money-creating function. Thus, adjusting the *reserve requirement* was one way of regulating the supply of money.

Banks have always borrowed from one another when they are in need of funds. This practice is especially important when more people appear to redeem their notes or to withdraw their savings. If the interest rate charged by one bank to another is higher than the borrowing bank would realize from interest on money that it has loaned to its commercial customers, it will force that bank to maintain larger reserves. Thus, raising this *discount rate* that banks charge one another is another method for reducing the supply of money.

A third way to affect the amount of money that banks will make available is by making it more desirable for them to loan their money to the government. This is the principle behind *open market operations*. Here, a bank's decision to buy government securities once again puts potential money to work in servicing the government's debt rather than in expanding the money supply.

The actions that affect the supply of money can be summarized as follows: To *expand the supply of money* in the economy,

1. Reduce the reserve requirements that a central bank imposes on its member banks.

2. Lower the discount rate—the interest charged by a central bank to those banks that borrow from it.

3. Have a central bank allow banks subservient to it to sell governmental securities that they hold, thereby freeing up the assets of those smaller banks.

To contract the money supply simply reverse these actions:

1. Increase the reserve requirements of correspondent (or "member") banks in the Federal Reserve system from, say, 10 percent of their assets to 12 percent.

2. Raise the discount rate—the interest charged by the central bank to banks that borrow from it—by, for example, 1/2 percent—from 8 3/4 to 9 1/4.

3. Require the member banks to buy government securities on the open market, thereby tying up assets that might otherwise be loaned to private people or businesses.

These three methods for managing the money supply by regulating the banking system have been understood for generations. They were practiced by the Bank of Amsterdam at the beginning of the seventeenth century and by the Bank of England since its creation at the end of the same century. They are the methods that the U.S. Federal Reserve system has employed since its creation in 1913, but they were used by Nicholas Biddle's Second Bank of the United States in the 1820s and 1830s. The most important advantages modern monetary policy managers have over their institutional forbears are improved communication and vastly better methods of measurement .

BANKS AND MONETARY POLICY IN U.S. HISTORY

A fundamental function that all governments perform is providing a medium of exchange. This function was problematic in colonial America, for hard money was in short supply. Reliance was placed on coinage from England and the Spanish possessions in Florida, but barter was often used out of necessity. Since money can be nearly anything that satisfies its three definitional conditions, tobacco was found to be wholly serviceable as a medium of exchange in Virginia. The short supply of money forced some colonial governments to print paper money. During the Revolution, paper money was widely used to pay the debts of the states to their soldiers and military suppliers, and the Continental Congress also adopted paper currency— the famous Continental dollars. Although history has ridiculed the congressional currency with the expression that something is so worthless that it is "not worth a Continental," no less a figure of frugality than Benjamin Franklin was a proponent of paper currency. Arguably, the Revolution could not have been won without resorting to the expediency of paper money.

The role that banks play in creating money emerged after the colonial period. The first commercial banks in the United States appeared only after independence—the Bank of North America, chartered by Congress on the last day of 1781, and the Bank of Massachusetts, organized in 1784. As part of his ambitious plans for national economic development, Alexander Hamilton, the first secretary of the Treasury, realized the need for both a source of capital and for an institution that could serve as a depository and fiscal agent for the new government. On December 13, 1790, Hamilton submitted his report on a national bank to the House of Representatives. Although Jefferson, in Washington's cabinet as secretary of state, adopted a strict constructionist interpretation that any bank would be unconstitutional because Congress was not specifically empowered to charter it, Hamilton argued that it was constitutional under congressional power to collect taxes and to regulate commerce. Hamilton's views won. Headquartered in Philadelphia, the national capitol during the 1790s, the Bank of the United States was chartered for a period of twenty years. It had eight branches, and its notes were generally accepted throughout the country. Its holdings in coin made it a central bank of last resort for the smaller banks that were springing up—a bank that could exercise a certain degree of financial control through deposit requirements and manipulation of the discount rate. The Bank of the United States was organized as a mixture of public and private enterprise. State-chartered banks rose from thirty in 1801 to eighty–eight by 1811.

Almost from the first the Bank of the United States was the subject of political controversy. William Branch Giles, a Jeffersonian Republican from Virginia, charged its organizers with corruption and mismanagement in 1793; and John Taylor of Caroline, Virginia, contended that the monied interests had come to dominate Congress and, through it, the bank as well. By 1811 the movement to recharter this first bank was caught in the snarl of the peculiar politics of the Madison administration—personal hatreds, party factionalism, and regional rivalry. The administration, through Treasury Secretary Albert Gallatin, supported the bank's renewal, but the "Old Republican" faction of the president's party opposed it for several reasons. One was animosity toward the Swiss-born Gallatin himself. Another was the very same strict constructionist arguments that had been offered two decades before—arguments that were offered because of the growth of state-chartered banks, which sought to obtain all the business the national bank would leave behind if it were allowed to die. Calling the bank a vestige of Federalist power and noting that two-thirds of the bank's stock was held by British interests, the anti-British hysteria that had grown intense since the Chesapeake Affair of 1807 was additional fuel on the fire. So the bank died. The irony was, of course, that the bank would have been very useful in the ensuing War of 1812—a war that Congress was glad to declare but was never disposed to support financially.

The War of 1812 proved to be a financial nightmare. The credit of the country suffered and the government only narrowly escaped bankruptcy. As a result of the political leadership of those who had weathered the financial storms of the war's last year, people like Treasury Secretary Alexander Dallas and John Jacob Astor, a second bank was chartered in 1816. Once again designed as a mixed corporation with central banking functions, this bank suffered at first from the mismanagement of a Republican politician named William Jones. Set right under the leadership of former Congressman Langdon Cheves, the bank's political and economic fortunes were tied to those of Nicholas Biddle, a financial genius with keen understanding of banking. Leading the bank after 1823, he oversaw an aggressive expansion. Bank notes in circulation rose from $4.5 million in 1823 to $19 million in 1831, and the bank increased its presence in the South and West. Its use of "documentary bills," or promissory notes, amounted to a variety of short-term commercial paper, which provided an elastic currency that could be expanded or contracted with economic conditions and as the bank saw fit. Its contraction of this money supply in 1832 probably brought on a depression, which was seen by its advocates as an attempt to stem inflation and by its adversaries as a vindictive plot against interests loyal to President Jackson.

The battle to recharter this Second Bank of the United States, and the Biddle-Jackson conflict, was one of the classic confrontations of American political history. Under Biddle's leadership, the second bank had supplied capital for business and reduced the threat of inflation from the disorganized currency then in circulation, which was supplied by an undisciplined system of small banks. Opposition to it came from many quarters, however. A policy of branch drafts caused state banks to reduce the quantity of their notes in circulation and was a tight money policy that angered debtors everywhere, especially those in the West and South. Martin Van Buren and New York interests friendly to him were rivals of Philadelphia's financial preeminence, which was traced to the presence of the bank in that city. The state banks were also closed out of the opportunity to be depositories for federal money, and many of them became states' rights advocates who reopened the issue of the bank's constitutionality.

Into this mixture came Jackson, who in his first State of the Union address gave voice to these objections and indicated his own preference for a wholly government-owned institution largely confined to holding deposits. Although the bank's charter was not due to expire until 1836, a tactic of early renewal seemed prudent to Biddle, but the bill that would have brought it about was vetoed by Jackson. Now the stage was set for one of the most vitriolic elections in history. The election of 1832 was seen as a campaign of privilege, monopoly and monied aristocracy against the president and "the people." The ticket of Jackson and Van Buren received 56.5 percent of the two-party vote over Henry Clay, the Whig candidate, and an overwhelming victory in the Electoral College. The stage was set for the bank's final battle.

The president saw his reelection as a mandate to end the bank, while Biddle followed a tight credit policy to embarrass the administration. Over the objections of Whig opponents in the Senate, Jackson took steps to withdraw all federal deposits. There was even dissention in his own cabinet, and Treasury Secretary William Duane resigned over the issue. Nevertheless, by the end of 1833 some twenty-three state banks—"pet banks" in the eyes of the opposition—began to receive public funds. Despite intense senatorial opposition from Clay and Calhoun, the bank failed to secure a new charter. Chartered instead as a state bank, it became the Bank of the United States of Pennsylvania, but thereafter financial leadership in America gradually swung from Philadelphia to New York.

From this time until the Civil War, American banking and monetary policy were afloat in uncharted seas. A few radical Jacksonians preferred abolishing all banks, and during the 1840s and 1850s nine states did made all banking illegal (Robertson, 1968, p. 23). But the opportunity for profit from state banks was so great that their number and capitalization increased dramatically. The flood of demands on legislatures for charters, plus the spread of the democratic ideal of opportunity for all, led to "free banking"; that is, anyone in compliance with certain minimal standards could start a bank. The opportunities for fraud were particularly vast in Michigan under that state's Free-Bank Act of 1837 and in the many states that emulated it.

Not all states were undisciplined, however, and the New York law became a model that was copied by many states and by the United States itself during the Civil War. Although New York also facilitated entry into the banking business, it allowed banks to issue banknotes only in the amount equal to that of national, New York, or similarly approved other state bonds on deposit with the New York comptroller of the currency. The comptroller was empowered to liquidate the assets of any bank that failed to redeem its notes on demand. New York banks were also required to keep specie reserves of at least one-eighth of their outstanding notes.

Elsewhere state governments themselves—Ohio, Missouri, and South Carolina—were shareholders in their own banks until the Civil War, when nearly half the states had banking regulations similar to those of New York. The notes of these state-chartered banks constituted the entire paper currency of the nation from 1836 to 1860, when 1,500 banks issued six denominations of notes, on the average, or 9,000 different kinds of paper money (Robertson, 1968, pp. 22–29.) There were publications that tracked all this currency, however, and most banks were fundamentally honest. The American economy probably could not have expanded as it did without them.

The impetus for a uniform national currency and for uniformity among the banking structure itself came from what is so often a force for reform—wartime necessity. When the Lincoln administration assumed power there was little money in the Treasury, and Secretary of the Treasury Salmon P. Chase was adverse to raising taxes to pay for rapidly expanding expenses. During the summer of 1861, with the Union defeat at Bull Run hanging heavily in the air over Washington, Congress authorized the Treasury to pay government salaries with paper currency. This was fiat money or, more technically, non-interest bearing notes. Later, the Legal Tender Act of February 1862 was the basis for the issuance of nearly $.5 billion dollars in currency by the war's end. Printed by the Bureau of Engraving and Printing, the bills were black on one side and green on the other. As might be expected, the purchasing power of these "greenbacks" depreciated against gold prices, going as low as thirty-five cents on the dollar as Union fortunes waned. With victory in sight by 1865, however, it returned to eighty cents.

More than greenbacks alone were needed to finance the war, and Secretary Chase put forward a companion plan for national banking. Eventually a system of nationally chartered banks was brought forward in June 1864. The bill was sponsored by Senator John Sherman (R–OH), but it would not have passed without a grass-roots newspaper and insider lobbying effort by financiers Jay and Henry Cooke. Their work would have done credit to any lobbying campaign today.

Under the law, national banks were required to maintain one-third of their capital in interest-bearing U.S. government bonds and to issue currency in amounts up to 90 percent of these assets. A new agency, headed by the comptroller of the currency, would issue uniformly engraved notes to member banks, and a total of up to $300 million was authorized to be apportioned among the states by population. Nine months later a tax on state bank note issues forced 700 state banks to become national banks and ensured a uniform national currency.

The return to peacetime conditions reduced federal attention to monetary issues. The Public Credit Act of 1869 provided that public debts would be paid in gold, in accordance with the sound money policy of the Grant administration. Four years later, on the heels of silver discoveries in the West, which easterners feared would fuel inflation, the Coinage Act of 1873 eliminated silver coinage and made gold the sole standard of monetary value in the United States. Called the Crime of '73 by silver backers, this action was seen by "soft-money" advocates as a conspiracy. A money panic later that year did force the government to issue a small quantity of greenbacks, but the Specie Resumption Act of 1874 provided that gold-based payments would be restored by 1879. The silver issue would not go away, however, and hard times caused the enactment of the Bland-Allison Act in 1878, which provided for the Treasury Department to buy from $2 million to $4 million in silver each month. This was not enough for the Greenback Labor party, organized in Toledo, Ohio, in 1878; but the accumulation of gold by the Treasury bolstered confidence in the greenback, which sold on a par with gold by year's end.

As we have already seen, monetary policy returned as the leading issue of American politics after the late 1880s and continued to be troublesome until the creation of the Federal Reserve system during the Wilson administration.

THE FEDERAL RESERVE SYSTEM

The creation of the Federal Reserve system in 1913 was a continuation of policy-making as a consequence of crisis conditions. Indeed, the panic of 1893 had caused a pair of eastern bankers to put forth a scheme calling for an association of banks that could issue currency backed by bank loans to businesses—by bank assets—rather than by gold or silver. Called the Baltimore plan, it was introduced at an American Bankers' Association meeting in 1894. The idea surfaced again at the Indianapolis Monetary Convention three years later, but the return of prosperity laid it to rest until the panic of 1907—a dramatic downturn in the economy that yielded the creation of a National Monetary Commission headed by Senator Nelson Aldrich (R–NY) and Representative Edward Vreeland. Using the Baltimore plan, as embellished over the years, as a point of departure, Aldrich and a group of bankers met at exclusive Jekyll Island, Georgia, to formulate a revised blueprint for money and banking in 1910. It called for a national association to hold a part of member bank reserves, to set discount rates for borrowing, to buy and sell financial instruments on the market, and to issue currency.

Democrats won a majority in the House of Representatives in 1910 and controlled all of Congress and the White House, too, after 1912. Representative Arsene Pujo (D–LA) held hearings on "the money trust" and the great concentration of wealth among America's leading banks. With Aldrich gone from the Senate, leadership in monetary reform shifted to Representative Carter Glass (D–VA), to the House Banking Committee, and to President Woodrow Wilson.

Conflicts over the structure of the new Federal Reserve system were just as important as those concerning its methods of operation. Geographically, there was a need to separate control from both Wall Street and from Washington. Within the banking community itself there was rivalry between eastern bankers, who were at ease with a greater degree of centralization, which they felt they could control, and western bankers, who feared domination by that same eastern establishment. From the perspective of political parties, Democrats insisted on enough governmental authority to counterbalance the weight of the bankers. Thus, the 1912 Aldrich plan called for direction by a forty-six-member National Reserve Association, only five of whom were appointed by the president. Clearly, the private bankers would have been in control. The plan put forward by Carter Glass a year later called for a thirty-six-member board, now with *six* presidential appointees, but also with a nine-member executive board that would have included all of the presidential designees. The final arrangement was a compromise among Glass, President Wilson, and the various banking interests: a *seven*-member board of presidential appointees (with the secretary of the Treasury and Comptroller of the Currency as ex officio members), not more than one member from any single Federal Reserve district, overlapping tenure to prevent presidential packing of the board, and an advisory council of bankers with the right to meet at least quarterly with the board.

Today's Federal Reserve Board closely resembles that of 1913, but there are important differences (see Figure 10–2). The Secretary of the Treasury and Comptroller of the Currency were removed by the Banking Act of 1935 in an effort to make the board more independent of presidential influence. Twelve regional federal reserve banks are located across the country: Boston, New York, Philadelphia, Cleveland, Richmond, Atlanta, Chicago, St. Louis, Minneapolis, Kansas City, Dallas, and San Francisco; each is memorialized by name and Federal Reserve district number on each piece of U.S. currency that it issues.

While the Federal Reserve is at the center of monetary policy, it also has a major role in the regulation of banks and financial institutions. It shares this responsibility with the Comptroller of the Currency, the Federal Deposit Insurance Corporation (FDIC), and state bank regulators, but it has lead responsibility in issuing a host of regulatory rules. It was in developing rules governing bank reporting on money laundering that a glimpse of disarray could be seen among the governors, as when Governor Martha Seger worked independently of other governors, the Treasury Department, and the House Banking Committee to promote the banking industry's point of view. The Federal Reserve also serves in a more strictly administrative capacity by performing many functions that provide services to banks.

The Federal Reserve's seven governors, as with any group of strong-willed people, display several decisional dimensions. The governors, among them Chair Alan Greenspan, Vice-Chair Manuel Johnson, and Martha Seger, had their ups and downs during the 1980s.

THE POLITICS OF MONETARY POLICY

Politics is about who gets what, when, why, and with what effect—which means it is about relationships among groups of people. Monetary policy has

Figure 10-2.

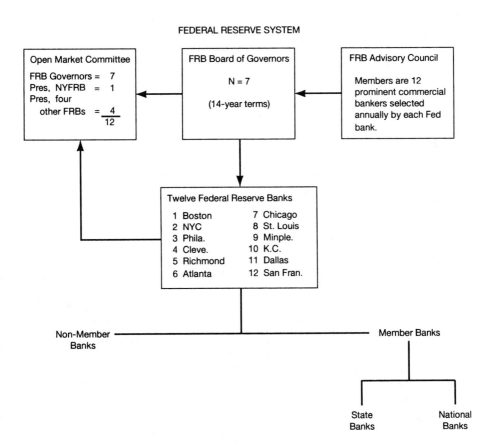

FEDERAL RESERVE SYSTEM

always separated people by groups. Particularly important have been regional alignments, such as the conflict between financial centers in the East (or
in major cities) versus those in the West and South (or at a distance from the
regional city bank) who must rely on those centers for money. There are
also obvious rivalries between debtors and creditors, for those who owe
money would prefer to pay with inflated dollars whereas creditors would be
only too happy to be repaid in dollars worth even more than those they
loaned out. Financial institutions themselves are rivals. Commercial banks
and savings and loan associations occupied different niches until the deregulation of 1982, though since then the image of S&Ls has not been good.
Deregulation has also come to mean that smaller banks are often arrayed
against money-center banks with which they must compete or by which they
may be bought out. And historically, there are differences among occupational groups. Those who borrow are the natural rivals of those who lend.
This was true when the farmers and promoters of Jackson's time opposed
Biddle's Bank of the United States, and we see it today in the concerns about
tight money policy that are voiced by the housing and automobile industries.
These inevitable group conflicts inevitably spill over into the Federal
Reserve, where, in John Woolley's (1984) words, it will "inescapably" favor
"certain societal interests over others" (p. 2).

Although monetary issues today do not command the intensity of interest that they have at certain historical times, there are a number of points of
enduring importance to those who constitute the attentive public in this
area of economic policy. Occasionally they bubble to the surface, and the
Federal Reserve and its policies become current news—as they did in controversies over the decision to increase the discount rate in 1965, as they did in
allegations about increasing the money supply in many presidential election
years, or as they did during the months of the tight money policy of the
Volcker leadership after 1979. For the attentive public, especially those in
interest-rate-sensitive sectors like home building and automobiles, the
Federal Reserve always harbors a number of important issues. Let us consider just a few of them. The most fundamental issue is the economic orientation of the key policymakers themselves—the seven governors of the Federal
Reserve, the presidents and board members of the twelve district banks, and
the orientations of the professional staff members of the system.

Confidentiality is a second enduring issue. We commonly assume that
secrecy is necessary for matters of national security and perhaps, too, in personnel matters; but it is called for in economic policy matters as well. For
example, crop forecasts by the U.S. Department of Agriculture (USDA) are
carefully guarded and are not released to the public until late on Friday
afternoon, when the commodity markets have closed for the weekend. The
minutes of the Federal Open Market Committee are not available until thirty days after the monthly meeting. In the short term this practice can lead to
the wrong signals being sent to the public about Federal Reserve intentions,

as occurred in 1989. An inadvertent signal by the Fed that it was loosening credit by injecting funds into the system triggered the Friday the 13th stock market crash (Wessel and Herman, 1989, p.C1;5). The conflict over Federal Reserve secrecy boiled over the following weekend in a heated exchange between Chairman Greenspan and Manuel Johnson (Murray, 1989, p.C1;6). This is a particular problem because the agency's policy has not been conducted steadily, and it seems first to say one thing and then to do quite another (Woolley, 1984, p. 1) In the long run, the Federal Reserve has the reputation of dealing harshly with former governors or other insiders who have revealed details about the inner workings of the system, as it seems to have done in the case of a book published by former member Sherman Maisel in 1973. As political scientist Woolley (1984) has written, " it seems as if the System has been unnecessarily preoccupied with confidentiality *per se...*" (p. 202).

Third, there are issues associated with the independence of the Federal Reserve system from its environment—from the president, from Congress, and especially from the private financial community. Presidents seek to make wise public policy, but they are also solicitous of their standing in the opinion polls. Understandably, their popularity falls when the economy declines, but perversely for presidents, it also lags behind when prosperity returns. Thus, presidents need to nominate people who share their own or their economic advisers' monetary and economic views and who share a vested interest in maintaining acceptable economic performance. Three major agencies within an administration are relevant to monetary policy, each of them more closely attuned to advising the president or to carrying out his decisions: the Council of Economic Advisors and the Office of Management and Budget, both within the Executive Office, and the Treasury Department. It is only natural that these offices would hope for close relations with the Federal Reserve—to make its chair, together with the director of the OMB, the chair of the CEA, and the Treasury secretary, a part of "the team." But this bonding does not always happen. The extreme example was the way in which Paul Volcker's rigid policies to bring inflation under control contributed to Jimmy Carter's defeat in 1980. Public criticism early in the Bush administration by OMB Director Richard Darman made it clear that Alan Greenspan was pursuing a more restrictive monetary policy than the administration wanted.

Conflict between the administrative triumvirate of Treasury, CEA, and OMB and the Federal Reserve is most likely to occur late in the business cycle. When prosperity seems likely to end, the administration may wish to see a lower discount rate or the sale of government securities in order to expand economic activity. The existence of the political business cycle (PBC), however, suggests that cooperation between the president and the Federal Reserve can go too far. In its clearest manifestation, the PBC would slow money growth a year and one-half or two years before a presidential election to reduce inflation and then expand the money supply during election years to induce an artificial prosperity. The objective is to increase the electoral chances for the incumbent party's presidential candidate. The existence of the PBC has been suggested by anecdotal evidence for many years, but the possibility that monetary policy was an instrument in electoral politics seemed to be confirmed by correspondence showing Federal Reserve chair Arthur Burns's willingness to help the reelection of Richard Nixon in 1972 by appropriate monetary expansion.

The empirical literature on the PBC is large, with its advocates and doubters arrayed on both sides. In one review of the literature, for example, Nathaniel Beck (1987) concluded that the PBC really does not exist—at least not because of any purposeful Federal Reserve action. In his view, the Federal Reserve lacks the tools necessary to effectuate such a program. Even if it could, the "efficient markets" school would argue that the public would discount in advance any expected monetary increases, thereby making futile such a purposeful policy. A more recent analysis by Kevin Grier (1989, pp. 376–389), however, has found a significant four-year cycle in M1 growth from 1961 to 1980, even while controlling for interest rates, income levels, and budget deficits.

If the agency's independence from the president has its ups and downs, its relative freedom from congressional control seems more secure. Although created by Congress and charged with regularly reporting to the Senate Banking Committee through its chair, the system has strong resources of its own. Because its budgetary income is generated entirely from services rendered to member banks, it is immune from the power of the purse that is so crucial to effective oversight. On a personal level, the towering, cigar-chomping figure of Paul Volcker was the equal of the acerbic committee chair Senator William Proxmire (D–WI)—himself as formidable a congressional infighter as any on Capitol Hill at that time.

Former Chair William McChesney Martin said that it was the Federal Reserve that always had to take away the punch bowl just as the party was getting interesting. This fact leads to calls for reforming the agency by making it more responsive to the administration and to Congress. Among the proposals under consideration by congressional committees recently have been changing the term of the chair, shortening the term of the governors, eliminating the presidents of the Federal Reserve banks in decision making, returning the Secretary of the Treasury to the board (as he was before the Banking Act of 1935), auditing the agency by the General Accounting Office (an arm of Congress), putting its expenditures into the budget, and requiring prompt publication of its minutes.

To many people, the greatest cause for alarm is the agency's freedom from domination by its attentive public and client groups—the financial community. In the late 1960s the movement for deregulation generally was driven by the perception that independent regulatory agencies often were least independent of those they sought to regulate. People moved through "revolving doors," from private life to government and back again, typically with hefty salary raises and renewed access to those who remained in power. This practice, coupled with half-hearted oversight of businesses that seemed to be contributing to higher prices, inflation, and substandard service, led to reduced regulation in many areas and to the outright abolition of the Civil Aeronautics Board. How insulated is the Federal Reserve today from similar patterns of control by private financial interests?

Under the Federal Reserve system the issue of cooptation by financial interests arises in two ways. The first is in the selection of members of the Board of Governors, especially in the nomination of the chair. Party is rarely of great importance. What is important is for successful nominees to have experience and technical expertise and to be acceptable to three client groups: prominent mainstream bankers, businesspersons, and economists. Democratic administrations, as well as Republican ones, are attuned to the veto power that these groups exercise. President Kennedy reneged on a promised nomination of Seymour Harris because of his unacceptability to these important constituencies; and President Carter appointed Paul Volcker as chair, against the advice of his still-trusted adviser Bert Lance, only because he was acceptable at a time of growing financial difficulty. No one who is very far from the mainstream of orthodox thinking is likely to be appointed to the board. The second concern about the ability of the banking community to coopt the Federal Reserve involves its influence on the selection of regional bank boards and subsequently the policies of the Federal Open Market Committee.

There is also the politics of public opinion. Greider (1987) has argued that unlike earlier generations, the public today seems unconcerned with monetary issues because they seem too difficult. Only during recessions or periods of severe unemployment does the Federal Reserve enter the mind of the average person. This is a result of purposeful action to mythologize monetary policy, to take it above "mere politics," and to assure Americans that all is well because of the competence of all-knowing public servants. Because of the lack of class consciousness in America, even the middle-class conservatism of the union movement since the time of George Meany, there is a great aversion to inflation. The Marxist might raise the issue of false consciousness—that the masses do not understand that with inflation their debts would be easier to pay. A better view might be that the popularity of presidents does not increase with inflation but rather decreases with declines in real income (Woolley, 1984, p. 4).

SUMMARY

Of all of the issue areas involving governmental intervention in the economy, none is of earlier date than those that involve the quantity and quality of money. Issuing coinage was a fundamental act of governmental sovereignty, but probably from the very first there were attempts to debase the circulating medium by shaving off the edges ever so slightly, with the goal of amassing a significant pile of shavings of one's own. From earliest times there has been contention between those who seek a stable money supply that is a reliable store of value and those wanting to ensure a sufficient quantity of money to allow economic growth and prosperity, perhaps at the expense of inflation. Arguably, too, there have been those who purposefully seek to inflate the currency to undermine the wealth of the rich.

With the development of a banking system after the American Revolution came the issue of who would regulate it and how it would provide a medium of exchange. These rivalries soon manifested themselves in sectional, occupational, and party-based conflict, as the United States vacillated across long temporal swings between centralized control (1791–1811, 1816–1836, and 1861–1873) and uncontrolled laissez-faire (especially the era of "free banking" between 1837 and the Civil War). Although there had been serious panics in 1819 and 1837, the boom-and-bust cycles that followed the Civil War and the long-term deflation that characterized the period generated a level of concern that spawned third party movements like the Greenback and Populist parties and the Bryanite, western, silver-bug wing of the Democratic party in 1896.

Synoptic change in American politics usually is the consequence of crisis, and it was the panic of 1907 that eventually gave rise to the Federal Reserve system that remains among us today. Unfortunately, the creation of the Federal Reserve system in 1913 did not guarantee healthful monetary policy. The mistakes of the 1920s contributed their share to the stock-market crash of October 1929 and to the subsequent Great Depression. Since the Banking Act of 1935, however, the actions of the agency have been freer of presidential influence and less partisan than before; they have also been more professional, if also more bureaucratic. The growth of the economics profession has enabled central authorities to control the nation's money supply with far greater certainty. Although exogenous shocks such as those resulting from the oil crises of 1973, 1979, and even 1990 can be destabilizing, the variations in amplitude that long characterized monetary issues have been greatly muted.

Five clusters of political issues are latent in monetary policy. First, there are concerns associated with the differing economic schools of thought among the seven governors of the Federal Reserve system as well as between the board itself and the twelve regional banks. These differences become particularly important when they are played out in the monthly meetings of the FOMC. Second, there are the confidentiality and secrecy of the system's decision-making processes—particularly when the nation's financial markets misinterpret those actions, with disastrous consequences for the stock market. Third, there are the several facets to the issue of institutional independence. The ability of a president to influence monetary policy is a function of at least his own professional skills and those of the Federal Reserve chair, but questions relating to the board's independence from the White House seem greatest with regard to the PBC. Although congressional leaders like Senator Proxmire (D–WI) have a legitimate stake in monetary policy, interference from Congress seems less of a problem than that from 1600 Pennsylvania Avenue. To populistic critics of monetary policy, however, the greatest threat to democratic politics comes from the financial community, which is positioned in so many ways to influence Federal Reserve activities. Fourth, there is the image of monetary policy as the product of bureaucratic decision making. It is at the Federal Reserve that the view of the civil servant as the most significant determinant of public policy may be validated. Finally, there is the question of monetary policy as an aspect of public opinion. It has been said that banking works only when people choose to forget what it is that banks do—that the depositors' money is loaned out again as fast as it comes in. In like manner, the Federal Reserve remains free from political controversy only when people choose to disbelieve that it makes conscious choices about what it does. Greider (1987) has painted an intriguing image of central bankers as mystical figures in templelike settings who give the impression that they are merely the earthly agents of some all-knowing monetary deity. In fact, in the years since the monetarist ascendancy under Volcker, monetary policy is the product of an alliance between a bureaucratic elite and a financial community with a major stake in preserving money as, first, a store of value; second, a measure of value; and only third, a medium of exchange.

DISCUSSION QUESTIONS

1. How can the three uses of money (medium of exchange, store of value, and standard of value) work at cross-purposes politically?

2. What were the political issues underlying opposition to the First Bank of the United States in 1811? To the Second Bank during the Jackson administration?

3. What was the basis of conflict between using gold or silver as the monetary base after the Civil War? What was bimetallism?

4. What chain of events brought about the passage of the Federal Reserve Act in 1913?

5. How have banks and bankers often been perceived in American political life? Why?

6. How unified are economists on issues of monetary policy? What are the views of the several schools of thought today?

7. What sorts of groups approach the Federal Reserve, and how do they do it? How efficacious are they? What groups are the normal clientele of the Federal Reserve?

8. What have been the ups and downs of the Federal Reserve's relations with presidents since World War II? With Congress? What causes monetary politics to heat up occasionally as a political issue?

9. What is the political business cycle, and what is the weight of evidence about it? Is it imaginary?

10. What is meant by the term *late phase conflict*, as it relates to the president's relationships with the Federal Reserve?

11. What are the economic schools or orientations of the governors of the Federal Reserve? What other bases for dissent are there besides a monetarist or post-Keynesian outlook?

REFERENCES

Beck, Nathaniel. 1987, February. "Elections and the Fed: Is There a Political Monetary Cycle?" *American Journal of Political Science*, 31, 194–216.

Greider, William. 1987. *Secrets of the Temple: How the Federal Reserve Runs the Country.* New York: Simon & Schuster.

Grier, Kevin B. 1989, May. "On the Existence of a Political Monetary Cycle," *American Journal of Political Science*, 33, 376–389.

Maisel, Sherman. 1973. *Managing the Dollar.* New York: W. W. Norton.

Meiselman, David. 1984, January 10. "The Political Monetary Cycle," *Wall Street Journal*, p. A32;1.

Murray, Alan. 1989, November 29. "Oct. 13's Stock Slide Shows Fed Officials' Differences."*Wall Street Journal,* p. C1;6.

"Reserves, Money Stock, Liquid Assets, and Debt Measures." 1993, January. *Federal Reserve Bulletin,* 79, Table A4.

Robertson, Ross M. 1968. *The Comptroller and Bank Supervision: A Historical Appraisal.* Washington, D.C.: Office of the Comptroller of the Currency.

Wessel, David, and Tom Herman. 1989, November 29. "Should Fed Hide Its Moves, Leaving Markets Confused?"*Wall Street Journal,* p.C1; 5.

Woolley, John T. 1984. *Monetary Politics: The Federal Reserve and the Politics of Monetary Policy.* New York: Cambridge University Press.

PART FIVE

SUBSTANTIVE
ECONOMIC POLICIES

This group of chapters examines three different areas of political economy. The first, which is concerned with the maintenance of the marketplace, is crucial for the capitalistic, mixed economy of the United States. Since markets are central to capitalism, keeping them free of monopoly manipulation is vital. But as Adam Smith pointed out, although competition is the guiding hand of capitalism, competitors search for ways to mitigate its uncomfortable effects. Loose combinations had early origins, but the trust as a device for tight business combinations arose in America in the 1880s. The Sherman Act of 1890 was more concerned with mitigating the structural characteristics of the marketplace, and the Federal Trade Commission Act and other statutes expanded the government's focus to include fair business practices as well as organization. Today, there are concerns over whether or not our historic antimonopoly policy is only a lost cause of reform and whether new directions in world markets have made it obsolete.

Far more people work for wages and salaries than act as owners, managers, or entrepreneurs. Thus, as discussed in Chapter Twelve, the posture that government assumes toward the working man and woman is especially important to the participants in any economic system. Prototypical labor unions were organized by craft from the earliest times, and national labor brotherhoods existed even before the Civil War; but it wasn't until the age of industrialization that bitter struggles between owners and workers became a feature of the American economic landscape. Propelled by industrialization, wartime personnel demands, and the New

Deal, the acme of union membership and political strength was reached by 1945, when nearly 36 percent of the nation's work force was unionized. The numbers of union members have declined steadily, however, and today only 14 percent of America's workers claim union membership. The decline in union political strength may have been proportional.

International political economy, the third chapter in Part Five, is distinctive in the way that it cuts across each of the areas of economic life that have been considered to this point. It touches (or is itself affected by) the government's regulatory and supportive policies, by its fiscal and monetary policies, and by its antitrust and labor programs. Although foreign trade has always been consequential in American politics, the perception that the world is becoming a smaller place has increased its importance. The enactment of the Trade Expansion Act in 1962 confirmed the importance of multilateral trade negotiations and the importance not only of the European Common Market but of expanded trade with other parts of the world as well. In the 1990s, the North American Free Trade Agreement has introduced a new direction in barrier-free trade among Canada, the United States, and Mexico. Although this still-developing "North American Common Market" may indeed become the world's most populous trade union, it has also unleashed a host of political concerns in the United States and Canada that are still being played out.

CHAPTER ELEVEN

STRUCTURE AND PERFORMANCE IN THE MARKETPLACE: MONOPOLY AND ANTITRUST POLICY

Just as one-person rule is anathema to democracy, so too is monopoly contrary to theories about market economics and mixed capitalism. That it was wrong for single firms or groups of individuals to restrain competition was a view that was held in the ancient world; and for more than a century, antitrust has been one of the cornerstones of American public policy. It is an issue that has staying power. Our major political parties have included platform planks that proclaim support for a strong antimonopoly policy in election after election. An "antitrust community" of lawyers, academic specialists, and governmental administrators has grown up, along with a vast body of legal and economic writing on the subject. Given the great degree of economic concentration in many industries, however, as well as the merger and hostile takeover activities of the past dozen years, Michael Lewis-Beck has argued that antitrust policy has become the lost cause of American politics. But could it also be possible that antitrust policy has seldom if ever enjoyed universal acceptance and that half-hearted enforcement has been the norm historically?

This chapter begins by considering some economic concepts that define the competitive marketplace. Next, it examines the development of antitrust and monopoly policy and the circumstances surrounding the passage of the Sherman Act as a source of ambiguous cues about subsequent antitrust policy. We then review the initial use of the law and the statutes that have been developed to supplement it, followed by the arguments against large-scale enterprise and the contrarian views of the Chicago school. We next consider the way in which antitrust enforcement has been carried out by the Department of Justice under Reagan and Bush, and finally, we summarize the issues that are found in the antitrust political arena today.

MONOPOLY AND MARKET STRUCTURE

Because monopoly means "one seller" and "trusts" were legal devices for bringing about the unified behavior of formerly competing firms, any discussion of monopoly and antitrust policy must begin by considering the number of producers or sellers in the marketplace. Hypothetically, at least, there are four types of markets: pure competition, monopolistic competition, oligopoly, and monopoly.

Monopoly is the easiest of the four market conditions to describe. The word comes from the Latin *mono* (or "singular") and the Greek *polion* (or "right to sell") and means "sole selling rights." Apparently the word itself was first used by Sir Thomas More in *The Utopia* in 1516 (Thorelli, 1955, p. 14). Monopolies were privileges awarded by governments to favored subjects to supplied needed products or services, as well as conditions that grew up wholly apart from governmental involvement. A monopoly is said to exist when (1) there is one producer or group of producers who agree among themselves to fix prices, control quantities produced, or divide up geographical market areas. Monopoly also involves (2) a product or service for which there are no near substitutes and (3) an ability to control prices by controlling the quantity produced. Virtually by definition, (4) entry into the monopolized marketplace by potential competitors is blocked by insurmountable barriers that are the consequence of economic, technological, or legal factors. These factors are exemplified by prohibitively high costs of entry; by skills or patent rights held by the monopolist; or even by laws that limit production to a particularly named firm, as in the case of a regulated public utility. Finally, there is the matter of advertising. When old-time monopolists advertised, they did so for reasons of public relations or political strategy. Today's regulated monopolies, in contrast, seek to increase demand for gas or electricity in order to realize even greater economies of scale. Examples of monopolies can be found in the regulated public utilities, but after more than a century of antitrust policy it is difficult to find many today in the unregulated sector. Instead, monopoly policy is directed at various forms of anticompetitive behavior and at proposed mergers that would bring about unacceptable levels of concentration within a market.

Pure competition is at the opposite end of the spectrum in terms of numbers of competitors. It is often the idealized view of what a market economy is, and it is said to exist when there are (1) a great number of firms producing a product, (2) no significant differences that identify the product of one producer from that of another, (3) no ability by any one producer to affect either the price or the quantity of the total product by withholding his output from the market, (4) relative freedom of entry into the market for those who want to compete (as well as unnoticeable effects when any one producer quits), and (5) an absence of nonprice competition that would justify any efforts at advertising.

Examples of pure competition should be abundant in any market economy, and the typical case that is put forward is in agriculture: thousands of wheat farmers, grain that is indistinguishable by grower, no noticeable effect on the overall quantity or price of wheat if one farmer decides to grow soybeans next year, low entry costs (in comparison to auto manufacturing), and no advertising to distinguish one person's product from another's. That pure competition is only an idealized model becomes apparent upon close inspection, however. Pure competition entails many producers, but just how many firms equals "many"? Although they may offer a standardized product, producers will seek to distinguish their breed stock, for example, as being superior to that of a competitor. And continuing with the farming example, the high price of land and equipment relative to the return on investment constitutes a formidable barrier to anyone wanting to pursue it. Throughout the past century the proportion of Americans in farming has declined from nearly 50 to only about 4 percent. This decline underscores the fact that markets characterized by pure competition are rugged places in which to compete.

Monopolistic competition is the term applied to markets one step removed from pure competition, in which producers seek to distinguish themselves in various ways. Here too we see large numbers of independent producers, but they point to differences in quality or service that distinguish themselves, although these differences may be more perceptual than real. Individual firms exercise limited control over price, depending on the degree of product differentiation; but entry into the marketplace may be relatively easy, with added costs resulting from a need for advertising or for research and development to establish a slightly different product. It is advertising, with vigorous nonprice competition, that especially characterizes monopolistic competition. A glance at the yellow pages of any telephone book reveals that monopolistic competition abounds in the American mixed economy, ranging from automobile dealers to grocery stores and from plumbing to television repair.

In an *oligopoly* there are few sellers, with "few" meaning three or four competitors or perhaps six or eight, within a relevant market. There is product differentiation in some oligopolistic markets, such as automobiles or high-priced electrical appliances like washers and dryers; or there may be none at all, as in steel beams, aluminum ingots or building materials. But it is in the control that individual firms can have over prices that we see one of the most singular features of oligopoly. The small number of competitors makes it easier for them to track one another's prices; and typically one firm emerges as a price leader—as the seller most likely to be the first to initiate an increase in selling prices. Typically too, as the "kinked demand curve" illustrates, price decreases are known to precipitate price wars as all firms seek to match reductions—an unhappy circumstance for any oligopolist. As a result, prices in oligopolistic markets tend to change slowly on the down side. The few sellers in oligopolistic markets can be an invitation to collusion, which combined with the tendency of their prices to move in concert, makes oligopolists targets of antitrust scrutiny under even innocent circumstances.

There are problems with each of these four market models. First, although each begins by considering the number of sellers—one, a few, or a great number—there is disagreement over how many firms it takes to constitute "many" and how few firms equal "a few." Does oligopoly begin with fifty firms, with a dozen, or with only four? Second, there are geographical considerations. Although there may be many lumber suppliers nationwide, for example, there may be only one within a 50-mile radius. Third, there is the problem of product similarity, or of identifying the industry in which the product is offered. When DuPont manufactured all the cellophane in the United States, it was argued by its customers in the tobacco industry that it reaped monopoly profits. But cellophane was subsequently ruled to be only one category of "flexible wrapping materials" that include waxed paper, plastic wrap, and brown paper. Thus, DuPont was not a monopolist. The concept of interindustry competition is important, too, for the broader the definition of an industry, the more difficult it is to contend that monopoly exists. If only a single railroad serves an area, it is not a monopolist if trucking, canal barges, or air freight are seen as alternative modes of transportation. More than nine out of ten metal cans are produced by only two firms— Continental Can and the American Can Corporation. It can be argued, however, that the appropriate market definition should include glass and plastic containers as well as metal ones.

Market concentration is an important concept in the American economy. It can be measured as the percentage of output controlled by the largest four, six, or some other small number of firms; and one of the seminal analyses of market concentration was made by the Temporary National Economic Committee (TNEC) during the 1930s. Today, two firms produce 80 to 90 percent of all the metal cans in the United States (American Can and Continental Can). Three firms provide the same proportion of aluminum production (Alcoa, Kaiser, and Reynolds) and military and commercial aircraft (Boeing, McDonnell-Douglas and General Dynamics). Seventy to 80 percent of pharmaceuticals are produced by four firms (American Home Products, Merck, Pfizer, and Eli Lilly) and the same percentage of all rubber tires by three firms (Goodyear, Bridgestone, and Uniroyal). Indeed, many of the best-known American industries are oligopolistic.

Other ways have been developed to assess the degree of market concentration. One of them is the Gini Index of Concentration, a number that ranges from zero for pure competition to 1.00 for pure monopoly. More recently the Herfingdahl-Hirschmann Index (HHI) became a favored measure during the 1980s by the Antitrust Division of the U.S. Department of Justice. Under this scheme, proposed mergers between firms in an industry with an HHI of 1,000 were to be closely scrutinized for their anticompetitive effects, and those with an index of greater than 1,800 were to be disallowed.

MONOPOLY AND RESTRAINT OF TRADE

In A.D. 483, the Emperor Zeno recognized that monopolies were driving up the prices and undercutting the quality of supplies being purchased for the Roman army at Constantinople. In his edict to the Praetorian Prefect of Constantinople, he prohibited monopoly practices in the purchase of clothing, fish, or other food. The penalties to be paid for violating this rule were heavy fines, forfeiture of property, and perpetual exile.

Important principles of antitrust policy have come to us from English practice. As Hans Thorelli (1955) has pointed out, forestalling, engrossing, and regrating were three similar medieval practices for controlling the distribution of commodities at the wholesale stage. The goal was to corner the market by buying up all available grain before it was harvested or all of a day's catch of fish before it arrived at the town dock. These practices of middlemen were seen to serve no purpose in the primitive markets of the time other than to increase retail prices, upset local shopkeepers, and prevent the collection of tolls that farmers or fishermen would have paid when their goods came into town. Parliament legislated against these practices as early as 1266; but when national markets developed because of improved transportation and when the notion of freedom of contract had been established, the last of the laws against forestalling was repealed by 1772.

Another antimonopoly development under common law was a reaction to granting "letters patent" by the monarch. The granting of patents was a historic prerogative of royalty, and one type was given to guilds to confirm their long-standing privileges or to confer new ones. Guilds were professional trade associations and social organizations—social units with powers of their own. In *Davenant* v. *Hurdis*, the *Merchant Tailors'* case (1373), the London tailor's guild had required that every member who "sent work outside," or subcontracted it, must send at least half of it to fellow guild members. Lord Edward Coke, Davenant's lawyer, argued that under this arrangement the guild members were not required to provide good, workmanlike service. In finding against the guild, the court initiated the concept that monopolies were contrary to the public good.

Other types of patents were granted to individuals outside of the guild system for carrying on trade overseas or in the domestic economy as well as for inducing the immigration of foreign artisans. Rather than contributing to monopoly, such royal grants may have encouraged competition in manufacturing by reducing the power of the guilds. By the time of Queen Elizabeth I, however, the selling of patents to courtiers had become a way to raise revenue. By 1600, there were patents for the production and distribution of soap, salt, glass, iron, paper, and other products. Protests against these abuses echoed throughout Parliament. In 1601, the Queen conceded that there had been abuses in the system and that all patents were subject to the common law. Two years later, in *Darcy* v. *Allein* (1603), it was ruled that a patent grant to the plaintiff for the exclusive right to manufacture playing cards had resulted in raising their price and lowering their quality. The award was voided because it violated the rights of others to carry on the trade.

Still, controversy over patent-based monopolies continued, and in 1623 Parliament enacted a Statute Against Monopolies. In serving also as the basis for modern patent law, the statute was the "high water mark of English antimonopoly policy," (Thorelli, 1955, p. 26) but it proved to have too many loopholes to be effective—a record that would be repeated in the decade that followed the enactment of the Sherman Act in 1890.

Monopoly was not an immediate problem in the young United States. To the extent that the American colonies were subject to mercantilism, English patents (especially involving grants of land) and legal doctrines were present. But the lack of a manufacturing base, plus the abandonment of the common-law tradition in the wake of the Revolution, dimmed our concerns with it. American animosity to the special privilege that monopoly yields meant that there would be a wellspring of opposition to it, as there was at trading posts and forts by frontier radicals. By the time of Andrew Jackson's Farewell Address in 1837, however, "the monopoly problem" had taken on a life of its own in the form of the Bank of the United States. By midcentury, the growth of commerce and manufacturing, the impact of railroads, and the economic forces unleashed by the Civil War had prepared the ground for major monopolistic abuses.

When monopolies began to appear in the mid-nineteenth century, they typically took the form of "loose combinations"—gentlemen's agreements and "pools" that would ensure profits for all by minimizing cutthroat competition. In a Louisiana case, a price-fixing agreement among eight firms that sold material for wrapping cotton bales was broken by one of the participants, who saw an opportunity to make an even quicker profit. When the other seven participants brought suit for breach of contract, a state court held that the agreement was not enforceable because it had been a restraint of trade, and restraints of trade were contrary to the public order. This line of reasoning was used a decade and a half later, when five Rochelle, Illinois, grain dealers had combined to fix prices and divide profits. After the death of one of the participants, his heir sued for his share of the profit pool. Here, too, the court refused to require the payment of the ill-gotten gains. Fifteen years later, a combination in Ohio had cornered 95 percent of the candles made in the United States. Although at regular intervals the participants were to receive a share of the profits, a member who decided to leave the cartel was denied the share that was owed to him and a court refused to require payment of these monies. But although the common law refused to assist monopolists in their internecine squabbles, it lacked a mechanism for declaring monopolies themselves to be illegal.

"Tight combinations" appeared in the decades after the Civil War and took several forms. One was the trust, the classic example of which was the Second Agreement of 1882, a device created by John D. Rockefeller that established the Standard Oil monopoly. Under this scheme, the stockholders of fourteen corporations, plus groups of shareholders in twenty-six other firms and forty associates of Rockefeller himself, exchanged their stocks for "trust certificates" in Standard Oil that were worth a par value of $100 apiece. All decision making was surrendered to a nine-member Board of Trustees, which coordinated production and pricing decisions for the participating companies, admitted new corporations to membership, and dominated the emerging oil industry in America. It was a business innovation of devastating power, and soon it was copied by trusts in cottonseed oil, linseed oil, sugar, whiskey, cordage, lead, and dozens of other commodities. And economically inclusive devices they were, too. The sugar trust included seventeen of the twenty-one leading refiners and dominated 95 percent of all production. The American Cotton Oil Trust controlled 88 percent of that product. Eighty-five to 90 percent of production in its field was governed by the whiskey trust in 1887. With the trusts seemingly beyond the control of the courts, other, even tighter combinations were being formed by outright mergers and buy-outs. It was time to seek statutory relief.

Demands for controlling monopolies had been increasing for years. The Patrons of Husbandry, or Grangers, were a farm organization that had attacked "chartered monopolies"—particularly railroads—as early as 1868; and in 1871 Illinois had created a railroad and warehouse commission to establish fair minimum rates. This action was upheld by the U.S. Supreme Court in *Munn* v. *Illinois* and related *Granger* cases in 1877 as legitimate uses of the "police power of the state" in regulating businesses "affected with a public interest." The challenge had been made on the grounds that the regulation was a denial of the "substantive due process of law" guarantees of the new Fourteenth Amendment, as well as because the regulated activities were in interstate commerce. This claim was of little help, however. For one thing, the Granger laws dealt with only a part of the monopoly problem. For another, the newly emerging trust arrangements were a unique organizational device. And finally, within a few years the Supreme Court became hostile to state-level attempts at regulation.

The case of *San Mateo County* v. *Southern Pacific R.R.* (1882) was the first Supreme Court consideration of whether corporations were entitled to the same constitutional protection as human beings under the new Fourteenth Amendment. The Court found that they were. Four years later, in *Santa Clara County* v. *Southern Pacific R.R.*, Chief Justice Morrison Waite encouraged the use of "substantive due process of law" as a defense for corporate property rights. Later in the same year, *Wabash, St. Louis & Pacific R.R.* v. *Illinois* nearly overturned the *Munn* case of 1877 and suggested that there was a zone of commerce where neither the states nor the federal government could constitutionally regulate. Finally, eight years later in *Reagan* v. *Farmers' Loan and Trust* (1894), the Court asserted for itself a role in protecting corporate property rights from all governmental regulation. Clearly, the U.S. Supreme Court had dramatically changed course between 1877 and 1894.

Soon demands for monopoly control moved into the mainstream of American politics. Several states enacted antimonopoly statutes, and the two major parties took over the demands for national legislation that previously had been voiced by the Greenback party in 1876, the Anti-Monopoly party in 1884, the Knights of Labor, and the Populists. In his State of the Union address in 1887, President Grover Cleveland, a Democrat, asked Congress to take action. Soon the Republicans, to counter their ties with interests associated with Gould, Vanderbilt, and Astor, developed an even stronger antimonopoly stand.

THE SHERMAN ACT

Enacting good statute law requires a clear definition of the problem, but this was no easy task in antitrust legislation. The trust problem was new; but taken together with other changing business practices, the problem of market structure was a moving target that was hard to hit. There was disagreement about the causes of trusts. Were they only a defense against the periodic panics of the time? Were they normal in certain industries but improbable in others? Low-tariff advocates, for their part, were convinced that trusts were the consequence of high import taxes, but protectionists like Senator William B. Allison (R–IA) pointed out that there was no tariff wall protecting Standard Oil or the beef and whiskey trusts. Most critics of trusts were sure that they were nothing more than devices for maximizing profits at the public's expense, whereas their defenders—and there were many—saw them as a legitimate search for efficiency.

There also was disagreement about who the miscreants really were. Whereas business combinations were the target of farmers and those from the West and South, others saw agricultural cooperatives and labor unions as unfair competition and restraints of trade. The sorts of remedies that could be applied also engendered disagreement. Legislation that would only forbid the trusts the right to use federal courts would do nothing more than codify the ancient common-law approach, and removing tariff protection from trust-made goods would spare the majority of trust excesses. Since corporations were the creatures of the states, there seemed to be nothing that the federal government could do to revoke old charters or circumscribe new ones. At the other extreme were those who wanted to prohibit trusts from carrying on any interstate commerce whatsoever, even though it was unclear just what "commerce" meant or where it began or ended. Perhaps, some said, a constitutional amendment was in order; but what would it say?

The most detailed account of the Sherman Act's passage is by Hans Thorelli (1955, chap. 4, pp. 166-232). In July 1888 Senator John Sherman (R–OH) introduced a resolution empowering the Senate Finance Committee to explore antitrust legislation. This committee was designated because, as its chair, Sherman could better control any bill that was prepared under its jurisdiction. He also seems to have agreed that at least some monopolies were based on tariff protection (or rather on *excessive* tariff protection since he himself was a protectionist) and his committee had jurisdiction over tariff law. Sherman also saw the general taxing power, delegated to Congress by Article I, Section 8, Clause 5 of the Constitution, as an appropriate foundation on which to base his attack on the trusts.

Unfortunately, the bill that emerged was imprecise. By being aimed at all "persons or corporations" that tended to "prevent full and free competition" or to "advance the cost to the consumer," it could be construed as moving against groups as diverse as labor unions, agricultural cooperatives, and even the Women's Christian Temperance Union, as much as against corporations. More succinct bills were forthcoming, however, and by January 1899 the phrase "in due course of trade" had been added in order to base Sherman's bill on the commerce clause. Perhaps because commerce was not within his committee's jurisdiction, Sherman reverted to grounding his bill on the taxing power only a few months later. In all, there were six antimonopoly measures introduced in the Senate and thirty-four in the House during the 50th and 51st Congresses (1888–1889 and 1890–1891) (Thorelli, pp. 164-166).

Carrying the symbolic designation of S 1, the bill that was to become the Sherman Act was hammered out in March and April 1890. Prairie radicals like John Ingalls (R–KS) and Richard Coke (D–TX) wanted to prohibit speculation in agricultural options and futures, which they equated with ancient forestalling. There were challenges to grounding the bill on the taxing power and assertions that the commerce clause would be a superior constitutional foundation. Although only William Stewart (R–NV) denounced the bill in debate, others like Senator Orville Platt (R–CT) were not friends of S 1. There were amendments from friend and foe alike, most of them serious and some specious—a typical feature of the legislative process and an illustration of why important legislation cannot be written on the floor.

Because of the constitutional issues involved, the bill was routed back to the Judiciary Committee and reported back to the full Senate in a wholly redrafted form six days later. George Edmunds (R–VT), the chair, wrote the most original parts—Sections 1, 2, 3, 5, and 6. William Evarts of New York contributed the phrase "in the form of trust or otherwise" that was inserted in Section 1. James George (D–MS), the Senate's leading constitutional lawyer, wrote Section 4. The contribution of George Hoar (R–MA), to whom some later attributed the authorship of most of the bill, was limited to Section 7 alone, and Ingalls provided Section 8. Although George Vest contributed no language, he was an influential force in the committee's deliberations. And what about John Sherman? Although he was not on the committee and did not write the final version, his had been the moving spirit behind it. The bill was approved by a vote of fifty-two to one on April 8 (Thorelli, 1955, p. 212).

Nearly all the work had been done by the Senate. Despite doubts about its likely effectiveness, the only change in the House was an amendment by Richard Bland (D–MO) to get at "transportation monopolies" exercised by Armour & Co. The bill passed 152 to 72, with 103 not voting. After two conference committees that centered around the Bland amendment, the bill was finally approved as it had originally passed the Senate. President Harrison signed "a bill to protect trade and commerce against unlawful restraints and monopolies" on July 2, 1890.

If antitrust policy has been a lost cause of American reform politics, some of the problems are traceable to this original statute. First, antitrust policy seems to have been only moderately important in comparison to other business that was before Congress: the Force Bill, Union Army pension legislation, the Sherman Silver Purchase Act, and the McKinley tariff. In addition, there were conflicting factions in Congress: radicals like Ingalls and Coke who wanted a more far-reaching statute, legalists like George who focused on how to base the bill constitutionally, and opponents like Stewart and Blodgett. Legitimate differences of opinion among the members seems also to have caused some of the parties to impute dark motives to their opponents. Even Sherman's own motives have been questioned. There was a lack of economic theory about the causes of monopoly as well as rapid change in the nature of abuses, and these factors resulted in ill-defined terms like *trust, combination,* and *restraint* in the statute. The intent was to leave implementation to the courts; but when a legislature does not define its terms, the courts will. The bill's authorship was in doubt for years because its importance increased so slowly (Clark, 1931, p. 43; cited in Thorelli, 1955, p. 212).

The statute itself was extensive. Section 1 was aimed at business performance, or *practices.* It prohibited agreements among parties that *unreasonably* restrained trade—which means there must be undue restraint or an intent to do so. Certain types of behavior have come to constitute per se violations that are illegal in and of themselves: price fixing by competitors; dividing customers or markets; agreements among competitors to boycott any third party; and tied-in sales, in which a seller requires customers to purchase some additional product in addition to the one really wanted. There is a "rule of reason," however, that will allow some conduct in restraint of trade if there is good business purpose for doing so and there is no intent to do harm.

Section 2 was directed at business *structure*. It prohibited any single firm from actually monopolizing or attempting to monopolize a relevant market, where "market" has either a geographic or a product meaning. An ability to control prices or exclude competition is the test, but the courts have avoided stipulating the percentage of market control that would be offensive. Both Sections 1 and 2 can be enforced through criminal penalties of a fine of up to $100,000 for each violation or by imprisonment of up to three years or both.

Section 4 set out procedures by which the Justice Department could use civil suits to prevent violations by injunction or restraining orders to end unfair business practices. Section 7 privatized the act by allowing injured private parties to bring suit against offenders and to receive treble damages if successful. As a result, 90 percent of all antitrust cases are between private-party litigants.

APPLYING THE SHERMAN ACT

Enforcement of the government's portion of the Sherman Act was to take place through the Department of Justice, although there was no separate appropriation or organization for antitrust activities until 1903. Because the department had only eighteen lawyers among a staff of eighty, only seven suits were filed during the two remaining years of the Harrison administration. There were eight more during Cleveland's second term and three while McKinley was president. These figures contrast with the forty-four during the Roosevelt years and the eighty-nine during Taft's administration.

For more than a decade after its enactment, the Sherman Act faced significant barriers from the judiciary. Its first Supreme Court test came five years after its passage in *U.S.* v. *E. C. Knight Company* (1895). At issue was the legality of the combination that controlled 90 percent of the table sugar produced in the United States at that time. Although Congress finally had grounded the law on the commerce clause, Chief Justice Melville Fuller echoed the reservations of Senator George when he wrote the opinion for an eight-to-one majority: The trust was not a commercial entity but was engaged in manufacturing. Manufacturing might be antecedent to commerce, but it was not commercial action in itself, and only the states might constitutionally regulate it. Stung by this opinion, the statute's defenders retorted that Attorney General Richard Olney as well as President Cleveland himself were lukewarm to the spirit of the Sherman Act and had done a poor job of presenting the government's case. Not only did the decision seriously impair attempts to control monopolies, but it actually had a stimulative affect in the creation of new ones.

The first use of the Sherman Act in a labor dispute reached the Supreme Court shortly thereafter. During the Pullman Strike of 1894, the government had sought an injunction under the act against the leaders of the American Railway Union for interfering with the flow of mail. Although the Court eventually held against the union on broader grounds, the actions of Olney, Cleveland, and the judiciary in *In Re Debs* (1895) showed that the law might not enjoy the future that antimonopoly reformers like Ingalls, Coke, and Sherman had envisioned.

It was not until the end of the decade that the Court accorded a measure of respectability to the statute. *Addystone Pipe and Steel Co. v. U.S.* (1899) concerned six regional iron pipe firms that were clearly as involved in selling their products as in manufacturing them. In refusing to overturn a lower court decision, the Supreme Court invalidated a marketing scheme that was clearly in the stream of commerce. Still, in 1908 the antilabor thread that lay within the act was found again in *Loewe v. Lawlor* (1908), the *Danbury Hatters'* case. In the wake of a prolonged strike against hat manufacturers, labor had called for a secondary boycott. A unanimous Court held that this was a conspiracy in restraint of trade, as defined in Section 1.

During the administrations of Theodore Roosevelt and of William Howard Taft, however, the posture of the government toward trust-busting changed dramatically. The first major antitrust success came in *Northern Securities Co. v. U.S.* (1904), when a narrowly divided court held that the railroad holding company was an illegal combination in restraint of interstate commerce. In an ironic footnote to history, the newly appointed Associate Justice Oliver Wendell Holmes, Jr. (who went on to a distinguished career on the Court), argued in dissent for a "rule of reason" that would have allowed the trust to continue. Roosevelt, who had nominated Holmes to the Court, fumed that he could find a jellyfish with more backbone than Justice Holmes had shown! Additional victories for the government soon followed. The beef trust was dissolved in 1905 in *Swift & Co. v. U.S.*, with Holmes developing the "stream of commerce" idea under which local business agreements were held to be integral parts of interstate commerce and subject to federal regulation.

In companion cases initiated by the Department of Justice in 1906, John D. Rockefeller's Standard Oil of New Jersey and James Buchanan Duke's American Tobacco Company were both declared to be illegal monopolies. Rockefeller's organization had been blatantly heavy-handed, even by the standards of that time. In 1904, his affiliate in Kansas reduced crude oil prices to undercut independent producers and drive them out of business. Progressive author Ida Tarbell attacked the action, and the following year the Kansas congressional delegation pressured Congress to institute a survey of the oil business. The Justice Department brought suit in St. Louis on November 15, 1906. After 12,000 pages of transcript and 400 witnesses, the 4-judge panel unanimously found that the 37 subsidiary companies were guilty of monopolization and restraint of trade. It was this finding that the Supreme Court upheld in *Standard Oil Co. of New Jersey, et al. v. U.S.* (1911).

OTHER ANTITRUST LAWS

The lessons revealed by the Pujo Committee about business practices and the loopholes punched in the law by Supreme Court findings yielded additional antimonopoly legislation in the Progressive era. The Clayton Act (1914) was a series of amendments to the Sherman Act designed to close gaps opened by the judiciary's use of the rule of reason, as well as to respond to evolving business practices. Its Sections 2 and 3 were primarily aimed at business practices, just as the opening portion of the Sherman Act had done twenty-four years earlier. Section 2 dealt with *price discrimination*, or differences in selling price used by a wholesaler to injure a local retail seller. Section 3 restated prohibitions against *tying contracts*, because of a 1912 Supreme Court ruling, and sought to outlaw exclusive dealing arrangements in which a firm is forced to agree not to deal with its supplier's competitors. In the years since the Clayton Act, however, the courts have usually tolerated both of these practices unless the seller controls a substantial market share and the effect of these practices is to lessen competition.

Section 6 revisited an issue that had received considerable discussion during the consideration of S 1 during the 51st Congress: the posture of organized labor under antitrust law. New wording stated that labor is "not a commodity or article of commerce" and was inserted to overrule the Court's findings in the *Danbury Hatters'* case.

Sections 7 and 8 of the Clayton Act were directed at *business structure*—the topic of the Sherman Act's Section 2. Section 7 recognized that mergers had replaced trusts as anticompetitive devices after the *Knight* case. Thus, this new provision prohibited corporations from *acquiring stock* in competing firms when the effect was to lessen competition. The firms must be engaged in interstate competition for the prohibition to apply, however, and this provision did not forbid companies from acquiring one another's stock solely for investment purposes. Finally, Section 8 sought to limit the *interlocking directorates* that the Pujo Committee had found so prevalent in investment banking. The law prohibited people from serving as director of two or more large corporations that were competitors.

The Federal Trade Commission (FTC) Act was a statutory companion to the Clayton Act. It lengthened the list of illegal behavior to include trade boycotts, mislabeling, and adulteration of products, and it created an independent regulatory commission that could implement parts of the Clayton Act and seek civil remedies through the courts. Under Section 5, the commission was empowered to take action before wrongs occurred. This statute goes further in attacking more varieties of unfair business practices even today than any other antitrust law.

There are several additional major sources of antitrust law. The Webb-Pomerene Act of 1918 was the consequence of European trade practices that had become apparent during World War I. It authorized exporters to organize trade associations without fear of antitrust law violations—which shows that foreign trade considerations have been a continuing problem for America's antitrust policy.

Antitrust legislation was eclipsed during the 1920s, for "the business of America was business." Even President Coolidge said so. When the finger pointing about the causes of the Great Depression began, however, economic concentration and predatory business practices were prominent targets. But even when the New Deal was flailing about for solutions that might get the country moving again, antitrust law was also buffeted. The National Recovery Act (NRA) set aside important antitrust concepts in the belief that the problem was not too little competition but too much. The Robinson-Patman Act (1936), then hailed as the Chain Store Act, was a product of the hard times of the 1930s. Representative Wright Patman (D–TX), later the long-time chair of the House Banking and Currency Committee, was one of the last populists. His bill harkened back to the days before chain stores had entered into competition with family-owned shops. It fortified Section 2 of the Clayton Act by prohibiting unjustifiable discounts to larger purchasers than to smaller ones, unless those differentials could be justified on the basis of lower costs. The Wheeler-Lea Act (1938) was aimed at suppressing "unfair or deceptive acts or practices" in food and drugs. Although it was an amendment to the FTC Act, it broke new ground by making the commission responsive to harm done directly to consumers rather than only to harm against competing firms.

The Celler-Kefauver Anti-Merger Act, passed in 1950, has had a telling effect on reducing mergers between large firms by rebuilding the Clayton Act's Section 7. Although it had forbidden the acquisition of one firm's stock by another when the effect was to lessen competition, the courts had gradually opened loopholes by allowing the acquisition of assets (as opposed to stock) and by allowing purchases of stock to proceed if they occurred before the FTC complained about them. Enacted during a new wave of post-World War II mergers, Celler-Kefauver narrowed the definition of a market by calling it "a line of commerce" in any one part of the country, and outlawed stock acquisition if it would lessen competition substantially or tended to create a monopoly.

The Hart-Scott-Rodino Antitrust Improvements Act (1976) expanded the powers of the Antitrust Division for acquiring evidence from third parties. It also stimulated antitrust action below the national level by authorizing federal courts to hear cases brought by state attorneys general on behalf of their residents. Moreover, the law has been particularly useful for allowing premerger clearance to proposed amalgamations between large firms. Because it has always been difficult to stop a merger once it has been consummated, this statute now requires notice to be given to the Justice Department and FTC at least thirty days before they occur. Not only does this provision bring the government into the proceedings earlier, but it also allows the parties to know before completion of final action whether the merger will be challenged in the future.

Recent antitrust politics has emphasized the exemption of certain practices or industries from antitrust laws. For example, bills have been introduced that would allow the television industry to discuss guidelines concerning violence in that medium, that would coordinate airline scheduling, and that would allow joint ventures among competing minority-owned businesses. Easing the impact of antitrust law in foreign trade has been another important topic. During the 101st Congress (1988–1989) there were forty-two antitrust bills introduced in the House and forty-one in the Senate.

DOES BIG ALWAYS MEAN BAD?

A number of classical arguments have been raised against monopoly. One is that it yields overpriced, shoddy goods. This view was promoted in Zeno's Edict, the *Merchant Tailors* case, *Darcy* v. *Allein*, and Adam Smith's argument that competition will steadily improve quality and lower costs and prices. A second complaint is that monopoly destroys innovation, for in the absence of competition there is no driving need to create. A third argument derives from neoclassical economic theory: Monopoly gives rise to inefficient allocations of resources because price exceeds marginal cost. Fourth, monopoly concentrates wealth in society when a few profiteers become richer and the greater number of victims becomes poorer. This result is objectionable on the normative, distributive ground that argues against creating an impoverished underclass. This notion of concentration of wealth gives rise to a fifth objection: that economic stability is threatened by an inequitable distribution of purchasing power. In the Keynesian view, the Great Depression persisted because of the concentration of wealth that had brought it on.

By turning away from monopoly per se to a concern simply with the very large size that can characterize oligopolistic firms, two additional objections arise. First, there is the political argument that wealth derived from bigness yields undue political power. This view was put forward during the Progressive movement, motivated the Pujo Committee in 1912, and was a force in passing the Clayton and FTC acts in 1914. Second, there is the populistic view that small-scale enterprises are better than larger ones for a number of reasons. This view became embodied in the Robinson-Patman Act's hostility toward chain store growth. Although this preference for modest size persists in the notion of "small is beautiful," it seems to attract few advocates outside the environmental movement.

If critics of large-scale enterprises have long been in evidence, there is a large and growing number of defenders. The first line of defense is the notion of *economies of scale*. The costs of production in industries characterized by high levels of concentration are such that goods can be produced more efficiently in large enterprises. A corollary of this principle is the belief that innovation, far from being stultified, can often be supported only by organizations of very large size. For example, small enterprises cannot support basic research that may not pay off for years. Another aspect of this line of argument is that to be competitive in the international marketplace, American enterprises must be larger. This was the rationale for waiving normal antitrust requirements in the international arena through the Webb-Pomerene Act. It was by synthesizing all of these arguments that the Chicago school developed increasing efficiency as an effective defense against charges of anticompetitive behavior. In specifying where bigness and efficiency end and where monopoly and restraint of trade begin, economic reasoning confronts legalistic argument and the administration of antitrust laws becomes crucial.

ANTITRUST ADMINISTRATION

Antitrust policies are administered primarily by the Antitrust Division of the Department of Justice (DOJ), under the direction of an assistant attorney general. The types of violation concern *business practices* that restrain trade or reduce competition through monopolization and *business structures* that reduce competition through corporate mergers. Action by the DOJ begins with an investigation of possible antitrust violation through a preliminary inquiry. This step may call for a field investigation and the acquisition of information through a Civil Investigative Demand, or CID — which relies on the power to subpoena documents and other information. If adjudication is called for, there will then be grand jury proceedings, where 35 to 40 percent of the Antitrust Division's resources are expended annually. Sanctions for serious, purposeful violations, as decided by a court, call for criminal law penalties in the form of fines or imprisonment. Less serious, nonwillful violations are pursued under civil law, where penalties include injunctions against future actions and compensatory remedies undertaken by the offending company.

Antitrust administration moved to the right during the 1980s. First under William Baxter and then Charles Rule, the numbers of employees in the Antitrust Division, in conjunction with Reagan-era practices, declined from about 850 during the mid-1970s to about 700 by 1983. By 1989, the division had lost half its personnel, and arguably, the quality of federal lawyers had diminished as well. With a starting salary of $30,000 per year, bright young antitrust attorneys could begin at two-and-one-half times that amount in private practice.

More important, there were changes in the balance between attorneys and economists under Reaganomics. Previously, economic analysis had been secondary to statutory and case law expertise in bringing cases. During the 1980s, however, economic analysis led the way. Economists of the Chicago persuasion judged industry structures more by their potential for increasing efficiency than for increasing the concentration of firms within an industry. Some have argued that the measures used, like the Herfingdahl-Herschman Index, predisposed the economic analysis to be lenient in judging proposed mergers. It seems more likely, however, that it was the critical values of this index, rather than the tool itself, that contributed to greater toleration of mergers by the division. Indeed, the division often failed to move against mergers even when they did cross the threshold numbers.

The effects of administration could be seen as the decade unfolded. The most obvious impact was in a new wave of mergers that typified the 1980s, especially in the growth of leveraged buy-outs in which takeovers were financed with money borrowed in the form of junk bonds. As long as the economy was growing, as it did through the second quarter of 1990, corporate raiders could practice their trade at will. Fortunes were made by Carl Icahn, T. Boone Pickens, Robert Holmes a Court, and others, as well as by those in the financial community who received huge commissions by putting the deals together. Lax enforcement allowed mergers that would not have been proposed in earlier years. Not a single case of vertical price-fixing was brought during the Reagan years, and only three Sherman Act Section 2 cases were brought against attempts to monopolize—the lowest number for any eight-year span of time since 1900. The focus instead was on large horizontal mergers and agreements between direct competitors. The consequence of this practice was an increase in economic concentration in the United States. But although there was less enforcement, when the Antitrust Division did move, it did so through the more flamboyant criminal law sanctions rather than through civil proceedings.

The Bush era, under the direction of James Rill as assistant attorney general, seemed to break somewhat from the Reagan administration. A tougher image was projected toward proposed mergers, with the result that there were fewer. There were ten challenges during Bush's first year in office, one of them preserving Wilkinson Sword as a competitor to Gillette in the razor blade market. Despite the merger of Uniroyal Goodrich by Groupe Michelin and mergers among major accounting firms, the activity of the pre-

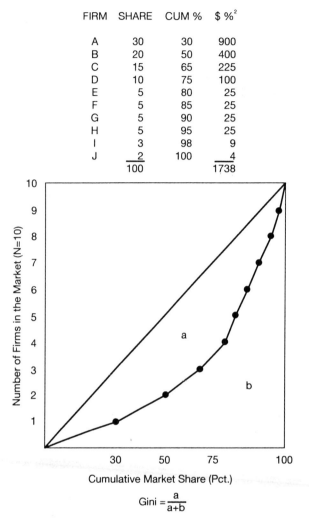

FIRM	SHARE	CUM %	$ %^{2}
A	30	30	900
B	20	50	400
C	15	65	225
D	10	75	100
E	5	80	25
F	5	85	25
G	5	90	25
H	5	95	25
I	3	98	9
J	2	100	4
	100		1738

$$\text{Gini} = \frac{a}{a+b}$$

Figure 11-1.

ceding years subsided. Actions have been brought against price-fixing by Ivy League colleges and by airlines, and there have been threats to prosecute foreign firms that violate American laws even if the actions took place overseas.

POLITICAL ISSUES IN ANTITRUST POLICY

In antitrust policy, as in all policy domains, there are many small, unique controversies that center on issues, viewpoints, and personalities of the people involved. But perhaps three areas of political dispute stand out today.

One is inherent in the issue of industry structure: "bigness" versus populistic opposition to large corporations. Chicagoists, emphasizing the potential benefits of efficiency, are less likely to challenge mergers than populists, who remain suspicious of great size, or legalists, who insist on either enforcing antitrust law or repealing it. A second issue is the politics of seeking exceptions from general antitrust law in the name of equity, especially in the face of competition from overseas. Third, there is the issue of the organization and administration of the Antitrust Division and the FTC. Enforcement of programs is directly affected by the quality of the bureaucracy in charge of it; but low levels of funding, sometimes defended by a need to shift Justice Department resources to the war on drugs, detract from the resources available to the Division.

Michael Lewis-Beck (1979, p. 191) thinks he knows why antitrust is the "lost cause" of American public policy. Contrary to the conflictual image of government as regulator, he believes that it is inherent in our pluralistic system for the government to be a facilitator and helpmate. The government normally provides subsidies and benefits to business, which means that neither the president nor Congress, neither the Democrats nor the Republicans, are committed to a robust antitrust policy. Maintaining competition, he asserts, "is in reality a very low priority" in American politics.

DISCUSSION QUESTIONS

1. Which of the four types of markets characterize automobile production, automobile sales, and automobile repair? What about tomato production, ketchup production, and ketchup sales? Electrical power generation, transmission, and sales?

2. What was the common-law approach to dealing with monopoly in the primitive markets of medieval England? What could statute law do differently?

3. Are all monopolies trusts, and are all trusts monopolies? Are all trusts and monopolies illegal today?

4. Should oligopoly be illegal?

5. What were the sorts of problems that were encountered by those who drafted the Sherman Act in 1890? Why were they so difficult to cope with?

6. Identify these legal concepts: (a) manufacturing and commerce in the *Knight* and *Addystone* cases; (b) stream of commerce in the *Swift* case; (c) rule of reason in the *Northern Securities* and subsequent cases before World War I.

7. Why are there so many antitrust statutes, and why are so many bills introduced in each Congress each year to amend our antitrust laws?

8. "Ours is a government of laws, and not of men." Discuss this homily in the light of changing Supreme Court interpretations of antitrust law before 1914 and in the light of the administration of the Antitrust Division during the Reagan administration.

9. What is meant by the phrase *economies of scale?*. Where do these savings come from, and are there any limits to them?

10. What do you make of Michael Lewis-Beck's assertion that policymakers today, regardless of party or branch of government, have little interest in developing robust antitrust law?

REFERENCES

Anderson, James E. 1986. "The Reagan Administration, Antitrust Action, and Policy Change." Unpublished paper presented at the Midwest Political Science Association, Chicago, Ill.

Armentano, Dominick T. 1982. *Antitrust and Monopoly: Anatomy of a Policy Failure.* New York: Wiley.

Barrett, Paul M. 1990, June 13. "Assistant Attorney General Rill Sends Message to Firms," *Wall Street Journal,* p. A16.

Clark, John D. 1931. *The Federal Antitrust Policy.* Baltimore, MD: Johns Hopkins Press.

Katzman, Robert A. 1979. *Regulatory Bureaucracy: The FTC and Antitrust Policy.* Cambridge, MA: MIT Press.

Kovacic, William E. 1989, October 10. "Steady Reliever at Antitrust," *Wall Street Journal,* p. A18;4.

Lewis-Beck, Michael. 1979, February. "Maintaining Economic Competition: The Causes and Consequences of Antitrust." *Journal of Politics,* 41, 169–191.

Posner, Richard A. 1979, April. "The Chicago School of Antitrust Analysis." *University of Pennsylvania Law Review,* 127, 925–948.

Schwartz, Warren P. 1981. *Private Enforcement of the Antitrust Laws: An Economic Critique.* Washington, D.C.: American Enterprise Institute.

Stigler, George J. 1985, January. "The Origins of the Sherman Act," *Journal of Legal Studies,* 14, 1–12.

Thorelli, Hans B. 1955. *Federal Antitrust Policy: Origination of an American Tradition.* Baltimore, MD: Johns Hopkins University Press.

Weaver, Suzanne. 1980. "Antitrust Division of the Department of Justice," in James Q. Wilson (ed.), *The Politics of Regulation.* New York: Basic Books.

Willis, Robert L., Julie A. Caswell, and John D. Culbertson (eds.). 1987. *Issues After a Century of Federal Competition Policy.* Lexington, MA: Lexington Books.

CHAPTER TWELVE

ORGANIZED LABOR: POLITICS, POLICY, AND ADMINISTRATION

The politics of organized labor has a different flavor than the other issues that have been considered to this point. Fiscal policy, antitrust, restraint of trade, and monetary politics all take place in the comparatively antiseptic arenas of polite, if sometimes vigorous, conflict. They involve economic abstraction and, in earlier times at least, comfortable surroundings, good food, and the occasional fine cigar. Although people like Daniel Shays, Huey Long, or Ralph Nader might upset the calm, most of those who are closest to the action wear expensive clothes, frequent the world of ideas, and are at home in the very best salons of Georgetown and Wall Street.

Labor politics is different. No policy area in America has engendered more conflict and bitterness than this one. There are personal struggles and sacrifices here, but there are also violence and organized crime. In no other democratic, economically developed nation have there been the levels of violence that have characterized the struggles of labor for two centuries. Racism and sexism of the worst kind are interwoven into labor politics, but there are also hands of friendship and solidarity that reach across the chasms of color and gender. There are people in the labor movement whose lives have exemplified personal nobility and selflessness—people like William Sylvis of the National Union of Iron Molders, Richard Davis (a

Black organizer), and "Mother" Jones, both of the United Mine Workers. And there are corrupt, self-serving people who violate their trust for personal gain. There have been fundamentally differing views within the labor movement itself over just what its objectives ought to be; and the very nature of organized labor introduces an issue with which the American political culture is very uncomfortable—the importance of social class.

This chapter will treat (1) political and economic considerations about labor organizations, (2) the development of organized labor, (3) state and federal laws governing organized labor, (4) the role of governmental agencies and of the National Labor Relations Board, (5) labor's approach to the political process, and (6) the issues that are prominent in labor and union politics today.

POLITICAL AND ECONOMIC IDEAS ABOUT ORGANIZED LABOR

American public opinion is ambivalent about labor organizations: It seems either to love them or to hate them. There is not much middle ground. Arguably, the balance of opinion has shifted away from labor since 1958, and union membership has declined from more than one-third of the work force in 1945 to about 14 percent in 1993. What are the reasons for this decline?

Some objections to organized labor are endemic to the American ethos, at least as it has existed since the end of the Civil War. In a sense, labor organizations contravene parts of the American ideology. In a culture that values individualism and private initiative, the idea of concerted action by working people seems wrong to many Americans. Adam Smith had argued that the wealth of nations was founded on the propensity of individuals, and not of collective groups, to truck, barter, and trade. Americans, and market systems generally, claim to value risk-taking, but it is the objective of unions to reduce the risks of lower wages and job loss. Unions are a feature of industry; yet Americans yearn, if not for a return to Jeffersonian agrarianism, at least for the green lawns of suburbia. Moreover, unions have a foreign element. Many of the organizers of the late nineteenth century were immigrants from Ireland or Germany, and often they championed ideas of socialism or syndicalism that were strange to North America. These people, with their notions of class conflict, were at odds with a historic strain of nativism.

Other reasons for labor's decline in popularity are more recent. As we move farther away from the struggles of the Great Depression, generational replacement means that those who were committed to the cause thirty years ago have left the work force. Meanwhile, they are being replaced by new workers who lack an appreciation of unionization. The simultaneous decline of manufacturing and rise of the services sector is a second factor. Whether craft or industrially based, manufacturing activities are easier to unionize than is the services sector, which has many of the characteristics of a secondary labor market. Then there is the drumroll of bad publicity during the past two decades. Public confidence in many institutions, including Congress and business, eroded during the 1960s; and television has been said to be harsher on public organizations than on public people. The pro-market opinion shift of the Reagan era, filtered through the media, has not been kind to labor organizations. Crime and scandals such as the Teamsters' Central States Pension Fund or the mysterious disappearance of Jimmy Hoffa have had lasting effect. Finally, the behavior of the National Labor Relations Board (NLRB) has changed. Between 1947 and 1980, the board seemed to be neutral or perhaps slightly prolabor; this posture changed after 1980.

There are important organizational or structural considerations about unions that should be noted. One is a distinction between craft and industrial unions. From the earliest decades of the new United States, associations were formed among men with skills that took years to master—trades like printing, boot- and shoemaking, carpentry, and fine cabinetmaking. With the introduction of machine-based manufacturing, which required much less skill and training, and especially with the rise of large-sized plants in ironworking, in assembly-line mass production, and in mining, there was a need to organize along industrial lines. The acceptance of less-skilled industrial workers into the brotherhood of labor was slow in coming. The development of amalgamated unions, which preserved craft jurisdictions within plants but coalesced for purposes of collective bargaining, was an important breakthrough for labor solidarity.

A second distinction must be made between independent unions and the "company unions" that emerged at about the turn of the last century. Often developed in the wake of great strikes and a feature of the American plan in labor relations, they have been scorned by union men and women for generations. Company unions, now rare, gave a semblance (and sometimes a reality) of workers' participation in labor-management relations.

There is an orthodox economic balance sheet on unions. Most neoclassical post-Keynesians recognize that unions are important for several reasons. On humanitarian grounds, they help to reduce the grinding poverty of the coal fields, the factory towns, and the urban centers. Unionized employees, or nonunion employees who work under conditions of union representation, enjoy significantly higher incomes than unorganized workers, although the fact of unionization alone cannot account for all of the difference in wages. Also, unionization has a stimulative effect on the economy by putting purchasing power in the hands of consumers. At the systemic level, labor's economic gains disarmed the threat of class conflict and the specter of revolution that at times seemed very real. The increased welfare of workers increases the equity and equality of the social system as a whole. Indeed, union successes at the level of the individual worker had reached the point by 1979 that George Meaney, president of the AFL-CIO at that time, could gladly point out with a certain pride that the American labor movement had become both middle class and conservative.

There are arguments against labor organizations as well. In seeking higher wages, shorter hours or increased benefits, they increase the costs of production, which in turn reduces the employer's profits by lowering efficiency. To the extent that wage increases for unionized employees are inflationary or draw down the money designated for the payroll, nonunionized employees may suffer a loss in their own real wages. Closed shops, by requiring all the workers to join the union or at least pay a representation fee, invoke a specter of coercion that flies in the face of individualism. There is also the argument that unions spawn their own bloated bureaucracy. Certainly unions came to realize the need for specialized assistance by the end of the nineteenth century, whether to process thousands of membership applications or to maintain an office for the local business agent. To many people, however, the most threatening facet of unionism is violence. Violence, in the form of smashed windshields or bloodied heads, can be a byproduct of a strike. An even greater problem is the violence from organized crime, which recognized unions as easy targets for extortion once the profits from bootlegging dried up at the end of Prohibition.

THE DEVELOPMENT OF LABOR ORGANIZATIONS

Ronald Filippelli contends that the majority of workingmen and women in colonial America arrived as bound labor, whether as indentured servants or black slaves. But for the indentured, at least, the development of America placed a premium on their skills as carpenters, joiners, smiths, shoemakers, or stonemasons. At first the demand for their services gave them more status and financial reward than they had enjoyed in the lands of their birth; but as the eighteenth century wore on, wealth became more concentrated in the hands of a few in Boston, Philadelphia, and other towns. With the approach of the Revolution, the working classes were in the forefront of the movement for independence, and organizations like the Sons of Liberty were based heavily on the artisan classes. But as Filippelli (1984, p. 12) has said, the issue of "home rule" for America was accompanied by the question of "who would rule at home."

The beginning of industrialization is found in the first half of the nineteenth century. During the colonial period an artisan might be employed in the small shop of a master craftsman to work on custom-ordered goods. Perhaps he was an itinerant journeyman touring the countryside. With progress came the merchant capitalist who supplied the funds and marketing skills for clusters of masters—now styled as managers—and dozens of journeymen. And not long after that, first with water power and then with steam, came machinery and the sequential performance of tasks, which allowed workers with far less skill to do the work of eight artisans in one-eighth the time. The first factory, a Pawtucket, Rhode Island, textile mill, was followed by the first large-scale use of female labor, in Lowell, Massachusetts, in the 1820s and 1830s; by 1850 the cotton textile industry was the first to be wholly mechanized. Conditions in the factories and mill towns may not have been as grim as in Europe. American mills did not widely adopt the English practice of hiring entire families as workers. Still, as Filippelli describes, from one-third to one-half of the New England work force in the 1830s was made up of children under the age of sixteen. The factories were poorly ventilated and heated—hot in summer and cold in winter, with clouds of lint hanging in the air—and operated from twelve to sixteen hours per day, six days a week.

This was the milieu in which labor organizations appeared in early America. There were associations of skilled masters in trades like shipbuilding and house carpentry, barrelmaking, cabinetry, printing, and leatherworking that resembled medieval guilds by monopolizing the supply of labor in a particular trade. Some were prosperous, and the Carpenters' Company of Philadelphia constructed and owned the building where the Continental Congress first met—Carpenters' Hall. There were also combinations of workers, indentured servants, and even slaves who struck or rebelled for higher wages—treasonous acts punishable by death—such as Bacon's Rebellion of 1676. Sadly, there were combinations to bar black workers from engaging in certain trades, but Revolutionary era associations like the Sons of Liberty were crucial organizations in the struggle for independence. Early strikes were often aimed at local governments that had set wages too low; and with the end of the Revolution there were walkouts by New York shoemakers in 1785, Philadelphia printers in 1786 and 1794, and cordwainers (shoemakers), in 1789. Although many of these early strikes centered on wages, other issues included hours of labor or control over apprenticeship training and thus the number of future workers in a trade.

The government was more often the friend of capital than of labor. Framers of the Constitution like Gouverneur Morris and high Federalists like Fisher Ames had feared "the mobocracy." Although the equation of strikes with treason ended with independence, early strikers soon became subject to prosecution for engaging in illegal conspiracies under common law. In a series of cases involving cordwainers' and shoemakers' unions in Philadelphia and New York between 1806 and 1815, the ancient Tudor Industrial Code was invoked as a common-law precedent. English law, which had sought to balance the interests of workers (against exploitation) with the interests of employers (having an adequate labor supply) was interpreted so that strikes were a conspiracy against the law. At a time before Joseph Story had redeemed the common law in the federal jurisdiction, these conspiracy cases were grist for battle between Federalists and Jeffersonian Republicans.

In 1824, the first known strike by women occurred among the weavers of Pawtucket, Rhode Island. In 1828 the Tariff of Abominations gave unprecedented trade protection to American-made goods, and banks and other state-chartered monopolies loaned money to workers at higher rates than those charged to industries. Although the political party of the left was more sympathetic to labor's concerns, it was Andrew Jackson who authorized the first use of federal troops against strikers when he put down a dispute over a closed-shop arrangement that involved Irish workers digging the Chesapeake and Ohio Canal near Williamsport, Maryland, in 1834. The leaders of skilled craftsmen saw industrialization and its hold on government as a threat to the ideals of the American Revolution.

Labor sought to organize not only for economic gains but for political ones as well. Individual craft unions banded together to form "city centrals" during the 1820s and 1830s, and there were efforts to abolish property qualifications for voting. Between 1828 and 1834, various labor parties sought to introduce such reforms as the ten-hour day, abolition of debtors' prisons and prisoner-made commodities that competed in the open market, and the end of the antiquated militia system that allowed the wealthy to buy their way out of service. Labor sought to introduce mechanics' lien laws that would make former employees the first claimants for payment when firms went bankrupt and refused to pay back wages. Labor objected to the monopoly problem of that time—banks in general and Nicholas Biddle's Second Bank of the United States in particular—and supported a system of free public education that could open the doors of opportunity. The results of all this activity were mixed. Some of these demands were realized, but most had to wait. Nor did labor speak with one voice. Whereas it generally supported Jackson in 1832, Clay benefited from labor's help in many quarters. In 1836, however, the Navy Department did establish a ten-hour day for the employees of civilian contractors.

Both success and defeat characterized attempts by labor to organize in the decade before the Civil War. With prices increasing 12 percent but wages only 4 percent during the 1850s, national-level associations began to appear. Railroad labor led the way, although today's brotherhoods are from a later period. The National Typographical Union was founded in 1852, followed by Hat Finishers (1854), Journeymen Stone Cutters (1855), United Cigarmakers (1856), Iron Molders (1859), and Machinists and Blacksmiths (also 1859). In a familiar scenario, however, the panic of 1857 threw many out of work, and the surplus of unemployed workers was fatal to many of the new unions.

Great fortunes were made after the Civil War— the Rockefellers in oil, the Vanderbilts and Stanfords in railroads, and Andrew Carnegie in steel. At that time the great monopolies and trusts were in bloom, and the workplace was in flux. A few individual plants that had employed 100 workers grew to more than a thousand factories that employed between 500 and 1,000 by

1900. The development of machine processing, division of labor, and time-and-motion management experts like Frederick W. Taylor heralded the decline of the old apprenticeship procedure and of the craft-based system that it nurtured. Meanwhile, poverty stalked the coalfields and the mill towns, where a rising tide of immigrants ensured a steady supply of cheap labor. Labor's response was to organize. After all, as Filippelli (1984, p. 58) quotes one trade unionist of the 1890s, workingmen were just as entitled to a monopoly as were businesses.

The first attempt to create a single national labor organization occurred after the Civil War in the form of the National Labor Union (NLU). Its philosophy was communalism, according to which unionization was only one step to the ultimate creation of producers' cooperatives. As its founder, William Sylvis, saw it, there could be no individual freedom for workingmen as long as they labored for factory owners. Working in tandem with eight-hour leagues and other reformers, the NLU succeeded in securing an eight-hour day for federal employees in 1868. The organization was deeply wounded by the death of Sylvis, however; and soon the loss of working-class leadership, the panic of 1873, and disagreement over the admission of blacks and women ended its effectiveness.

With the demise of the NLU, the field was left to the Knights of Labor. Begun in the Philadelphia garment trade in 1869, its membership was open to the skilled and the unskilled alike, as well as to women and blacks. Many of the Knights' local assemblies were old craft unions that were riding out the effects of the 1873 depression, but a "mixed assembly" emerged as the organizational spine of the Knights. Terrence V. Powderly, politician and small businessman, became its president in 1879; seven years later 60,000 blacks and 50,000 women were enrolled. It was clear that raising the pay of blacks and women would reduce their threat as cheap competition for men in the workplace. The political agenda of the Knights included the restriction of Chinese immigration, and Congress accordingly prohibited the importation of Asian contract labor. But it was the failure of Powderly to champion the eight-hour day that was the Knights' undoing.

The formation of the American Federation of Labor (AFL) was the result of the rebirth of the eight-hour day issue, the resurgence of craft unionism, and the importance of organizational skills. A jurisdictional dispute between the Knights and various affiliated craft unions, including the Cigar Makers Union headed by Samuel Gompers, led to a national meeting in Columbus, Ohio, in 1886. The AFL was formed from this meeting attended by representatives of a dozen national unions, six dissident Knights craft assemblies, and seven independent, local unions.

Radicalism was a part of labor's history between the 1870s and World War I. The goals of craft protectionism and producers' cooperatives were taken up by socialists, Marxists, and anarchists, who were often immigrants from Germany and the British Isles. Those who were executed after the

Haymarket massacre, after trials that failed to link them with the actual bomb throwing, were German-born. Especially threatening to mainline politics and society at the turn of the century was the International Workers of the World (IWW), or Wobblies. Not only were they a force in manufacturing and mining; but also they developed a particularly strong following throughout the western states. Finally, the songs of the Swedish-born troubadour and organizer Joe Hill were silenced by a Utah firing squad in 1915 after he was convicted of robbery. Subsequent research casts doubt on Hill's guilt. Syndicalism, seen as a particular threat by the larger community, became the target of state criminal laws during World War I and the period of the Red scare.

The 1920s were hard for labor. The recession of 1921 cut into many of the gains that unions had made during the war. Meanwhile, management and capital counterattacked. The Red scare justified attacks on labor during the period, and the American plan celebrated the notion that collective bargaining was un-American because it undermined each worker's individual right to bargain with his or her employer. The United Mine Workers (UMW) under John L. Lewis took heavy losses during the 1920s, when their membership fell from 500,000 to 150,000. When the Great Crash came in 1929, miners' families in Pennsylvania said that times were already so bad that they never noticed the Depression.

There is no period in American history that can compare with the New Deal era in terms of the growth of labor membership and political power. With unemployment rising and industrial relations rapidly worsening, the Norris-LaGuardia Anti-Injunction Act was one opening for labor. Section 7-A of the National Industrial Recovery Act (NIRA), a creation of Roosevelt's First Hundred Days, was the first ray of hope from the new Roosevelt administration. But arrangements in NRA codes for boosting wages soon seemed to be hollow promises. By the spring of 1934, industrial violence like that at the Electric Auto-Lite strike in Toledo made it clear that more had to be done. The response was the Wagner Act—the National Industrial Labor Relations Act of 1935. In creating the NLRB, guaranteeing the right to organize, and defining unfair labor practices by management, the Wagner Act was the single most important piece of labor legislation in the nation's history.

The emergence of the Congress of Industrial Organizations (CIO) was the major development of the 1930s inside organized labor itself. Since the time of Samuel Gompers, the AFL had been concerned primarily with the problems of the skilled crafts and had shown far less interest in the worries of workers employed at giant factories. John L. Lewis of the miners' union and Sidney Hillman of the garment workers sought to organize on a broader scale and in 1935 formed the Committee for Industrial Organization within the AFL. Then, in an action reminiscent of Powderly's mishandling of the eight-hour day issue, AFL president William Green expelled the new group. Renaming itself the Congress of Industrial Organizations and acting under the protection of the Wagner Act, the CIO soon perfected the sit-down strike as a bargaining tactic and had great success in organizing the automobile, steel, rubber, textile, and shipbuilding industries. Hillman enjoyed access to the Roosevelt administration as a political operative, and Roosevelt's phrase "Clear it with Sidney" symbolized labor's access to the highest circles of power. The amalgamation that yielded today's AFL-CIO in 1955 was fifteen years away.

America has seen a decline in the fortunes of organized labor since World War II (see Figure 12–1). When the end of Prohibition dried up the revenue sources of the newly organized crime families, the thugs were able to attack a soft target by infiltrating the labor movement. By the 1950s and 1960s, crime and racketeering were exposed in the Teamsters Union, first with Dave Beck and later with Jimmy Hoffa. Problems within the Teamsters have continued, not the least of which was the embezzlement of the Central States Pension Fund. Labor's own leadership seemed to lose touch with the needs of the rank and file, particularly as generational replacement meant that fewer workers had personal experience of the hardships of the Depression. And to the extent that organizational efforts are inherently easier in manufacturing and mining, the decline in those sectors during the postindustrial era also accounts for the decline in union membership, not only in proportional terms, but in absolute numbers as well.

Changing conditions in the political environment, such as the antilabor posture of the Reagan era, are also responsible for labor's decline. During Reagan's first months in office, the Professional Air Traffic Controllers (PATCO) struck over conditions of labor and compensation.

Figure 12-1.

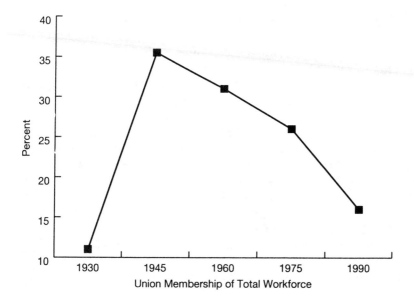

Union Membership of Total Workforce

The result was the firing of a major proportion of union members by their employer, the federal government. This signal, plus the proemployer posture of the NLRB, has had a deleterious impact on labor organization.

There are several themes in labor's long history. One is the rivalry of craft versus industrial unionism. The organization of workers by craft was natural until the arrival of mechanization, the lower level of skill needed to operate machines, and the appearance of the manufacturing plant with employees numbering in the hundreds. Within unions like the AFL, the prestige and power flowed easily to the craft affiliates—the carpenters and machinists. The struggle to organize by industry, regardless of the particular trade, could no longer be contained after the development of the assembly line. The CIO was immensely successful in organizing automobile and other assembly-line workers. Although the CIO merged back with the AFL in 1955, there is a sense in which the craft-industry rivalry lingers on in the attitudes toward unions that continue to be held by airline pilots, government workers, teachers, and others who fit uneasily into the union milieu of today.

A second theme concerns the place of women and minorities in labor organizations. Some industries, beginning with the Lowell textile mills in the 1820s and continuing in the garment trades and domestic service, were built around the availability of female workers. In the larger work force, however, women were usually seen as a source of cheap labor that would undermine the wages of men. That this was a justification for increasing women's wages was seldom recognized, and only the Knights of Labor welcomed women as both full members or auxiliary chapters. In the case of blacks, racial stereotypes led to the conclusion that "union standards" would not be upheld if they were allowed to join. But here again, it was the Knights almost alone who counted black workers among their numbers. This failure to accept women and minorities in leadership positions in organized labor continues today.

A third theme is violence, a feature of labor organization during the last quarter of the nineteenth century. More than had been the case with earlier depressions, the panic of 1873 had a dramatic effect on labor organizations because of the new industrializing society in which it occurred. A protest by unemployed workers gave rise to the Tompkins Square riot in New York City in 1874. Violence flourished in the Pennsylvania coalfields as Irish miners, the Molly Maguires, struck out at owners and other workers alike. A remarkable nationwide strike in the summer of 1877, early in the Hayes administration, closed down the country's railway and telegraph service for days; but the high degree of support that rail workers received signaled the resurgence of organizing activity that yielded fruit with the first national meeting of the Knights of Labor the following year. Still, the violence continued: the Haymarket massacre in Chicago in 1886; the Homestead massacre in Pennsylvania in 1892, in which industrialist Henry Clay Frick was both shot and stabbed (he survived). The Pullman strike in 1894 was marked by violence, as were coal strikes in 1902 and the Ludlow massacre in Colorado in 1914. Probably in no other country has the struggle for labor organization generated as much violence as in the United States.

Organized labor in America is also unique because of the failure of certain other themes to develop at all. One was the breadth of unionism's purpose. Reformers, from Robert Dale Owen in the 1820s to William Sylvis in 1866, and the cooperativists of the 1880s had hoped that unions would be a stepping stone to a new, cooperativist society. Those utopian ideas melted away in the face of what Samuel Gompers called "pure and simple unionism," in which union activism was directed primarily to workplace issues: wages, hours, benefits, and a relatively narrow but changing set of related concerns.

For other reasons, but certainly including the notion of "pure and simple unionism," another feature of unionism in other democratic nations failed to appear in America— the organization of an independent labor party. An idea that surfaced frequently throughout the nineteenth century was to remain apart from politics and to concentrate instead on the development of utopian societies or producers' cooperatives. It came to naught. Much more important was whether to create a separate labor party or to throw support to whichever of the dominant parties would serve labor best. The separate party concept met with fleeting success in Jacksonian times, and it was an option that was exercised frequently during the Gilded Age. Among them were the Greenback Labor party in 1878; the Independent Labor party, which won the Milwaukee mayoral election in the late 1880s; and various socialist and workers' parties in the generation that followed. The culmination was Eugene Debs's remarkable candidacy in 1920, when he won nearly a million votes while in the Atlanta Federal Penitentiary after his conviction under the Espionage Act of 1918.

LABOR POLICY

Early labor law existed only at the state level, the descendant of colonial practice and English common law. Most of it was adverse to workers' organizations. Between 1806 and 1815, strikes by shoemakers' unions in Philadelphia and New York were prosecuted as illegal conspiracies. The decisions in these cases were based on a "creative" use of the common-law notion of conspiracy, and it was not until 1842, in *Commonwealth* v. *Hunt*, that Chief Justice Lemuel Shaw of Massachusetts ruled that unions were legitimate and strikes were not illegal. Aside from reforms regarding such issues as imprisonment for debt, however, it was not until the twentieth century that the first positive laws concerning labor began to appear. The first workmen's compensation law was adopted by Maryland in 1902. The first limitation of the workday for women, on grounds of health, was passed by

Oregon in 1903 and upheld by the U.S. Supreme Court in *Muller* v. *Oregon* (1911). Unemployment insurance did not appear until 1932, in Wisconsin. But the speed of reform varied widely from state to state, and it was not until after World War II that Mississippi became the last state to adopt workmen's compensation.

The earliest federal intervention in labor activity occurred during the presidency of Andrew Jackson, on January 29, 1834, when a strike by Irish laborers working on the Chesapeake & Ohio Canal in Maryland spurred the first use of federal soldiers in a labor dispute . After the Civil War, the U.S. Army was an occasional participant in labor disputes. President Hayes employed federal troops during the unprecedented nationwide railroad strike of 1877, for example, and Grover Cleveland used them in Illinois during the Pullman strike of 1894. For the most part, however, when troops were used in labor disputes they came in the form of state militias, for example, the Pennsylvania National Guard in the Homestead strike in 1892, the Colorado National Guard in the coal strike of 1902, and the Ohio National Guard in the Electric Auto-Lite Strike in Toledo in 1934.

Federal involvement in labor often took a more positive role, as it did in establishing shorter workdays and higher wages. Soon after the C&O dispute, the Navy Department instituted the first ten-hour day at its docks in Philadelphia in 1838. By 1860, the ten-hour day had become nearly standard because of state statutes. Later, in 1868, Congress shortened the day to eight hours for workers employed by the government or by government contractors—an important milestone on the road to the eight-hour day for all.

Some of labor's first successes with Congress, ironically, were in the area of immigration. The Emigrant [sic.] Contract Labor Act of 1864 was designed to increase the flow of workers from abroad during the Civil War. But in 1885, the repeal of the contract labor law, particularly as it applied to workers from China, was a major lobbying success of the Knights of Labor.

Because the federal concern with interstate commerce was most recognizable in railroading, it was in this industry that important developments in federal labor legislation appeared at the end of the nineteenth century. A framework for creating ad hoc mediation commissions was enacted in 1888, but it proved to be ineffective in the Pullman strike. Because of the germ of antiunionism in the Sherman Act, the first significant application of that statute was directed at labor's role in the Pullman dispute. Still, symbols are important in politics, and about this same time Congress in 1894 designated the first Monday in September as Labor Day.

Federal railway labor legislation began to have more effect with the Erdman Act of 1898, which created a mediation board comprising the chair of the ICC and the commissioner of the Bureau of Labor. The board recorded a number of successes in the following decade and played a role in settling sixty-one disputes in the last eight years of its life alone. The Newlands

Act of 1913 created a successor four-person Board of Mediation and Conciliation. Eventually a nine-member board, with representatives from management, labor, and the public, was authorized by the Esch-Cummins Act of 1920. The Act of May 20, 1926, then imposed a Board of Mediation, which in turn was superseded by the Railway Labor Act of June 27, 1934. Throughout it all there was a gradual march from providing only "good offices" for mediation (Erdman Act), to imposing an eight-hour day and extra pay for overtime (Adamson Act), to powers just short of compulsory arbitration (Esch-Cummins Act), to upholding the right of employees to organize for collective bargaining (Railway Labor Act). There had been more federal involvement between 1898 and 1932 than in all of American labor history.

World War I deserves special attention for the stimulus that it gave to centralizing tendencies and the growth of presidential power. Beyond the special case of railroads, where labor was concerned, the war was the occasion for the creation of a Mediation Commission in 1917 and a National War Labor Board in 1918. With the dissolution of these wartime labor agencies at war's end, there was a dramatic increase in strike activity. A wartime requirement that federal suppliers must bargain collectively with their employees had the effect of creating something despised in the world of labor: the company union. Company unions continued to grow after the war, and their membership reached 1.4 million by 1926 and 2.5 million by 1935.

The 1920s saw the decline of labor on most fronts. In 1912, a Massachusetts law that created a commission to establish minimum wages for women was found unconstitutional by the Supreme Court in *Adkins* v. *Children's Hospital* (1923). Attempts at outlawing the products of child labor in interstate commerce were overturned in the courts, and the 1924 Child Labor Amendment failed to obtain the approval of the requisite number of states for ratification. The one labor victory was the Railway Labor Act of 1926. Still, given the euphoria of the day, it was a booming decade until Black Thursday, 1929.

Although depressions always had been disastrous for unions, labor's greatest gains occurred during the 1930s with the aid of the federal government. In the midst of the Depression, the Norris-LaGuardia Anti-Injunction Act of 1932 forbade judicial injunctions to maintain antiunion "independent contracts," which were a device to impede union organization. Nor would there be injunctions from federal courts to outlaw strikes and picketing, the law said. The New Deal, perhaps surprisingly even to Roosevelt, was the champion of labor. The National Industrial Recovery Act, passed during the hectic First Hundred Days, created a National Recovery Administration (NRA) that sought to stabilize wages through its "industry codes." By the time the Supreme Court overturned the law in the *Schechter Poultry* case of 1935, however, labor had come to regard the agreements reached under Section 7a as inimical to its interests.

Now the way was clear for the Wagner Act, labor's most important legislative achievement. Based on the commerce clause and building on the commission concept, Congress created a three-person National Labor Relations Board (NLRB) with powers more favorable toward labor than ever before seen in the United States. The board and its staff could act in two broad areas. One was in labor representation—the process of petitioning for and holding elections for collective bargaining and recognizing unions as bargaining agents. The other area concerned unfair employer practices in the workplace and in the negotiating process. The Wagner Act's impact on labor was dramatic. The CIO in particular was able to exhibit startling success in organizing on an industrial basis. In 1937, only a month after the President had gone on radio with his scheme to pack the Supreme Court, the law was upheld in *NLRB* v. *Jones and Laughlin Steel Corp.* by a vote of five to four, when the Court gave an expansive definition to the meaning of interstate commerce.

Labor won another major victory with the Fair Labor Standards Act of 1938. Generally, the statute established a minimum wage of forty cents per hour (to be phased in gradually over eight years from a base of twenty-five cents and a forty-hour work week and outlawed labor by children under the age of sixteen. However, there were important limitations. The law exempted agricultural workers, much of the service industry, and all who were not in interstate commerce. In the half century since its establishment, the politics of labor legislation has often focused on both increasing the minimum wage itself and expanding the number of workers who are covered by it.

1938	$0.25	1974	2.25
1946	0.40	1989	3.35
1949	0.75	1990	3.85
1961	1.25	1991	4.25
1968	1.60		

World War II, when America was the arsenal of democracy and unemployment fell to nearly zero, was when organized labor approached its zenith. Still, forces that saw labor as a threat were never far from the battle. There was the return of the Red scare. Radicalism was part of labor's early history, and some of the best organizers during the 1930s really had been Communists. In the emotionally charged atmosphere of the Cold War, the loyalty issue emerged as part of the antilabor rhetoric, and the requirement of loyalty oaths was a perennial topic in Congress.

Management had chafed under the Wagner Act after 1935 because it seemed too prolabor. The unfair practices of Section 8, for example, enumerated wrongs that might be committed only by employers, not by labor. Inflation was blamed on wages that had "spiraled" during the war. When the GOP returned to power in the House and Senate in November 1946, the 80th Congress moved quickly to amend the NLRA through the Taft-Hartley

Act. The revisions outlawed the closed shop, allowed employers as well as workers to sue for contract and strike damages, allowed eighty-day injunctions for "cooling-off periods" for any strike that might threaten the national interest, and required union officials to take loyalty oaths. It also expanded the NLRB to five members and established a new Federal Mediation and Conciliation Service. It was a far-reaching bill that was passed over the veto of President Truman, and parts of it continue to be grist for labor politics even today.

Labor legislation has also focused on organized crime. The bureaucratization of unions had concerned many who had developed the old craft unions, and the emergence of the union business agent provided a point of centralization where power, influence, and money might converge. With the end of Prohibition, labor unions were recognized as soft targets by mobsters seeking to replace profits that were no longer available from bootlegging and associated rackets. Some unions and their leaders were strong enough to throw out the thugs who had suddenly become established in their organizations. Others were not so fortunate. Investigations of the influence of organized crime within labor unions were carried forward by senators like John McClellan (D–AR) and Estes Kefauver (D–TN); and the Labor Management Reporting and Disclosure Act of 1959 (Landrum-Griffin Act) was aimed at protecting union members from gangsterism, corruption, and unfair elections within their own unions. Still, the activities of Dave Beck and Jimmy Hoffa, the looting of the Teamsters' Union's Central States Pension Fund, the murder of dissident UMW member Jock Yablonski, and a host of other misdeeds have marred the public's perception of unionism during the past generation.

Other legislation has been aimed at discrimination by unions. With occasional exceptions, the civil rights record of the labor movement was seldom admirable. The successes of black Americans were usually restricted to specific industries, as in the Brotherhood of Sleeping Car Porters under the leadership of A. Phillip Randolph during the 1930s and 1940s. Women have usually been relegated to traditional industries as well and excluded from union leadership positions. The Civil Rights Act of 1964 forbade discrimination not only by employers but also by unions, and this provision was reinforced by the Equal Employment Opportunity Act of 1972.

It would be expected that a president who attracted supply-side economists and whose name became linked with conservative economic policies would be no special friend of organized labor. Some of the changes of the 1980s were small or subtle, such as the termination of annual surveys by the Bureau of Labor Statistics of the number of people in organized labor. Other actions, such as the president's behavior during the PATCO strike in his first months in office, were more palpable. The controllers, employees of the Federal Aviation Administration (FAA), had walked out over low wages, hectic working conditions in the control towers of the nation's airports, and lack of vacation time. The president adopted a "get tough" position toward the union and, after a back-to-work order was ignored, fired those who remained off the job. Eventually a whole new group of controllers was hired and trained, although the conditions that brought on the strike changed little. However, many in the labor movement believe that changes at the NLRB have been the most important factor in the continued decline of union membership.

ADMINISTRATIVE ORGANIZATIONS

Many federal organizations are active in the labor field, including the Department of Labor's Bureau of Labor Statistics and the workplace inspections of various safety-related agencies. But it is the NLRB that is of foremost importance to the right to organize.

The NLRB, created in 1935 by the Wagner Act from the various mediation boards that had preceded it, has the characteristics of IRCs generally. Administrative agencies are empowered with a blend of rule-making, administrative, and adjudicative functions—with legislative, executive, and judicial authority. Adjudicatively, they offer economies of scale because, operating within specialized areas of jurisdiction, they can mass-produce decisions, bring the insight that generalist judges might lack, and (presumably) hold down litigation costs. Administratively, they can provide services such as conducting representational elections. Legislatively, IRCs can create rules pursuant to statutory guidelines laid down by Congress.

During its first decade of operations the NLRB probably did comport with management's belief that it was avowedly prolabor. A study of its actions between the Taft-Hartley Act and the Reagan era shows, however, a long record of general impartiality between 1948 and 1979. By recording the votes cast by each member against business under Section 8-A of the National Labor Relations Act and against labor under Section 8-B, Terry Moe (1985, pp. 1105–1106) was able to calculate the orientations of the twenty-five people who served on the board during this time. His findings show that the annualized scores for the five-member NLRB, where a score of .500 would indicate complete neutrality, never went below the .438 of 1954 (a probusiness posture) or above the .549 of 1978 (a prolabor position). There did seem to be a very slight trend toward the labor position across the thirty-two year time span, however.

Although there has been no comparable analysis of NLRB voting since 1980, a number of indicators suggest that the board's orientation was probusiness under Reagan-Bush. One aspect of this shift was the quantity of cases handled by the board. The administration was slow in filling vacancies when they occurred, and for this and other reasons the backlog of cases processed each year grew larger while the annual numbers of completed cases became smaller. And because labor law allows appeals to the federal courts, the growing litigiosity of public life in America means that employers can file actions that can take years to settle. Meanwhile, firms can fire workers who are union sympathizers, organize antiunion campaigns, or hire replacement workers when strikes occur.

The other shift in NLRB action has been in the quality of its decisions. Board decisions during the 1980s made it easier for a company to move its operations if it could show that the reason for the relocation was not to avoid a union (*Milwaukee Spring* case). It reduced protection for an employee who protested against unsafe working conditions unless he or she acted "in concert" with other employees (*Meyer Industries* case). Union organizing was made more difficult by giving employers more freedom to question employees about union-organizing activity (*Rossmore House* case) and by prohibiting union solicitation during working time (*Our Way, Inc.*). At bottom, says Gregory LeRoy (1990) of the Midwest Center for Labor Research, the reason for the decline in union membership "has nothing to do with Americans' interest in joining a union [but] everything to do with the corruption of the [NLRB]" (p. 23).

LABOR'S APPROACH TO POLITICS

Organized labor has long been politically important, but its participation has been peculiarly American. Unlike many Western democracies, there never has been a viable labor party in the United States. There were stillborn attempts to develop them during the Jacksonian era and at the end of the nineteenth century, of course, as well as attempts as recently as the 1920s to link labor with one of the socialist traditions. But socialism has never been acceptable in America, and labor has overwhelmingly followed one of the admonitions of Samuel Gompers to pursue "pure and simple unionism"—to concentrate on job-related issues while eschewing utopian visions, cooperative associations, Fabian socialism, and a distinctive labor party.

Another of Gompers's strategies was for labor to adopt a balance-of-power strategy that would prevent the two major parties from taking it for granted. Supporting the party or candidate that is its friend of the hour would make the most of labor's modest numbers, but this prescription has broken down since Gompers's time. Although individual unions like the AFL and UMW might toy with taking their support elsewhere, most of labor became allied with the Democratic party after the realignment of 1932. A notable exception has been the Teamsters Union since the Senate investigations of the 1950s. In the eyes of labor's leadership, at least, the Democratic party is the party of choice.

More problematic for labor politically has been its inability to deliver a solid column of votes in presidential elections. There has been a noticeable erosion in support for Democratic candidates among the union rank and file since the 1950s, especially among those who are not convinced union members. Reagan had a special appeal to labor's rank and file; so despite labor's influence in securing the Democratic nomination for Walter Mondale in 1984, individual workers supported the Republican ticket in embarrassing numbers. As real wages continue to fall from their levels of 1970, labor may regain its electoral solidarity. But if labor's great contribution is the number of votes it can deliver on election day, this asset becomes depleted as the number and proportion of union members in the electorate diminish.

Although labor's electoral support remains significant, its lobbying activities may be more important today. Labor developed the political action committee (PAC) device in response to the prohibition of political contributions that was part of the Smith-Connally Act of 1943. Later, in the wake of the Watergate scandal of the Nixon era, labor's PAC idea was taken up by corporate lobbies to finance electoral campaigns. As long as campaign contributions through PACs remain a cornerstone of electoral politics, labor can maintain access to the corridors of power.

ISSUES FOR ORGANIZED LABOR TODAY

The most fundamental issue that confronts organized labor today is its ability to organize collectively. Although the basic principles of the Wagner Act of 1935 remain intact, there has been an erosion in their application. The belief that the gains of organized labor are inflationary because they are not accompanied by concomitant increases in productivity, the unsustainable idea that American labor costs are so high that they reduce our ability to compete in international markets, and a decade of antilabor rhetoric from conservatives in and around the Reagan administration are among the reasons for a decline in the proportion of the work force that is unionized. In addition, the NLRB is seen by many in the labor movement as promanagement, both in its decisions and in its failure to treat labor disputes in a timely manner.

There are also issues that endure across the decades, including the nature of work rules, benefit packages, and safety on the job. Work rules, which govern which trade does what work inside the plant, are one variety of job guarantees. The requirement that only a union electrician, for example, can plug in a spotlight helps to ensure that there will be work enough for all. Early retirement, such as "twenty and out," also means that there will be vacancies in the work force for a new generation. Rising medical costs mean that health insurance is important at the bargaining table, and cost-of-living adjustments for retirees are part of the package.

The peculiarities of the postindustrial era, with its increases in technological expertise and increased flow of international trade, have put a new face on yet other issues. Higher technology, plus lessons learned from Japanese managerial methods, have engendered a new spirit of workplace cooperation. Quality circles and other vehicles for utilizing the practical insights of workers on the production line emerged in the 1980s. Often this new spirit of labor-management cooperation has been approached as cautiously by labor as by management. But although tenuous at the beginning, cooperation within the plant is a departure from the confrontational approach of the past.

This new cooperation between labor and management also appears when there is a threat from foreign competition (see Table 12–1). As the proportion of the economy associated with international trade grows, the idea of having "a level playing field" becomes important. There must be as much opportunity to sell American-made goods overseas free from trade restraints as there is for foreign-made goods to enter the market here. Thus,

TABLE 12–1.
Industrial Competitiveness
Some people argue that greater unionization in the United States unleashes forces that yield trade deficits with other countries. Indeed, there was a slight tendency for the levels of unionization to be lower in the dozen countries with which the United States had a trade deficit in 1988. (Pearson's $r = -.12$) At the same time, however, the U.S. trade deficit was greater with those countries having higher wages ($r = .12$), and the correlation between levels of unionization and domestic wages in those twelve countries was .32. None of these correlations is statistically significant.

Country	Trade deficit with U.S. 1988 U.S. Dollars	Hourly Wage (U.S. Dollars)	Percent of workers unionized
Japan	52.1	13.14	30
Taiwan	12.7	2.71	18
West Germany	12.2	18.07	34
Canada	11.7	13.58	31
South Korea	8.9	2.46	10
Brazil	5.0	1.49	50
Italy	4.8	12.87	42
Hong Kong	4.6	2.43	15
Mexico	2.6	1.57	35
Sweden	2.3	16.85	90
France	2.1	12.99	20
Switzerland	0.4	17.94	20
United States	120.9	13.90	18

For purposes of comparison, the U.S. trade deficit for 1988 was $121 billion, the average hourly wage was $13.90, and 16 percent of the workforce was unionized.
Sources: OECD Monthly Statistics of Foreign Trade, April 1989; *The (Toledo Ohio) Blade*, December 28, 1990.

labor and management jointly approach congressional delegations and the Representative for Trade Negotiations in search of protection from imports.

The new alliance between labor and management breaks down over disinvestment and outsourcing. As American firms transformed themselves into multinational corporations after World War II, they often began to manufacture products in countries where labor costs were lower. By the 1970s, American firms began manufacturing component parts "offshore"— typically in Southeast Asia or Mexico—with a proportionate decline in high-er-paying jobs in the American labor force. Outsourcing also denotes the manufacture of components from lower-cost states and localities within the United States, at the expense of workers in industrial states.

DISCUSSION QUESTIONS

1. What were the origin and importance of the distinction between craft unions and industrial unions in the United States?

2. Differing views emerged concerning how labor should seek its goals. What were these world views? Which ones won out and why?

3. Was government a friend or a foe of early labor organizations? Which branches of government? At what times? Why the changes?

4. What factors brought about the passage of the National Labor Relations Act, or Wagner Act, in 1935?

5. What were the major provisions of the Taft-Hartley Act of 1947? How did orga-nized labor react to them?

6. What have been the trends in the percentage of America's work force that is unionized? Why the recent decline?

7. Discuss the relationship between organized labor and the Democratic party in the New Deal realignment. What has been labor's relationship with the Republican party in the Reagan-Bush era?

8. How "independent" is the NLRB as an independent regulatory commission?

9. What are the major issues on the agenda of American labor in the 1990s?

10. What organizations and ideas stand in opposition to *organized* labor today?

REFERENCES

Filippelli, Ronald L. 1990. *Labor Conflict in the United States: An Encyclopedia.* New York: Garland Publishing

_____. 1984. *Labor in the U.S.A.: A History.* New York: Knopf.

Foner, Philip. 1974. *Organized Labor and the Black Worker, 1619–1973.* New York: Praeger.

Howe, Louise Kapp. 1977. *Pink Collar Workers: Inside the World of Women's Work.* New York: Putman.

Kortz, Robert F. 1970. *Statutory History of the U.S.: Labor Organizations.* New York: Chelsea House.

LeRoy, Gregory. 1990, September 3. Quoted in *The* [Toledo, OH] *Blade,* p. 23.

Moe, Terry. 1985, December. "Control and Feedback in Economic Regulation." *The American Political Science Review,* 79, pp. 1094–1116.

Morris, Richard B. 1946. *Government and Labor in Early America.* New York: Columbia University Press.

Ross, Phillip. 1965. *The Government as a Source of Union Power.* Providence, RI: Brown University Press.

Taylor, Benjamin, and Fred Witney. 1979. *Labor Relations Law,* 3rd ed. Englewood Cliffs, NJ: Prentice Hall.

Zwerdlin, Daniel. 1980. *Workplace Democracy.* New York: Harper & Row.

CHAPTER THIRTEEN

POLITICAL ECONOMY IN INTERNATIONAL PERSPECTIVE

International economic issues have always been important in American politics. During the colonial period America supplied raw materials that were exchanged for finished English products, and a large proportion of the ships of the British merchant fleet were American-made. Shippers and merchants were important people in early America, and after the loss of British naval protection after 1776, they turned their attention to China in search of new markets. Ensuring the safety of its trading interests in the Mediterranean drove America to create its own navy in the 1790s. It was during the last century that U.S. economic interests in Central America, often with the support of military power, gave rise to its unfortunate reputation as the "Colossus of the North"; and the annexation of Hawaii was the story of how economic interests brought about the end of Hawaiian sovereignty. After 1945, the United States became the world's leading economic power and the dollar served as the western world's reserve currency; during the 1980s, however, its unfavorable balance of trade has made it the world's largest debtor nation.

This chapter examines four topics of international political economy. First, it describes the laws of absolute advantage and comparative advantage—the rationale for international trade itself. Second, it traces American policy toward tariffs and trade. Third, it considers the international monetary regime. Finally, it examines the North American Free Trade Agreement (NAFTA), which has become a particularly contentious study in international trade among Canada, Mexico, and the United States.

THE RATIONALE FOR WORLD TRADE: THE LAWS OF ABSOLUTE AND COMPARATIVE ADVANTAGE

The law of comparative advantage, first recognized by the classical economist David Ricardo, is a powerful justification for unimpeded international trade. First, consider a hypothetical international system where only two countries (the U.S. and Japan) contemplate either trade or self-sufficiency in two commodities (agriculture and electronics).

	Agriculture (Vegetables)		Electronics (TVs, VCRs)		Country Maximums
United States					
Specialization	50	or	30	—>	50
Self-sufficiency	(25)	+	(15)	=	(40)
Japan					
Specialization	40	or	60	—>	60
Self-sufficiency	(20)	+	(30)	=	(50)
Commodity	50	+	60	=	110
Maximums	(45)	+	(45)	=	(90)

If the United States were to specialize in one commodity or the other, it could produce either 50 units of vegetables or 30 units of VCRs. Alternatively, the United States might seek self-sufficiency in each commodity. By doing both, only half as many productive resources can be employed in either endeavor, so we would end up with 25 units of vegetables but also 15 units of consumer electronics. The Japanese, for their part, could also concentrate in either vegetables (producing 40 units) or VCRs (60 units), or they too could seek self-sufficiency by simultaneously producing 20 units of vegetables and 30 of consumer electronics.

Notice what happens to the country, commodity, and world totals if each country specializes in producing the product that it makes best. If the United States sticks with agriculture and the Japanese eschew vegetables for electronics, both countries in this example will be better off. With specialization and free trade there will be 50 units of agricultural products and 60 of VCRs, or 110 units in all. Under a regime of self-sufficiency, however, there would be only 90 units in all (25 + 15 + 20 + 30 = 90). There is no magic in this example, for specialization means only that each country produces the commodity that shows the higher number of units (i.e., 50 rather than 30 in the American case), and the larger number will always be greater than the average of the sum of that number plus a smaller one. In this example, the United States has an absolute advantage over Japan in agriculture (50 units are greater than 40), and the Japanese enjoy a 60-to-30 advantage over the United States in making electronics. International trade makes obvious good sense in cases of absolute advantage.

Ricardo's contribution was in recognizing that trade continues to be mutually beneficial even when one partner fails to have an absolute advantage in either commodity. Let us rearrange the numbers in the preceding example so that the Japanese enjoy an advantage in both product lines.

	Agriculture (Vegetables)		Electronics (TVs, VCRs)		Country Maximums
United States					
Specialization	40	or	30	—>	40
Self-sufficiency	(20)	+	(15)	=	(35)
Japan					
Specialization	50	or	60	—>	60
Self-sufficiency	(25)	+	(30)	=	(55)
Commodity	40	+	60	=	100
Maximums	(45)	+	(45)	=	(90)

The outcomes would not be as advantageous as before, but under self-sufficiency the United States would produce 35 units and Japan 55, for a world total of 90. With specialization in that which each nation does relatively better, the United States produces 40 units and Japan makes 60, for a world total of 100.[1]

The laws of absolute and comparative advantage are based on the notions of specialization and differential costs in the factors of production. The Hecksher-Ohlin principle has gone further by explaining that nations will export items that are more intensive in the factor in which the country is endowed—raw materials, climate, managerial skill, physical capital, and so on. For example, the United States might do better in agriculture because of cheaper land, optimal mechanization, and greater agricultural knowledge from years of research. The Japanese may do better in electron-

---

1.Ricardo's example contrasted the ability of England and Portugal to produce wine and textiles. It was premised on the costs of production, as indicated by the hours of labor per unit:

	Wine	Textiles
England	120	100
Portugal	80	90

He concluded that even though Portugal was the lower-cost producer of both wine and textiles, it should concentrate on winemaking, where it had an advantage of 80 versus 120, and to import cloth, where it enjoyed a narrower margin of 90 to 100. (Ricardo, 1817, pp. 135, 404).

ics because of more skillful managerial methods and manufacturing techniques.

The theory of comparative advantage holds for localized economies as well as for international ones, and it is true regardless of whether production decisions are made through central planning or by markets.

Ricardo's theory of international trade does raise two sets of problems, however. One group of issues is most directly in the domain of economic analysis and economics as a field of study. What units of analysis should be used—hours of labor, profitability measures, or something else? How complex can these models become—how many countries and how many commodities? In opposition to an all-the-eggs-in-one-basket approach, what mixed strategy for commodity protection is appropriate given the uncertainties of overseas markets? As one abandons a fifty-fifty split to move toward specialization, it is not unreasonable to maintain some degree of local production. What mixed strategy should there be: seventy-five to twenty-five, ninety to ten, or what? What happens when the market for that commodity in which a country specializes collapses? What do buggywhip manufacturers do when automobiles come along?

Other problems are more political in nature. (1) Given the strategic needs of national defense or some other emergency that threaten a foreign supply line, where it is desirable to retain some sort of domestic production and just how large should that share be? Similarly, what happens when a product is offered solely for matters of prestige, such as a national airline? (2) What happens when one trading partner follows a regime of free trade but the other adopts a protectionist stance? (3) What deviations from a regime of free trade can be expected as a result of political pressures brought about by those whose welfare is threatened because of the loss of their occupations? How can our less productive "factors of production"—our people—be made more mobile so that they can move into a more productive industry? What do we do for those displaced workers who, for whatever reasons, simply are not mobile resources? (4) Who makes these trade-related decisions, and who decides who these deciders will be?

TARIFFS AND TRADE

Tariffs, or taxes on the importation of goods, are one of the oldest aspects of governmental involvement in international trade. Initially, in one of the first laws passed by Congress, the objective was to tap into the flow of commerce as a convenient source of revenue. By 1791, however, Treasury Secretary Alexander Hamilton's ideas for promoting manufacturing had resulted in an increase in the import tax for an avowedly protectionistic motive. But despite Hamilton, the rates were low enough until the War of 1812 that the amount of protection they afforded was relatively modest. The war was important, however, for in its desperate search for revenue, the import tax was raised to 25 percent. These high rates were the entering wedge for the protectionism that surfaced soon afterward. Beginning with average rates of 25 percent in the tariff of 1818, the effect of the tax nearly doubled by the tariff of 1828—the "Tariff of Abominations"—to average rates in the 45 to 50 percent range.

For a century the tariff was a perennial issue of American politics (Taussig, 1967). Once protectionism surfaced as a policy goal, the economic differences among the regions were a cause of conflict and bargaining. Between 1818 and the Civil War, the South opposed tariffs not only because they lacked manufacturing of their own but also because tariffs impeded their ability to export cotton and tobacco to Europe. Occasionally the shipping interests of New England also were tariff opponents. After 1865 the developing and consuming West added its opposition to high tariff rates. Throughout the period the Democrats were the low-tariff party, and the Whigs gave way to the Republicans as the party of protectionism. It was not mere coincidence that the Republican party adopted a high-tariff plank in 1860 to ensure its victory in Pennsylvania. To South Carolina, the reascendancy of a high-tariff party, on top of the issue of slavery, was the straw that lit the gun batteries that were trained on Fort Sumter.

It is difficult to compare the levels of protectionism of tariff laws across the years (see Figure 13–1). When ad valorem (or percentage) rates vary by commodity, should a grand mean be taken for all of the, say, thirty commodities, or should an overall average be estimated by taking into consideration the proportion of imports affected by each rate of tax? When tariffs are levied as "specific duties" (or fixed dollar amounts) fluctuations in the price of those commodities will affect the actual percentage of tax. If, while iron is being taxed at $5 per ton, the price of iron doubles, then the rate of the tax will fall by one-half. Comparisons are also hindered by variations in the breadth of the duty-free list—as when the list of items free from tax is expanded. Finally, there are also problems with estimating a tariff's impact on the raising of revenue. To the extent that protectionism achieves its goals, lower tariff revenues might indeed be the result of higher rates of tax.

An important change in tariff policy occurred when rate setting was removed from direct congressional action and delegated to the executive branch. This switch was first attempted during the 1880s, when Republican Secretary of State James G. Blaine negotiated several bilateral treaties in hopes of reducing tariff levels. Being treaties, however, these agreements had to be taken to the Senate for ratification, and they failed to pass. A half century later, the high rates of the Smoot-Hawley Tariff were being blamed for the persistence of the Great Depression.

Secretary of State Cordell Hull, a Tennessean and former member of the House Committee on Ways and Means, brought with him both the southern Democratic preference for low tariffs and the belief that nations

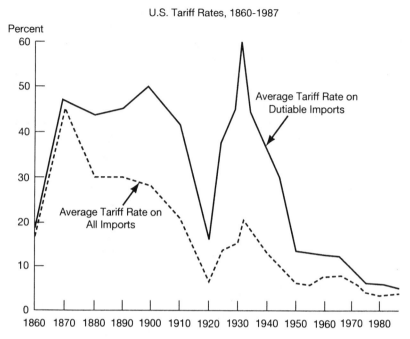

Figure 13-1. Source: *Annual Report of the Council of Economic Advisers* (January 1989) Pr40.9:989.

that traded together would have less reason to go to war. Under Hull's plan, bilateral executive agreements between heads of government could be the rate-reducing vehicles. Being executive agreements, they would not need senatorial concurrence; but the power to negotiate would have to be granted by the whole Congress. The Reciprocal Trade Agreements Act of 1934 authorized the Department of State to bargain with other nations, one by one, to raise or lower tariff rates over a three-year period by as much as 50 percent from those of 1930. This authorization was renewed in 1937 and at regular intervals thereafter; and as tariff rates would be cut in half, the base year from which future reductions were to be made would be updated. Renewals of the State Department's bargaining authority were often accompanied by congressional charges that foreign nations were unfairly "dumping" products in U.S. markets at below their cost of production, that vital industries were being undermined by foreign competition, or that U.S. negotiators were being outmaneuvered by foreign diplomats. By focusing attention on the overall issue of renewing bargaining authority, however, and avoiding separate votes on specific rates, the logrolling pressures that had yielded high tariffs for a century were blunted.

The movement for freer world trade accelerated gradually after World War II. The General Agreement on Tariffs and Trade, or GATT, was concluded among twenty-eight nations at a conference in Geneva, Switzerland, in 1947. Additional countries joined in the arrangement in 1949 and 1951, while the United States granted concessions on hundreds of items. During the 1950s, the European Common Market emerged, as did the growth of nontariff barriers like quotas, and domestic content requirements limited the flow of goods. Even in the United States, where tariff rates on dutiable items fell from 59 percent in 1932 to only 12 percent by 1961, the proportion of all imports that were taxed actually increased over the same time period from 33 to 60 percent.

Perhaps the first congressional victory of President John F. Kennedy was the passage of the Trade Expansion Act of 1962. It was a significant increase in the movement toward freer trade by arguing that future trade negotiations would be multilateral and that the negotiating would be removed from the State Department and placed in the Executive Office under the direction of a special representative for trade negotiations, who would be of ambassadorial rank. A series of bargaining conferences, beginning with the Kennedy Round in 1963 and continuing most recently through the Uruguay Round of 1989–1993, has nudged U.S. rates down to an average of 5 percent.

Today it is far more common to speak of trade policy than of the tariff. The balance of trade is said to be favorable (or positive) when exports out of the country are greater than imports into it. An unfavorable balance of trade is just the opposite—a situation in which imports are greater, as with the American trade balance vis-à-vis Japan in recent years.

Several factors can cause changes in a nation's balance of trade. There may be relative changes for better or worse in levels of productivity, in efficiency, or in the quality of production. Take levels of compensation, for example. The Japanese have been critical of the high levels of compensation of many American chief executive officers (CEOs), who may make as much as one hundred times more than the average worker. This same ratio is only about ten to one in Japan. Trade balances also can shift because of changing international demand. Tastes may change because of heightened environmental consciousness or because invention may make products obsolete. Or trade can be affected by barriers such as tariffs, quotas, or the *keretsu* agreements that allegedly keep American auto parts suppliers from gaining a foothold in Japanese markets. And as we shall see shortly, balances of trade can shift because of changes in the value of national currencies.

Trade balances also are affected by changes that have transcended national boundaries during the past two or three decades. Although multinational corporations are not new, their proliferation since World War II, plus developments in transportation and international finance, have come to mean that products carrying an American label can be assembled from components manufactured or assembled offshore in Asia, Central America, Mexico, and certainly in Canada. It is not improbable to question whether the modern nation-state—not all that old as human history goes—will be supplanted by new forms of organization within a few generations.

Two features of the American political landscape are striking in the politics of tariffs and trade. One of them is the inversion of the historic position of the major parties on the ideal of free trade. Protectionism, at least in part, was one of Alexander Hamilton's objectives, and it was usually a plank in the Republican platform through 1932. Interestingly, it was George Bush who carried the banner for free trade in the 1990s, whereas Democratic heirs of Hull and Roosevelt—people like Representative Richard Gephardt (D–MO)— have become skeptical of the liberalized trade policies of the past two generations.

A related shift has occurred among group interests. Manufacturing executives of a half century ago were usually protectionists. Today, with the growth of offshore manufacturing, many businesses with a multinational character have become free traders. And not long ago it was labor (either wearing its hat as a consumer of lower-cost foreign goods or optimistic about its ability to compete with foreign workers) that was internationalist. Now, however, labor tends to protectionism because of what it says is no longer a "level playing field." Among the economic sectors that are most threatened today are automobile manufacturing and those with high labor costs. Among products that have become extinct are television sets (Zenith was the last to end production in American plants) and eyeglass frames.

Activities of the GATT highlight problems in international trade. One is the conflict between trade and environmental policy. Under the Marine Mammal Protection Act, the United States has prohibited the importation of any tuna taken with fishing practices that are known to kill unacceptable levels of the porpoises that travel with tuna in order to feed on them. Mexican fishing interests, which use massive drift nets known to kill dolphins, brought an action before a special tribunal of the GATT, charging that the American environmental rules are a violation of GATT provisions. Late in 1991, the tribunal found in Mexico's favor, and the United States was said to be leaning in the direction of overlooking its own environmental requirement. During the 1989–1992 Uruguay Round of GATT bargaining, a concern of American representatives was the sanctity of intellectual property, particularly trade in pirated computer software and musical recordings bearing U.S. copyright protection.

A concern for the future is the European Community (EC) as it moves haltingly, if not inexorably, toward a multistate economic bloc. Given the important cultural, economic, and nationalistic interests of the participants, there may be strong pressures within the EC to develop the sort of logrolling politics that typified American tariff policy before 1934. France in particular has been successful in obtaining special protection for its agricultural interests. In 1992, the United States threatened to impose a severe tariff on French white wine, saying that subsidies paid to wine makers constituted an unfair trading practice. French farmers immediately rallied to protest in Paris and elsewhere against the American threat. The EC may be more interested in intramural trade with its member states than in world trade with Japan or with the United States, Canada, and Mexico—a triumvirate that may itself consist of a trading bloc.

INTERNATIONAL MONETARY POLICY

The functions of money in the international arena are similar to those we have already seen domestically. Its task of providing the liquidity needed for international trade and the movement of capital assets among nations is precisely that of serving as a *medium of exchange.* It is far more convenient to rely on money to smooth out a business transaction between New York and Hamburg than it would be to conduct barter arrangements, in which a shipload of wheat, say, might be exchanged for a hundred tractors, with a few bolts of cloth thrown in to sweeten the deal. (During the international currency crises of the 1930s and in pursuit of its economic policy of autarchy, Nazi Germany concluded many such barter arrangements, to the chagrin of the U.S. State and Treasury Departments.) Similarly, money provides a *measure of value* in comparing the utility of goods or adjusting imbalances in current accounts among the countries of the international system.

There are also dissimilarities between money in the domestic and international arenas, however. For example, the function of money as a stable *store of value* over time is ill served in the era of swiftly changing money relationships that the world has seen since the early to mid-1970s. A major problem of international monetary policy has been the volatility of relationships among currencies generally, especially the variations in the leading currency, the U.S. dollar. This instability has been called the dollar problem, although it has been two problems with a single name. Sometimes the dollar has been too weak (as it was in the late 1970s). Then again, it seems too strong (as it was in the early 1980s during the tight money policy of the early Reagan administration). In the judgment of many who study international money markets, it is stability that is important.

Politically speaking, there is nothing inherently good or bad about the strengthening or weakening of a currency. Instead, there will be categories of winners and losers when movement occurs in either direction, and it becomes a political decision about which set of interests one wants to foster. Consider what happens when the dollar becomes stronger against the yen, perhaps by moving from ¥150 per dollar up to ¥200. Because each American dollar then would buy more Japanese currency, Americans traveling in Japan would be able to do so less expensively. Meanwhile, Americans back home could buy a new Toyota for perhaps 25 percent less than before, if all things remained equal—which they seldom do. Americans who were travelers or car buyers would be winners, getting perhaps a quarter more in travel enjoyment or enhanced automobile purchasing power. At the same time, however, this stronger dollar would harm American automakers, as well as their workers and suppliers, by weakening car sales because of the lower price for imported Japanese cars. The stronger dollar (or weaker yen) would also depress services like the Hawaiian vacation industry because it would be more costly for Japanese tourists to visit there. Naturally, the fortunes of these winners and losers would be reversed if the dollar-to-yen relationship were to move in the other direction, with the dollar weakening by being able to buy, not ¥150, but only about ¥100. Auto workers would be gainers, but those hoping to buy Japanese products would complain. Understanding that different groups of people are differentially affected by currency movements is central to understanding the politics of the international monetary system.

The financial pages of most daily newspapers report currency exchange rates. The relationships among six leading currencies, as they stood on December 27, 1991, were as follows:

	$(US)	£	¥	DM	Franc	$(CAN)
Canada	1.161	2.187	0.009	0.770	0.225	—
France	5.155	9.712	0.041	3.428	—	4.440
Germany	1.508	2.841	0.012	—	0.293	1.299
Japan	126.5	238.2	—	83.85	24.53	108.9
U.K.	0.531	—	0.004	0.352	0.103	0.457
U.S.	—	1.884	0.008	0.663	0.194	0.861

In addition to instability, there are other important distinctions between international and domestic monetary systems. There is no truly "international" currency nor any international central authority analogous to the Federal Reserve that can regulate its value. Instead, there are only attempts at coordinating domestic economic policies among groups like the Group of Seven nations (G-7) in the hope of maintaining stability among currencies that are in common use. Another difference is that although there is usually a single most-used national currency that serves as a world standard, there are often competing currencies lurking in the wings. During the nineteenth century and up until World War II, the international money of choice was the British pound sterling. After 1945, with much of the world's industrial states in ruins and with the United States as the emergent leader of the free world, it became the dollar. In the 1990s, although the dollar remains the leading international currency, the Japanese yen and German deutschmark are joining it as "reserve currencies." These changes reflect alterations in trade patterns, in domestic economic health, and even in changing perceptions of world military security.

International money for most of history was either gold or silver or some denomination of paper currency that was redeemable in these commodities and issued by a reliable country. In the midst of the world economic collapse of the 1930s, international trade and commerce contracted because of an untrustworthy monetary system, the rise of national self-sufficiency in many regimes, repeated currency devaluations by countries seeking a trade advantage, and the descent of the industrialized world into the abyss of war once again. Seeking to learn from these events, it became an article of faith during the 1940s to believe that failures in the world's monetary system will undermine commerce and that nations that no longer trade in goods will instead trade in bullets and bombs.

Between the end of World War II and 1971, the world's monetary system was based on an arrangement that grew out of a conference held at Bretton Woods, New Hampshire, and came to be known as the Bretton Woods Agreement. In August 1944, some forty-four nations concluded that a stable monetary system, if married to free international trade, would foster a peaceful international system. Specie was to be replaced as a basis for international money by relying on the "Big Two," the United States and Great Britain, because the currencies of both were redeemable in precious metals. Certainly the dollar was "as good as gold," for it was exchangeable outside the United States at $35 per ounce, although individual Americans had been forbidden to own gold since 1934. The United States owned the seemingly vast sum of nearly $25 billion in gold, so the dollar could be held "on reserve" by the central banks of foreign nations. Participating nations in the Bretton Woods Agreement were to fix their own currencies in accordance with the dollar (and thus with gold) and committed themselves to maintain those valuations through exchange controls, short-term borrowing, and macroeconomic policies that would bolster not only their own domestic economies but their currencies as well. Underlying the Bretton Woods Agreement was the New Deal's faith in the efficacy of management and planning, as opposed to reliance on market forces alone, in yet another economic arena.

New Deal philosophy could be seen as well in the creation of two new institutions to facilitate international monetary policy and trade. One of them, the International Monetary Fund (IMF), was to be both a regulator and promoter. By design, it was to be the body for granting approval for the signatory nations to alter their exchange rates by more than plus or minus 1 percent from the norm. And it was to be a promoter of monetary stability as well by apportioning money and credit to ease the financial burdens of any participant in its balance of trade "current accounts"—burdens that would cause it to devalue its currency. The other new institution was the International Bank for Reconstruction and Development, more commonly known as the World Bank. The purpose here was to award long-term loans for capital rebuilding (as opposed to smaller sums for the balancing of current accounts) to the distressed economies of war-torn Europe.

The Bretton Woods Agreement soon operated quite differently than had been intended. Britain was unequal to the task from the outset because of its own economic problems. As England withdrew from its old colonial empire and turned inward to repair its damaged economy, the United States alone had to provide the benchmark currency. Then, with the rise of the Soviet military threat, American military aid to Greece and Turkey (the Truman Doctrine), American general assistance to Europe via the Marshall Plan, and American military aid to the NATO allies distributed the dollar on a worldwide basis. This act had the salutary effect of preventing a dollar shortage that would have hampered its use as a reserve currency. And in yet a different change in role, the World Bank became important in moving money to the developing Third World by the 1950s. Through it all, support for the American role in underwriting the international monetary system was maintained at home by the optimistic belief that given monetary stability and a healthy world economy, the United States would be a long-term winner because of the growth of world trade—trade in which we would inevitably enjoy competitive and absolute advantages.

Although it worked well for sixteen years, cracks in the Bretton Woods system were apparent by 1960, and its fall came a decade later. In 1960, for the first time, the amount of dollars held overseas was greater than the amount of gold reserves that the United States held to redeem them. This development had occurred because of years of military and nonmilitary aid, direct U.S. investment overseas, the toleration and even encouragement of trade barriers in other countries against American commodities, a failure to promote U.S. exports, and a decline in American gold reserves to $19 billion. In November 1960, the dollar's underlying weakness was signaled by a run on it by international speculators. Although a group of ten industrial nations was able to weather this storm, this was the signal that the postwar monetary regime was beginning to change. By 1968, the ten countries devised a system of Special Drawing Rights (SDRs)—an innovation that appears to have been the first time international money was created by an international organization.

The final end of the Bretton Woods system came in August 1971. There were several causes. First, there were economic weaknesses in America. The value of a nation's money is determined not only by its balance of trade or current account but also by perceptions of its economic health and military strength. The Johnson-era "guns and butter" policy of both fighting a war in Vietnam and building a Great Society, coupled with a lack of new taxes to support it all, weakened the economy. Second, there was the reemergence of Germany and Japan as powerful trading competitors. Third, this was the beginning of the remarkable interdependence that characterizes today's international economic life. By the 1980s these changes included computerized telecommunications, international banks of vast proportions, sophisticated trading schemes that operate in securities exchanges open day and night around the world, multinational corporations with large amounts of mobile capital, and large chunks of money in pension and other funds. Each of these developments contributed to the announcement by President Nixon on August 15 that thereafter the dollar would no longer be redeemable in gold; instead its value would be established by a freely floating market.

The floating currency system that replaced Bretton Woods was a rejection of the philosophy of direct management and a return to the idea of marketization. How does it work? Hypothetically, instantaneous price changes among world currencies should make for efficient markets and automatic current account adjustments among nations. Hypothetically, the price of a country's money—the dollar vis-à-vis the yen—is fixed by a closed system that returns to an equilibrium point. For example, a trade deficit at the first point in time (t_1a) (importing more than one exports) should result in a weaker dollar at the second point in time (t_1b), which in turn should cause increased exports (because our goods are relatively cheaper overseas) and decreased imports (because theirs are more costly) at t_1c which should reduce the trade deficit at t_2a and finally strengthen the dollar at t_2b. It should be a tidy, self-regulating system. In fact, however, the exchange rate of money is determined as well by domestic inflation (treatable with higher interest rates), internal political turmoil (caused by any number of factors), and external military security.

Since 1986 the Group of Seven (G-7) nations, consisting of the United States, Great Britain, Germany, Japan, France, Canada, and Italy, has met annually with concerns about trade and protectionism blending in with those about money management. The G-7 has sought to move away from the dollar as the reserve currency as the American balance-of-payments problem has grown and as Japan and Germany have sought to have their currency become a new world standard.

The floating system has had both positive and negative effects. On the one hand, the old gold-based system probably could not have survived because of the skyrocketing price of oil in 1973 and later because the currency would not have been sufficiently plentiful. Nor could it have survived the debt-payment problems of Third World countries in the 1980s. On the other hand, there have been wide fluctuations in currencies because of all the factors that brought on the end of the Bretton Woods system—telecommunications technology, international stock markets, sophisticated "players," and structural economic changes.

International monetary policy has a way of intruding on domestic politics now as never before. First, although the United States may be first among equals in international monetary circles, it is no longer preeminent. Indeed, it has not been so since 1971 or 1976 or perhaps 1980. If this realization comes as a psychic blow, it also is a justification for a less altruistic foreign economic policy. It will have an effect on the politics of foreign trade, which in turn will bear on deindustrialization, labor productivity, unionization, and welfare.

Second, the internationalization of money markets is beginning to have a significant impact on each country's ability to affect its own domestic monetary policy. When interest rates are lowered by the Federal Reserve in an attempt to stimulate the economy (as they were in 1991), large amounts of volatile capital may simply flee overseas in search of higher interest rates abroad. Conversely, high rates like those seen under Paul Volcker after 1979 can make the dollar too strong. This result can force other countries to raise their own interest rates, thereby restricting growth abroad, as occurred in the early Reagan years.

Third, trade dispensations given to other countries in the postwar era in an attempt to make dollars more available in the world community have outlived their purpose. Now, when the United States is no longer above the fray in terms of monetary interdependence, it may be time to insist on open markets and free trade.

Fourth, if the European Common Market proceeds with plans to issue its own currency—the Eccu—before the end of the century, its monetary policy could combine with tariff protectionism to make trade difficult for the United States. Finally, there is a trade-off between domestic and international policy goals that is more apparent now than ever before.

TOWARD NORTH AMERICAN FREE TRADE

One of the most striking developments in international trade policy has been the North American Free Trade Agreement (NAFTA), which developed in two stages. The first was through a bilateral accord reached with Canada in 1987–1988; the second was through a trilateral understanding that added Mexico in 1991–1992.

Consider first the Canadian agreement. The relationship with Canada began during the Reagan years with a ten-year phase-out of tariffs and other trade barriers in 1987. At that time, import duties imposed by the two countries were relatively low in ad valorem percentage terms: an average of 9 percent that Canada charged to U.S. imports and 4 percent on products flowing from north of the border into the United States. Still, fully three-fourths of all trade in both directions already had been entering duty-free.

As is usually the case, it was the nontariff barriers that were of greatest importance. Many of the benefits were mutual. Each country pledged to end discrimination against the other's suppliers of services like banking and tourism. A freer flow of agricultural commodities was ensured as well. In a number of individual instances involving the payment of subsidies, Canada was the clear winner. The Canadian government pays subsidies to many of its producers so that they can then reduce their selling prices and make themselves more competitive on the international market. These subsidies take the form of low "Crow's Nest Pass" rates for railroad shipments of wheat, for example, as well as payments to metal and uranium miners and petroleum producers. Surprisingly to those affected by them, the bilateral agreement allowed most of these Canadian subsidies to continue in effect. Also, building standards adopted by the Canadian Mortgage and Housing Commission that discriminated against American plywood were allowed to continue. Canada also won the creation of a new Canada-U.S. Trade Commission, which through its powers to issue binding decisions promptly promised to speed up a lethargic American appeals process. Surrendering control over domestic regulations that might be overturned as "trade barriers" to an international tribunal raises constitutional objections to those who see free trade as an indirect way to undermine the regulatory process. The United States was victorious, for its part, in one major way: gaining access to the vast Canadian electrical and petroleum reserves, thereby diminishing the threat to its energy supplies by the OPEC states.

The agreement that was signed by President Reagan and Prime Minister Mulroney on January 2, 1988, required the approval of each country's national legislature before it could be ratified. Even though Canada is America's largest trading partner, the trade agreement was not a major issue in the United States. Canada is, after all, relatively small, and Canadians are nearly indistinguishable from Americans in many ways. The two countries share a common language and culture and enjoy a similar level of economic development and standard of living. This is not to say that there was no opposition from American interests. There were outcries from western metal and uranium mining interests, from wheat farmers, and from lumber interests; but a feared coalition of westerners with eastern textile producers failed to mount effective opposition to the agreement in the Senate. The proponents, including the National Association of Manufacturers and the American Business Conference, carried the day.

A major reason for the success of the Canadian agreement was the arrangement in Congress. With a few notable exceptions, congressional leadership on both sides of the aisle was cautiously supportive, which in turn allowed the success of the "fast track" procedural device. Based on the all-or-nothing principle that underlies a "closed rule" in the House, "fast track" is designed to eliminate the opportunities for logrolling. Once a trade bill has been formally introduced, the two chambers have a fixed number of days (typically sixty or ninety) to go through the committee process, hold a debate, and vote the measure up or down. Although the House Ways and Means and the Senate Finance Committees are the leading panels, several additional committees (such as banking, agriculture, commerce, and foreign affairs) also process those parts of the bill that are relevant to their jurisdiction. No amendments to the bill are allowed to be made on the floor of either chamber. The House ratified the agreement by 366 to 40 in mid-August and the Senate followed suit by 83 to 9 a month later.

The ratification process was far more contentious in Ottawa. Canadians are traditionally wary of free trade with the United States for fear that the vastly more numerous Americans will overwhelm their markets and even their way of life. Despite sharing the longest undefended border in the world, with a dozen Americans for every Canadian, sensitivities are easily offended, especially north of the forty-ninth parallel. So, amid charges from the opposition that Prime Minister Mulroney had bowed to the wishes of the Reagan administration, party politics became an issue. Although the treaty passed the House of Commons in late August, it was held up in the Liberal party-controlled Senate until after a scheduled national election could be held. The trade agreement was the central issue of the campaign in which the Liberals held an early lead in the opinion polls. Mulroney's party emerged victorious, however, and the agreement was ratified on December 24, only seven days before it was scheduled to begin. In the midst of double-digit unemployment, the agreement continues to be contentious in Canada in the 1990s.

The second phase on the way to NAFTA came in 1990, when the Bush administration announced its intent to negotiate an agreement with Mexico similar to the one with Canada. Canada itself joined in the talks in January 1991. This time the motivation stemmed in part from the ponderousness of the so-called Uruguay Round of GATT negotiations. Impediments to freer trade had been posed by European interests such as French agriculture, as well as by Asian objections to maintaining copyright and intellectual property rights. But the lack of progress among the GATT conferees alone would not have made the opening to Mexico viable. It took the sudden willingness of Mexico to enter into trade negotiations. The determination of President Carlos Salinas de Gotari to move his country toward greater marketization, and the tempting visions of economic development that accompanied it, outweighed the historic Mexican antipathy to the Colossus of the North that is the United States.

Because of the great contrast between the U.S. and Mexican economies, the battle lines over trade became far clearer in this second agreement. With a 2,000-page document in hand, the major opponents to ratification in the United States were organized labor (which saw American jobs moving to Mexico), the environmental movement (which feared the cancellation of conservation requirements through the new International Trade Commission that would be created), and American fruit and vegetable growers (who objected to markedly cheaper Mexican produce). The administration and major business interests, however, saw the agreement in a positive light for many reasons. Because this was part of a general process of marketization in Mexico, it might have the effect of returning industries that had long been nationalized to the private sector. Developing the Mexican economy through enhanced trade also would be a substitute for foreign aid and would open new investment opportunities in Mexico. Development should also slow the pace of Mexican emigration to the United States.

Viewed from the perspective of any one country, each participant in trade bargaining seeks to grant fewer concessions than it receives in return. Viewed in its entirety, advocates of free trade insist that the overall result to all participants will yield a positive-sum outcome in which each country is a net winner. As a practical matter, three results seem possible: (1) Some countries will win more than others; (2) some countries will emerge as net losers; and (3) within any single country, those who win may be very different people with very different interests than those who lose.

Political controversy in the United States concerns the third possibility — that those who win and those who lose will be quite different individuals. Organized labor sees its members as net losers under NAFTA because of deindustrialization. American firms will move their manufacturing operations to Mexico, where tame labor unions have no impact, wages are one-tenth of those in the United States, and workplace hazards are largely unregulated. Simultaneously, the permanent loss of those American jobs will result in the creation of an underclass in the United States. As Walter Mead (1992) has put it, the fear of many is that the leading American export under NAFTA will be the loss of jobs to Mexico, while the leading import will be in bringing Third World living conditions to a nation that will resemble England in the age of Dickens.

The environmental movement, showing less solidarity than labor, divided on the NAFTA agreement. Some feared that the inevitable growth in Mexican manufacturing would occur along the environmentally degraded border region. Others were disturbed by the threat of imported foods grown in violation of U.S. Environmental Protection Agency (EPA) pesticide and fertilizer regulations. Eventually, however, the more moderate groups like the Audubon Society and the Natural Resources Defense Fund were convinced that environmental safeguards would be effective. Nevertheless, others see the International Trade Commission as a device that will be able to sweep away environmental and safety safeguards in the name of free trade. As Mead (1992) argues, the Bush administration's domestic agenda consists of using an international organization to make an end run around Congress and to negate the safety and environmental regulations that it has enacted during the last three decades.

Economically, the debate over free trade can be seen as fundamentally between those who emphasize supply (in the form of lower costs of production and lower prices) and those who emphasize demand (and who argue that no one will be able to buy those cheaper goods if their jobs have disappeared and have been replaced with minimum-wage employment). Will expanding international markets in Canada and Mexico open new customers for American products, or will the selective loss of jobs result in a new underclass in Canada and the United States?

Ideologically, NAFTA has been made possible by a conjunction in time of three like-minded regimes. Without the simultaneous existence of market-oriented regimes—of Reagan-Bush, Mulroney, and Salinas—the NAFTA agreement would not have been possible.

Ideologically, too, the historic preference of the Democratic party for free trade makes it unlikely that the movement toward free trade will be turned aside easily.

DISCUSSION QUESTIONS

1. Are present-day levels of trade with foreign nations unprecedentedly high for the United States? Are the political issues associated with foreign trade larger today than in earlier times?

2. What is the best course of action for a nation that lacks an absolute advantage in international trade?

3. Former Secretary of State Cordell Hull believed that nations that trade together will not go to war with each other. Conversely, he believed that the restriction of trade would lead to armed conflict. Do you agree or disagree with his position? Why?

4. What changes in the way that Congress participates in making trade agreements allowed the tariff rates to decline so markedly after 1930? Why would Congress have agreed to such a change in its role?

5. Liberals usually favored lower import tariffs during the 1930s, while conservatives often were protectionists. These ideological perspectives have been largelt reversed today. What can account for this reversal?

6. Given the law of comparative advantage, can there be any rational basis for organized labor to oppose the North American Free Trade Agreement (NAFTA)?

7. The U.S.-Canadian trade agreement of 1988 drew far less attention in the United States than has the NAFTA in the 1990s. Why has there been such a difference?

8. If European trade becomes concentrated among the Common Market, North American trade concentrated among the NAFTA participants, and Asian trade proceeds largely among the nations of Southeast Asia, then what will become of the economies of the third world countries of Africa and South America?

9. What are the causes of the daily fluctuations in the value of a nation's currency? Are they the same factors that cause fluctuations over a year, for example, or over a decade?

10. Is it always good when one nation's currency grows stronger relative to that of another? Is it always bad if a country's currency grows weaker? Good or bad for whom?

REFERENCES

Camps, Miriam, and Catherine Gwin. 1981. *Collective Management: The Reform of International Economic Organizations.* New York: McGraw-Hill.

Cassing, James, Timothy J. Mckeown, and Jack Ochs. 1986, September. "The Political Economy of the Tariff Cycle," *American Political Science Review,* 80, 843–862.

Destler, I. M. 1986. *American Trade Politics: System Under Stress.* New York: Twentieth Century Fund.

Gardner, Richard N. 1980. *Sterling-Dollar Diplomacy in Current Perspective: The Origins and Prospects of Our International Economic Order.* New York: Columbia University Press.

Gill, Stephen, and David Law. 1988. *The Global Political Economy: Perspectives, Problems and Policies.* Baltimore, MD: Johns Hopkins University Press.

Gilpin, Robert. 1987. *The Political Economy of International Relations.* Princeton, NJ: Princeton University Press.

Gowa, Joanne. 1983. *Closing the Gold Window: Domestic Politics and the End of Bretton Woods.* Ithaca, NY: Cornell University Press.

Mead, Walter R. 1992, September. "Bushism Found: A Second-Term Agenda Hidden in Trade Agreements." *Harper's,* 285, 37–43.

O'Halloran, Sharyn. 1991, April 18-20. "Congress, Parties, and the Tariff, 1878–1934." Unpublished paper, Midwest Political Science Association, Chicago.

Pastor, Robert. 1980. *Congress and the Politics of U.S. Foreign Economic Policy, 1929–1976.* Berkeley, CA: University of California Press.

Putnam, Robert, and Nicholas Bayne. 1987. *Hanging Together: Cooperation and Conflict in the Seven-Power Summits.* Cambridge, MA: Harvard University Press.

Ray, Edward J. 1981, February. "The Determinants of Tariff and Nontariff Trade Restrictions in the United States." *Journal of Political Economy,* 89, 105–121.

Ricardo, David. 1817. *On the Principles of Political Economy and Taxation.* Vol. 1 of *The Works and Correspondence of David Ricardo,* Piero Sraffa, ed. Cambridge: Cambridge University Press, 1966.

Schattschneider, Elmer. 1935, 1963. *Politics, Pressures and the Tariff,* rev. ed. Hamden, CT: Archon Books.

Taussig, F. W. 1967. *The Tariff History of the United States.* New York: Augustus M. Kelley.

CHAPTER FOURTEEN

GOVERNMENTAL FORMS AND ECONOMIC SYSTEMS

The concept of political economy, as you remember from our opening pages, entails two directions of causality. One is the effect that government has on economics, such as the central bank on the money supply or the FTC on the "creativity" of advertisers. The other is the impact that the economic system exerts on the political process, perhaps through pressure-group tactics or through the electoral impact of a period of recession. To this point we have considered these relationships at lower levels of aggregation and on a policy-by-policy basis, focusing on countercyclical finance, antitrust, labor policy, and international trade. Now, in this concluding chapter, we go to a higher level by asking about the relationships between the forms that governments assume and the kinds of economic systems that they have. Are democratic systems always associated with capitalism, or are they equally likely to foster alternative ways of making economic decisions, such as democratic socialism? Conversely, is a causal force exerted by the type of economic system a country has on its political regime? Does capitalism predispose a nation toward democracy, or is it equally likely to engender an authoritarian or elitist form of government? Are socialist economies predisposed to authoritarianism, or are they equally likely to be democratic? In other words, is there a correlation between economic systems and political systems, and if so, which comes first, the economic regime or the political one?

This chapter begins by reviewing the fundamental nature of democracy and capitalism. Next, we consider the relationship between the sort of mixed economy and pluralist politics that are found in the United States. Finally, we adopt an internationally comparative perspective to examine the relationship between capitalism and democracy on the international stage.

DEMOCRACY AND CAPITALISM

To clarify the relationship between democracy and capitalism we should reconsider briefly the meaning of these two concepts. *Democracy* means, literally, nothing more than that the "people" (the *demos*) are the holders of "power" (*kratos*). In classical Greek times, Aristotle feared that a "good" form of government that was controlled by the many—a system he called a *polity*— was likely to fall under the spell of a demagogic leader who would play on the cupidity of the poorest elements of society. The result would be mob rule—a government of the many of the bad form that he called democracy. Because of this terminology, *democracy* was a term of opprobrium in the early years of the republic. Not until well into the nineteenth century did *democracy* become the powerful, if ill-defined, catchword with the great symbolic value that it retains today, not only in the United States, but throughout the world. In our own century, countries have rushed to identify themselves as democracies, no matter how benighted or authoritarian they might have been.

The word *democracy* gives no guidance to just how the people should go about the business of self-governance. Democratic theorists have put forward three central principles that they believe must be present in any regime if it is to be truly democratic. The first concerns the principle of *majority rule* and typically emphasizes electoral phenomena such as levels of voter turnout, the electoral rules by which the government is selected, the proportion of the population that is entitled to vote, or perhaps the social characteristics of those who hold public office. It is to be hoped that a majoritarian conceptualization of democracy will go beyond voting alone by considering the breadth of different forms of political participation, both normal and extraordinary, that are tolerated. This moves us to the notion of respect for *minority rights*, the second crucial component of democracy. Whether these are minorities of race, religion, ethnicity, or opinion, there must be respect for the freedoms of speech, communication, and physical safety for true democracy to exist. Third, democratic theorists insist that there must be a similarity between the preferences of the public and the sorts of governmental policies that actually exist. It would hardly be democratic if, despite seemingly model electoral processes and minority freedoms, the actions of government were to reflect only the views of a small elite who actually made all of the important decisions. This, the correlation between *public opinion and public policy*, also seems crucial to the existence of democracy.

Under each of these three sets of criteria, the United States certainly qualifies as a democracy, although in some cases the fit is an uneasy one. It is well recognized that when rates of electoral participation are the measure, the United States ranks near the bottom of the world's democracies. Registration requirements and the lack of meaningful party-based competition discourage the American electorate from participating in elections. At the same time, however, the number and variety of forms of political participation that are accepted in the United States place America at or near the top of most scales of democracy. Whether the behavior is traditional, like lobbying and demonstrating, or nonsupportive, like protest marches and flag burning, few nations outpace the United States in the varieties of accepted political action. The match between opinion and policy also seems close, despite occasional important gaps, for example, in gun control. Still, critics like C. Wright Mills, William Domhoff, and Thomas Dye insist that public opinion is easily molded by a corporate or media elite and that what passes for mass attitudes is actually only a false consciousness.

Capitalism, too, is a complex concept. Grounded in notions of individualism, entrepreneurial self-reliance, private property, minimal governmental interference in the marketplace, and private ownership of the means of production and distribution, it also involves several corollaries. One is market-based choice with an acceptable number of alternatives; another is the principle of economies of scale, which leads to specialized tasks, to production lines in manufacturing, and to a need for fewer numbers of skilled craftspersons. But the capstone of capitalism is the accumulation of profits and their reinvestment in productive capacity.

DEMOCRACY AND CAPITALISM IN THE UNITED STATES

The United States is the modern world's oldest democracy, as well as its largest. It is also unmistakably capitalist, albeit the sort of "mixed capitalism" that is uniquely American and that includes considerable governmental regulation and economic support. But is there a causal relationship between the coexistence of these two systems, capitalism and democracy? To many Americans the answer is a resounding yes. Not only are democracy and capitalism compatible, but also they are interrelated and inseparable. Someone like Milton Friedman (1963) would argue that democratic notions of free speech and individual freedom of action are essential for the existence of a capitalist economy, while capitalism provides the essential supports that allow the maintenance of a democratic polity. But is this perception valid?

Consider first the development of democracy in America. If we center on the enfranchisement and voting aspects of democracy, it is very difficult to argue that democracy was present when the republic was created. Although most males in New England could vote for members of Congress in 1790, for example, the effects of property and gender qualifications, plus the fact of slavery, meant that only a few hundred people could vote for a U.S. representative in many southern states well into the nineteenth century, even though congressional districts had populations of well over 30,000. Many observers concur that something approaching democracy, at least for white males, took effect during the first thirty to forty years of the nineteenth century. The first modern mass political party was the Jacksonian wing of the Democratic party that had begun under Jefferson and Madison in the early national period and that was organized in the period leading up to the presidential elections of 1828 and 1832. Another milepost might have been passed by 1835, when Alexis de Tocqueville published his popular book, *Democracy in America*. Then there are those who argue that the first modern presidential election occurred in 1840 and who adopt that year as the birthdate of American democracy.

Democracy is an ephemeral concept that changes with experience and expectations. Populist writers of a century ago, as well as elite theory critics of today, have their own interpretations of America's democratic origins. Populists like Mary Elizabeth Lease (Hicks, 1961) held as an article of faith that self-determination had been lost after the Civil War, with the growth of industrial capitalism and monopoly, and that reform was needed to regain the hegemony of the people. Today's elite theorists, people like Mills (1959) and Domhoff (1983), are less concerned with the historical grounding of popular sovereignty than with the absence of it since World War II. All of this suggests that democracy is not a concrete "something" that arrived at a particular time but a series of behaviors that ebb and flow and are always in the process of "becoming" or of melting away.

If democracy was not present at the creation, neither was capitalism. Charles Sellers (1992) has argued that eighteenth-century America was, with a few noteworthy exceptions, a relatively egalitarian society of farmers and commercial interests until after 1815. Then the growth of manufacturing and markets in the North began to yield differences that had not existed before, differences in wealth, differences between farming and commerce, and differences between city and country. In the Deep South, where Eli Whitney's simple invention reinvigorated the slave-based cotton economy, a similar economic stratification grew between the few great plantation owners and the far more numerous small farmers. Viewing the contest between human rights and property rights as the basis for the rise of the Jacksonian Democrats and the Whig party, Sellers has concluded that democracy and capitalism were born, not as working partners, but under conditions of mutual tension.

Another interpretation of the development of the American political economy is that both the governmental and economic regimes are consequences of the nation's cultural values. In politics, governmental institutions reflect the dominant political culture, and both the political and the economic systems are the result of the cultural conditions that preceded them. Each of them has continued to evolve through time.

The American culture is a product of a series of attributes and events. The natural resources that awaited European settlement included vast tracts of land that seemed free for the taking, though there were always costs involved. These resources also included immense mineral riches, as well as forest and agricultural products, that could undergird economic development. The lure of these resources generated a frontier individualism. It also attracted immigrants who, with the important exception of African slaves, were pulled to America rather than pushed there, as had happened to so many of the population migrations of the Old World.

Equally important was the Whig tradition, which developed in England during the seventeenth century and conditioned the American thinking that led to the Declaration of Independence. It was based on the notion of strong parliamentary action and was marshaled against the Tories, or "king's friends." Following the Glorious Revolution of 1688, it fell to John Locke to defend the duty to revolt against tyrannical rule. Locke set forth ideas about governmental structures and functions that were taken up by the Baron Montesquieu, Jean-Jacques Rousseau, and others. The notions of personal rights to liberty and property also made the New World attractive to immigrants, blending especially well into the classical liberalism that was to reach its culmination by 1850.

Classical liberalism, recognizable today as the embodiment of modern conservatism, was an intellectual edifice that drew strength from both the Whig tradition and the new nation's massive resources. Augmented by the ideas of classical economists, particularly by Adam Smith and John Stuart Mill, its tenets were an accretion of what had gone before, culminating in a belief in the fundamental equality of all human beings, personal liberty, private property, and limited government.

Ideas like equality contributed to entrepreneurship in the economic sphere and to political enfranchisement in the political one. Personal liberty was important economically because it undergirded the freedom of contract, of speech, and of free travel that are so important to both political and economic freedom. And as for private property, what principle could be more central to capitalism? The sum of it all was an absence of class consciousness, which prevented the growth of socialism in the United States. A limited government calls on notions of civic duty to encourage popular participation in the governmental process, tolerance, and legalism. Clearly these are general tendencies, for there is no denying that distinctions of social class permeate many circles or that there is an intolerance of people who, somehow, are "not like us." Particularly vexing is a growing cynicism that, some feel, poses a threat to democratic institutions in this country as well as abroad.

Both the economic and political systems in America are the products of evolution from a civic culture that is unique to the United States. Every nation has its own culture. Canada, for example, has greater respect for collective action than does the United States. The English tradition carries with it important class distinctions, and that of France carries a socialist component that colors economic policies. Each country, whether Western, Third World, or emerging Eastern Bloc, is culturally distinctive, with the result that the political and economic lives of each will differ as well. Therefore, trying to export the American variety of a capitalist economy probably has little more hope of success than attempts to export governmental forms. Federalism did indeed take root in West Germany in 1949, but probably only because it coincided with historic regional patterns of that nation. In South Vietnam and Nigeria, however, attempts to transplant large parts of the American governmental model failed because of the absence of cultural support for the innovations that had arrived.

ECONOMIC AND POLITICAL SYSTEMS IN COMPARATIVE PERSPECTIVE

There is seldom enough variability within any single country to allow generalizations about the relationship between economic and political systems. As a consequence, we really need to consider the relationship between economics and politics in a comparative context. Although there have been ups and downs in the United States in the degree of reliance on markets as opposed to governmental decision making, as well as in the balance between popular influence and elite control, the degree of variability in either has not been large. There have been no complete rejections of either the political or the economic systems in the United States. Instead, there have been only incremental changes at the boundaries. This development has been fortunate for Americans, as well as for the British, Canadians, and a handful of other people, for all have avoided the bloody upheavals that normally accompany the expulsion of one regime and the replacement of it with another. If such major changes are useful for theory building in the social sciences, they have been tragically traumatic in the history of France, Germany, Italy, and Spain in the West, not to mention Russia, China, and many other nations in other parts of the world.

Europeans have given more attention to the relationship between economic and political systems than have the more pragmatic Americans. Joseph Schumpeter (1942) saw democracy as more of a threat to capitalism than a help. Wealth is always skewed, and the number of those below the arithmetic mean of income or assets always outnumber those above it. Schumpeter feared that the great mass of voters would support the use of the government's taxing power to redistribute wealth away from the "haves."

This act would make it impossible either to amass the amounts of capital needed for investment or to provide enough incentive to reward meritorious performance. This reasoning is used in the United States by a variety of conservative advocates, usually with the exhortation not to engage in an un-American class war. Then, too, it is asserted that there is so little concentration of wealth in America that radical redistribution would do little for the poor in any event. During the long hegemony of the laissez-faire Supreme Court, the principle of minority rights also carved out a haven for the minority that was wealthy. They could benefit from the curtailment of governmental regulation of the workplace.

Measuring economic variables in a comparative perspective is difficult. Even though social scientists often complain about never having quite the right data, they are accustomed to enjoying the use of a wide array of statistical information. Outside of the industrialized world, few nations can supply systematic and reliable economic information. Even when the data are similar, the base years for which they are gathered can differ widely. Base years for data vary from one nation to the next, and the definitions of even basic concepts in national income accounting demonstrate a wide range.

In spite of these measurement problems, there are several ways to operationalize the notion of capitalism in a comparative perspective. The simplest approach is to dichotomize all systems into capitalist and noncapitalist, the latter consisting of a mixture of socialist systems, barter economies, and preindustrial economies. This method seems unsatisfactory, for our own history suggests that democracy can develop and flourish in a preindustrial, "primitive" economy. We may be confusing industrialized and nonindustrialized with capitalist and noncapitalist. Alternatively, we might restrict our analysis to only developed economies, dividing them into those with decentralized, market-based decision making and those with centrally administered planning—into capitalist and socialist systems. Another approach might be to measure the magnitude of the private sector by assessing the percentage of total GNP minus the percentage of governmental activity.

Assessing democracy is no less problematic. Assuming the availability of data, one may pick from among indicators of voting, civil liberties and rights, or the correspondence of attitudes and policy. Bruce Russett (1967) used factor analysis of a number of indicators to develop overall assessments of political democracy in 124 countries for 1960 and 1965. Stuart Nagel (1984, pp. 124–127) used data from Ivo and Ruth Feierbend (1966) to categorize nations according to their levels of permissiveness; he concluded that free speech will improve the chances that truth will be discovered on a society-wide basis, that government will be honest and effective, and that higher standards of living will evolve.

A cross-tabulation of economic systems by political regime in the postwar world can help to define the relationship between capitalism and democracy (see Figure 14–1). If each variable is dichotomized, there is a strong preference for market economies to be democratic (cell a) and command economies to be authoritarian (cell d). Still, we find the dictatorial Pinochet regime in Chile and Franco's Spain as exemplary entries in cell b, the market-authoritarian match. And certainly, too, one finds Sweden as an example of a democratic regime that operates in a command economy. If we remove the Eastern Bloc nations that were under the control of the former USSR, however, the apparent preference of command economies to be authoritarian is attenuated markedly. Certainly there is a predisposition for democracies to be market-oriented, but there is also the phenomenon of democratic socialism.

Figure 14-1.

	ECONOMIC SYSTEM	
	Centrally Planned	**Marketized**
Autocracy	E. Germany	Franco Spain Pinochet Chile
Democratic	Sweden	United States

A preferable analysis would be diachronic, or one that compares political and economic conditions at an earlier time (at time t) with those at a later juncture (at time $t + 1$). But added to the concern over the specific measures that are used is the problem of how long the time lag should be. Whereas brief time intervals may be associated with significant change in the case of eastern Europe, for example, intervals of a generation or more may be required for other eras.

Advocates of particular economic and political systems might find reasons to argue that their favored regimes will yield preferred results, although the crucial empirical proofs of such relationships are yet to be found. In all likelihood, however, a nation's social culture probably will determine both its political and its economic life. Studies with titles that explore the governing of the Russian economy, the Chinese economy, or the fascinating economy of Europe in the years to come are yet to be made, but they will be fascinating to read once they appear.

DISCUSSION QUESTIONS

1. *Democracy* is a freely used and popular word. But what does it mean? Is it a variable, in that it ebbs and flows?

2. What are the defining characteristics of capitalism?

3. When did democracy begin in the United States? What are the criteria for your conclusion?

4. When did capitalism appear in the United States, and why do you select this particular year or decade?

5. Does capitalism ebb and flow as much as democracy does?

6. Many people have argued that the twentieth century has not been kind to democracies. How many twentieth-century democracies became authoritarian? What happened to their economic systems?

7. How many twentieth-century authoritarian countries became democratic? What happened to their economic systems?

8. Do you agree with Schumpeter that democracies are likely to lead to socialism? Why or why not?

9. What is meant by the terms *synchronic* and *diachronic analysis?* Which is preferable for social science?

REFERENCES

Bollen, Kenneth A. 1980, June. "Issues in the Comparative Measurement of Political Democracy." *American Sociological Review*, 45, 370–390.

Domhoff, G. William. 1983. *Who Rules America Now? A View for the '80s*. Englewood Cliffs, NJ: Prentice-Hall.

Feierabend, Ivo, and Ruth Feierabend. 1966. "The Relationship of Systematic Frustration, Political Coercion, International Tension, and Political Instability: A Cross-National Study." Unpublished paper, American Psychological Association. N.p.

Friedman, Milton. 1963. *Capitalism and Freedom*. Chicago: University of Chicago Press.

Hicks, John D. 1931, 1961. *The Populist Revolt: A History of the Farmers' Alliance and the People's Party*. Lincoln, NE: University of Nebraska Press.

Mills, C. Wright. 1959. *The Power Elite.* New York: Oxford University Press.

Nagel, Stuart. 1984. *Public Policy: Goals, Means, and Methods.* New York: St. Martin's Press.

Russett, Bruce M. 1967. *World Handbook of Political and Social Indicators.* New Haven, CT: Yale University Press.

Schumpeter, Joseph. 1942. *Capitalism, Socialism, and Democracy.* New York: Harper.

Sellers, Charles. 1992. *The Market Revolution: Jacksonian America, 1815–1846.* New York: Oxford University Press.

GLOSSARY

Absolute advantage. In international trade, this is the ability of companies in one country to supply goods and services at lower cost than competitors in other countries. Most world trade emanates from this ability, as in the case of Japan's exports of automobiles, America's exports of wheat, or France's export of prime table wine. Cf. **comparative advantage**.

Addystone Pipe and Steel Co. v. *U.S.* **(1899).** This was the first major antitrust victory for the government under the Sherman Antitrust Act.

Administered prices. This term refers to the belief that prices are set by the decision of executives in firms with monopolistic power rather than by the operation of supply and demand in an impersonal market. Proponents of the idea of free markets deny that administered prices exist.

Administrative law judge (ALJ). Approximately 1,200 people serve as hearing examiners in federal agencies and are important officials in independent regulatory commissions.

Ad valorem duties. These are taxes on imported goods that are levied as a percentage of assessed value. Although there are administrative problems in establishing just what assessed value might be, it is easier to record tariff rates by tracing changes in the percentage of duties across time than to work with specific duties.

Aggregate demand. An important concept in Keynesian economics, aggregate demand is the sum of spending for consumption, investment, government, and net exports (or exports minus imports): $D = C + I + G + (X - M)$.

American Federation of Labor and Congress of Industrial Organizations (AFL-CIO). A large labor organization, whose members are themselves national unions, founded in 1886; it merged with its offshoot, the Congress of Industrial Organizations, to create the AFL-CIO in 1955.

American plan. An aspect of anti-unionism of the 1920s, this saw unions as antithetical to the individual's freedom of contract. Employees should be happy to succeed on their own merits, so incentives were offered for the purchase of company stock while demands were extracted that employees would not join unions.

Australian ballot. Designed to reduce corruption and intimidation of voters, this reform of the 1890s required that the government would print all the ballots and that voting would be done in secret. It was one of a number of electoral reforms that weakened political party organization.

Automatic stabilizers. Built-in nondiscretionary fiscal measures respond to changes in the business cycle without direct governmental intervention. Spending for unemployment compensation and for welfare rises automatically during downturns without congressional action.

Bank of the United States. The first Bank of the United States was chartered for twenty years by Congress in 1791 at the behest of Treasury Secretary Alexander Hamilton. Partly public and partly private, it was America's first experiment with central banking and was allowed to die at the expiration of its charter. A similar Second Bank (1817–1837) expired after vitriolic conflict between its head, Nicholas Biddle, and President Andrew Jackson.

Behavioralism. A post–World War II movement to make the study of politics scientific; it emphasized quantification, computer analysis of data, a focus on individual political actors rather than on political institutions, and the need for explanatory empirical theory. Compare this process with positive economics.

Bimetallism. A late nineteenth-century movement of westerners and populists aimed at expanding the supply of money by backing it with silver as well as with gold.

Black Thursday. Investors typically refer to a particularly bad day on the stock exchange as "black"; but Thursday, October 24, 1929, was the day that stocks fell precipitously on Wall Street and the Great Depression began.

Bretton Woods agreement. At the U.N. Monetary and Financial Conference at Bretton Woods, New Hampshire, in 1944, forty-four nations established the International Monetary Fund and the International Bank for Reconstruction and Development (World Bank).

Business cycle. It encompasses the length of time from peak business activity through the following trough and back to the next peak. So-called Kitchin cycles average about forty months in duration, but there are also very long Kondratieff cycles of perhaps sixty years. The private National Bureau of Economic Research is the official arbiter of the beginning and ending of business cycles in America.

Canons of taxation. Adam Smith's five desiderata for a prudent system of taxation were adequacy, certainty, efficiency, ease of administration, and equity.

Capitalism. This economic system is premised on private ownership, market-based decision making by large numbers of buyers and sellers, and reinvestment of profits into the firm. The term *free-enterprise system* is preferred today.

Chicago school. The students or disciples of George Stigler, Milton Friedman, Friedrich von Hayek, and other economists at the University of Chicago; Chicagoists reject governmental intervention in the economy and have a strong preference for markets; they became important in such agencies as the Antitrust Division of the Department of Justice during the Reagan administration.

City central unions. In a number of cities during the 1820s and 1830s, individual craft unions found it useful to band together to form a single city-wide workingmen's organization. These city-based central unions were the step between the isolated craft unions of the early national period and the emergence of national unions in the 1850s.

Classical economics. It comprises early writers who first molded the study of economics. The classical period begins about 1776 with Adam Smith; embraces Thomas Malthus, Jean-Baptiste Say, and David Ricardo; and concludes about 1860 with John Stuart Mill.

Classical liberalism. Coming from *libertas*, meaning "liberty" or "freedom", this concept refers to freedom from control by government, tradition, or an established church. It typically celebrates the potential of the individual and is more the antecedent of today's conservatism than of New Deal liberalism.

Clayton Act of 1914. As an outgrowth of the Pujo Committee investigations, this Progressive-era legislation sought to supplement the Sherman Antitrust Act's antimonopoly provisions and to outlaw a wide variety of anticompetitive business practices.

Code of Federal Regulations. This code organizes thousands of administrative rules into fifty "titles" issued by the various departments and agencies of the federal government.

Committee on Industrial Organization. This committee was formed within the AFL in late 1935 in an attempt to organize along more "industrial" lines. Disagreement ensued, and most of its leaders either resigned from the parent union or were expelled by 1938, when it was reconstituted as the Congress of Industrial Organizations (CIO). The CIO and AFL merged in 1955.

Comparative advantage. David Ricardo demonstrated that individual nations and the world community both perform best if they specialize in producing and exporting that which they do best, even if they lack an absolute advantage. This argument is the justification for international trade.

Congressional Budget Office (CBO). Created in the Budget Act of 1974, it provides Congress with its own alternative, legislative branch-based fiscal policy projections and estimates.

Congressional casework. One of the activities of members of Congress and their staffs is working to solve the problems of their constituents. These efforts help to ingratiate members to the voters and are one of the reasons that most incumbents are reelected most of the time.

Consumer price index. A scale measures the price of goods in comparison with what they would have cost in some base year, such as 1913, 1967, or 1983.

Craft unions. Workers are organized according to their skills rather than to the industries that employ them. Machinists, for example, might be employed by railroads in the transportation industry or by camshaft makers in engine manufacturing. Craft unions are descendants of medieval guilds. The AFL's craft union members were inhospitable to lower-skilled workers, who clamored for industrial unions during the 1930s and who split off to form the CIO.

Critical period. This period refers to the years between the end of the American Revolution and the beginning of the new government under the Constitution (1783 to 1789). The nation was governed by the Articles of Confederation during this period, and although many textbooks recount a long list of public ills of that time, it was a period of accomplishment as well.

Current account. It is a statement of a nation's trade with other nations at any particular time.

Deficit. It refers to the difference that results when outlays exceed revenues for any single year. The national debt is the aggregation of these annual deficits.

Deindustrialization. This is the decline in the manufacturing sector and rise of the services sector of the economy. Since manufacturing jobs pay well, one consequence of deindustrialization is a decline in wages and the average standard of living.

Democracy. From the Greek words for "people" (*demos*) and "power" (*kratos*), this concept has no single meaning. Theorists distinguish between "procedural" democracy (which is concerned with activities like political participation, elections, and ways of taking power) and substantive policy outcomes (which are concerned with the educational, health, and economic consequences that government produces).

Deregulation movement. During the 1970s, it was felt that regulation more often served the interests of the regulated industries than those of the public. This belief, plus the uneconomic consequences of centralized route planning in the face of fuel shortages and inflation, caused both liberals and conservatives to dismantle many New Deal–era economic regulatory rules.

Devolution. The Reagan administration shifted responsibility for financing and administering many social programs to the state governments. Although the professed goal was to put government closer to the people, it raised an equity problem in those states that lacked the economic base for providing these services.

Discount rate. The percentage of interest that any of the twelve regional federal reserve banks charges to its member commercial banks for a short-term loan is called the discount rate because the lending institution's return already has been deducted, or "discounted," before the loan arrives. Given a loan for $100,000 at 6 percent, for example, the recipient would receive only $940,000.

Divided government. The phenomenon of Republican presidents and

Democratic Congresses has been common since 1953. This division in party control was blamed for the policy-making gridlock in Washington and in some state capitols as well.

Due process of law. This is a right guaranteed in the Fifth Amendment to the U.S. Constitution against unfair action by the national government and later extended by the Fourteenth Amendment against unfair state action. Initially it referred to certain prescribed *procedures* that had to be followed in arriving at a governmental action; but after the Civil War it came to mean that the very *substance* of a regulatory action had to meet some standard of fairness as well.

Economic determinism. The belief that all political issues or problems are caused by factors that are ultimately economic fallaciously ignores the independent effects of interpersonal conflict, race and ethnicity, religion, regional rivalry, or socialization.

Economic indicators. Being able to manage the economy implies the availability of useful and timely indexes of performance. Although there are hundreds of such measures, they are usually categorized as leading, coincident, and lagging indicators of performance.

Economic regulation. This regulation is designed to affect the price or availability of goods or services while leaving the production itself in private hands. After the Civil War it began with the regulation of railroads, then spread to banking and trade practices in the early part of the twentieth century. Economic regulation was the special target of the deregulation movement of the 1970s and 1980s.

Eighty-ninth Congress (1965–1966). A liberal, activist Congress was elected in the 1964 landslide defeat of conservative Republican Barry Goldwater. This was the Congress that enacted most of the Great Society social programs of President Lyndon B. Johnson.

Elite theory of politics. This is the idea that political power is held by a few influential people at the top of the social pyramid. In some conceptualizations this elite position derives from inheritance or some other nonmeritorious factor; in others it is derived from some institutional position and may be associated with merit. Either way, the decisions of elites do not reflect the wishes of those who are ruled.

Employment Act of 1946. This statute charged the president with managing the economy in order to attain full employment while minimizing inflation. The Council of Economic Advisers was created by this law to help meet these conflicting goals.

Energy crisis. Often applied to chronic conditions of low oil supplies and high oil prices, this term is especially appropriate for the seven years following the 1973 Arab-Israeli war. President Carter created the Department of Energy in 1977 in response to this problem, but the high cost of petroleum contributed to the stagflation that helped to defeat Carter in 1980.

Entitlement programs. Developed especially during the Great Society of the 1960s, these are benefits to which the recipient is entitled by right if certain criteria are met. Part of the "uncontrollable" part of the budget, most are in the welfare policy area. Their increases are said to be responsible for the increases in federal expenditures.

Federal Register. This is a daily publication of the federal government that reports forthcoming agency hearings, solicits requests for proposals from possible contractors and vendors, and publishes rules issued by administrative agencies.

Fellow Servant Doctrine. The principle that employers are not liable for injuries to an employee if the cause were the negligent action of a second employee. This doctrine has been largely superseded by workmen's compensation laws, under which costs for job-related injuries are paid from a state-administered fund regardless of who is at fault.

First Hundred Days. A whirlwind of legislative activity that occurred in a special session of Congress was called by newly inaugurated President Franklin D. Roosevelt, March 9 to June 16, 1933. New legislation dealt with banking, labor and unemployment, agriculture, and the securities market, among many other factors, and laid the foundation for the first New Deal. More recently, observers have closely watched the first one hundred days of every new president to gain a sense of his administration.

General Agreement on Tariffs and Trade (GATT). Created in 1947 as an agreement among twenty–eight nations to lower their trade barriers for one another, the GATT now includes most trading nations and has held ten multi-year bargaining "rounds," such as the Uruguay Round (1986–1993).

Gilded Age. Associated with a novel published in 1873 by Mark Twain and Charles D. Warner, this term refers to the ostentation and corruption in business and government that were rampant in the twenty years after the Civil War.

Gini index of concentration. This is a method for measuring the proportion of a nation's wealth that is held by the wealthiest elements of its population. Corrado Gini's index ranges between zero for a perfectly egalitarian society to 1.00 in a system in which all goods are held by a single individual.

Great Depression. Beginning with the Wall Street stock market crash of October 24, 1929, it continued for a much longer period than panics the country had experienced before. Although the unemployment rate fluctuated for the following decade, it was highest in the recession of 1937.

Gross domestic product (GDP). This measure is said to be an improvement over gross national product because it disregards the problem of the nationality of residents and nonresidents in accounting for international transactions. It was recently adopted in the United States for national income accounting. The GDP for 1991 was $5.678 trillion.

Gross national product (GNP). This is the value of all goods and services produced by a country per year, including overseas transactions. It varies slightly from GDP, has been more widely used in the international economic community, and has recently been adopted for most official reporting in the United States. The GNP for 1991 was $5.695 trillion.

Heckscher-Ohlin principle. It is believed that nations will export those things in which they are best endowed. The United States exports agricultural commodities because of its advantage in farmland, whereas some less developed countries export ores because of their mineral deposits. Some Southeast Asian nations export electronic goods because they have cheap labor that allows them to minimize their human costs of production.

Herfindahl-Hirschman index. A measure for assessing the degree of market concentration, this index is useful for the administration of antitrust policy. If the sum of the squared market shares of the firms in a given market exceeds some fixed quantity, such as 1,800, further merger activity might be disallowed by antitrust administrators.

Impoundment. The president refuses to allow an agency to spend monies appropriated by Congress.

Incidence of taxation. This is the specification of just who ultimately pays a tax. Whereas the personal income tax falls on the individual taxpayer, the incidence of other taxes depends on the elasticity of demand. The more inelastic the demand, the more likely it is that the tax is paid by the consumer.

Incrementalism. This is the notion that public policy is usually brought about through small, piecemeal alterations. Called "salami tactics" by William Safire, incrementalism is said to be typical of pluralism, where the many veto groups make it difficult to enact major synoptic change.

Independent regulatory commissions (IRC). Headed by boards of five or more commissioners appointed with the advice and consent of the Senate, a dozen agencies exercise a combination of rule-making, administrative, and adjudicatory functions. The oldest existing IRC is the Interstate Commerce Commission (established in 1887). The others were mostly created during the Progressive era (e.g., the Federal Reserve System and Federal Trade Commission) or the New Deal (the Securities and Exchange Commission and Federal Communications Commission). Each operates in an important area of economic policy; but one of them, the Civil Aeronautics Board, was abolished in 1985 as part of the deregulation movement.

Industrial unions. Different approaches for organizing workers were called for in very large plants that employed less skilled workers. In coal mining, automobile production, and the clothing industry, a more confrontational style seemed to be called for. Many in the craft union tradition of the AFL opposed this new style of organizing, and its Committee on Industrial Organization was forced out of the house of labor in 1938 (see also **Craft Unions**).

Industrial Workers of the World (IWW). Founded in 1893, the IWW (or Wobblies) had a particular appeal among the miners and unskilled laborers in the rural West. The execution in Utah of the Swedish immigrant organizer Joe Hill contributed to the folklore of the union, but federal prosecution of its leaders led to its end by 1920.

Inflation. The prices of goods increase over a period of time. It is measured by the consumer price index (CPI) and reported monthly, quarterly, or annually. Various indexes have existed to estimate price levels since colonial times.

Infrastructure. These systems of transportation, communications, and public utilities are believed to be crucial to a nation's economic competitiveness.

Institutional economics. This approach to economics focuses on the notion that the power of social organizations needs to be emphasized as well as the nature of the market.

Interlocking directorates. The placement of people on the boards of directors of supposedly competing companies became an important way to coordinate the activities of such firms and to build monopoly power. Such overlapping or "interlocking" membership was prohibited by Section 8 of the Clayton Act of 1914.

International Monetary Fund (IMF). The IMF, created at the Bretton Woods conference in 1944, coordinated the value of world currencies after World War II. The value of the dollar, which was the system's basic currency, was $35 per ounce. The fund made available a reserve of gold and currency from the participating nations that could be used to help with short-term balance-of-payments problems. American abandonment of the IMF came about in the two years following the Smithsonian Conference of December 1971, when the Nixon administration finally allowed the value of the dollar to float freely in world markets.

Interstate commerce. The power to regulate the flow of goods across state or national boundaries was awarded to Congress in Article I, Section 8, Clause 3 of the U.S. Constitution and became the legal foundation for many federal programs during and after the New Deal. At various times federal action has been nullified because the commerce in question was *intra*state or because the activity being regulated was deemed to be noncommercial in nature. See *U.S.v. E. C. Knight Co.* (1895).

Junk bond. This informal title was given to bonds often issued to finance a corporate takeover and characterized by high yield and high risk, with resulting concerns for both the issuing firm and the investor.

Keynes, John Maynard (1883–1946). An English economist, statesman, and mathematician, his book *The General Theory of Employment, Interest, and Money* (1936) legitimized countercyclical political economy by providing an analytical justification for increasing government spending and decreasing taxation during hard economic times.

Keynesian school. This economic school fostered Keynes's teachings, beginning with Alvin Hansen during the 1930s. Today, Keynesian ideas have been recast by neo-Keynesians and post-Keynesians.

Kondratieff cycle. A long-term cycle in business activity, perhaps sixty years in length, results from clusters of innovation whose effects gradually erode away. It is this underlying cycle on which such short-run phenomena as Kitchin cycles are superimposed.

Laffer curve. This geometric representation by the economist Arthur Laffer sees an inflection point above which greater increases in taxes result in reducing revenue because they discourage taxable activity.

Laissez faire. From the French expression for "to leave alone," this conservative notion holds that the government should have as little as possible to do with the economy because private ownership, market-based decision making, and free trade will optimize public welfare and raise the standard of living. This view was especially popular between the Gilded Age and the Great Depression.

Landrum-Griffin Act of 1959. The Labor Management Reporting and Disclosure Act was a bipartisan measure aimed at reducing gang influence within unions, promoting fair elections, and expanding the Taft-Hartley Act's prohibition of secondary boycotts.

Late phase conflict. The notion of John Woolley that conflict between the White House office and the Federal Reserve over appropriate monetary policy is greatest late in the business cycle—especially when the administration wants the Federal Reserve to stimulate the money supply as a recession wears onward.

Less developed countries (LDCs). These are the nonindustrialized nations of the Third World. Often they are former colonies of Western nations that rely on the export of raw materials to maintain a precarious prosperity.

Liquidity trap. During business downturns, reductions in interest rates have no effect if potential borrowers believe that the rates will fall even further. Interest rates may be so low that people prefer to hold their money rather than to borrow low-yielding securities. Keynes believed that this inadequacy of monetary policy necessitated the fiscal remedies of taxation and spending.

Logrolling. This political concept is based on American frontier experience: "I'll help you roll and stack heavy logs at your farm if you'll help me do the same on mine." Legislatively, Representative A agrees to support B's bill if B will do the same for A. This process occurs when the perceived benefits of receiving support for one's own venture outweigh the perceived costs of supporting the schemes of one's colleagues. The overall legislative result, however, usually is not what legislators individually would have supported.

Marshall Plan. The European recovery plan devised in 1947 was named for Secretary of State George C. Marshall. It was a program of massive American aid to postwar Europe so that free institutions could survive. Economic and military aid totaling $82 billion was extended between 1948 and 1961.

Mercantilism. A system for using the economy to enrich the state, mercantilism encouraged exports and discouraged imports to amass a surplus of gold. It flourished from the age of European discovery through the early nineteenth century and closely involved governments with their economies. Adam Smith's *Wealth of Nations* was an antimercantilist argument.

Misery Index (MI). This is an additive index such as that of the Teamsters Union: MI = $P + U + I$, where P is the prime rate of interest that banks charge their most creditworthy customers, U is the percentage unemployed, and I is the inflation rate. The index reached 36.87 in 1981, when the Teamsters opposed Jimmy Carter's reelection.

Mixed capitalism. This term is often used to describe the American economic system of private ownership, governmental regulation, and nonprofit activity.

Monetarism. This theory of fine-tuning the economy carefully matches the growth in the money supply to the growth of the economy. Conservatives are drawn to monetarism because it requires none of the clumsy intervention of Keynesian fiscal policy.

Monopolistic (or imperfect) competition. A market structure first described by Joan Robinson (1903–1983), it consists of many buyers and sellers, products differentiated by an identifiable characteristic or trademark, and vigorous competition promoted through advertising.

Monopoly. This is a market characterized by a single seller, absence of acceptable substitutes, and blocked entry. Monopolists may be a single private firm (e.g., the Aluminum Company of America before 1939), a regulated public utility (Columbia Gas of Ohio), or a number of sellers who act in concert for the purpose of maximizing profits at the consumers' expense.

Most favored nation. In this principle of international trade, one trading partner extends to a second the same low tariff rates that it confers to some third country with which it has its most unimpeded commerce.

Multinational corporations. These corporations do business in more than one country in order to reduce transportation or import tariff charges, protect patent holdings, or otherwise enjoy monopolistic advantages. Although known 200 years ago, they are a particular feature of the post–World War II period and are controversial because they owe no particular allegiance to any national state.

Munn v. Illinois (1877). This is one of several *"Granger* cases" in which the U.S. Supreme Court ruled that an Illinois regulation of grain storage rates was an acceptable exercise of the police power of the state for businesses affected with a public interest. This ruling was weakened in *San Mateo County v. Southern Pacific R.R.* (1882) and virtually overturned in *Chicago, Milwaukee & St. Paul R.R.* v. *Minnesota* (1890).

National debt. This money is owed by a government to its creditors. Whereas debt reported in absolute amounts may dull the senses (e.g., $4.123 trillion in November, 1992), it is more understandable if expressed in per capita terms ($16,400 per person) or as a proportion of annual **GNP** (70 percent).

National Industrial Recovery Act (NIRA) of 1933. A First Hundred Days measure aimed at affecting business structure, this statute created the National Recovery Administration, which sponsored codes of fair competition that sought to raise wages and eliminate cutthroat competition. Controversy swiftly followed concerning monopolization, code violations, and the conduct of the agency's head. Although the NIRA was found unconstitutional in *Schechter Poultry Co. v. U.S.* (1935), the president was not that unhappy to see its demise.

National Labor Relations Act of 1935. See **Wagner Act.**

National Labor Union. This was founded in 1866 as the first attempt to form a large national labor union. The creation of William Silvis, it ended with his death and as a result of the panic of 1873.

Navigation acts. Various mercantilist laws enacted by Great Britain between 1650 and 1767 sought to control American commerce on the high seas. These eventually became an additional abrasion between the mother country and the American colony.

Negative externalities. Also known as spillover effects, these are costs to the public because the selling prices of goods do not reflect the consequences of pollution or other liabilities.

Neoclassical economists. This name was applied to a group of economists who flourished from the mid-nineteenth century through the 1920s. This economic school included Leon Walras, Alfred Marshall, and Irving Fisher, and it embellished the teachings of the classical writers through the use of mathematics and greater attention on microeconomic phenomena.

Neoclassical post-Keynesianism. This term best describes the orthodox economic instruction provided in the United States today.

Neo-Keynesian school. This refers to a basic acceptance of Keynesianism but with modifications of its growth assumptions. The Harrod and Domar models exemplify this tradition.

New Deal. A rhetorical flourish in Franklin D. Roosevelt's first inaugural address became the label for the social programs of his administration in the 1930s.

New Institutionalism. This term was given to the amalgamation of the traditional and behavioral schools of political science about 1970.

Normalcy. A term used by the Harding-Coolidge presidential campaign of 1920, it denotes a desire to return to the "good old days" of pre–World War I America.

Normative economics. This orientation stresses humanitarian values in economic analysis as opposed to the hard realities of market analysis.

North American Free Trade Agreement (NAFTA). A trade agreement among the United States, Canada, and Mexico was championed by the Bush administration but opposed by those fearing the loss of manufacturing jobs to Mexico and the erosion of environmental safeguards.

North-South issues. These concerns divide the industrialized nations of the world (most of which are located in the higher northern latitudes) from the LDCs to the south. These concerns include prices paid for raw materials, the debtor status of many southern nations, and immigration.

Office of Management and Budget (OMB). This agency of the Executive Office of the President is responsible for developing the Administration's proposed budget. The director of OMB is one of the most important decision makers in an administration (see also **Congressional Budget Office**).

Okun's Law. Arthur Okun observed that a 1 percent decline in unemployment is correlated with a 3 percent increase in GNP. This principle was tracked carefully by President Ford's Council of Economic Advisers during the recession of 1975.

Oligopoly. This is a market structure with few sellers and many buyers that produces either a similar or a differentiated product and makes entry difficult. Because oligopolists are reluctant to engage in price competition, there is an opportunity for monopolistic profits to accrue to the few firms in the market; however, economies of scale may offset this process.

Open market operations. Federal securities are bought and sold in order to affect the money supply. When the Federal Reserve Bank of New York buys back Treasury bills, its money flows into the coffers of commercial banks. This act increases the banks' loanable reserves, allowing an increase in the nation's money supply.

Opportunity costs. Foregone opportunities are the consequence of having done A rather than B, C, or any of the other alternative courses of action. We never know for sure what those alternative actions might have brought about.

Oversight function. One of several activities of Congress, it consists of auditing the bureaucracy to see that its behavior adheres to the intent of the legislative branch of government. Seen as important by the framers of the Constitution, it is performed sporadically by the House and Senate.

Panic of 1857. One of many money panics that struck the United States during the nineteenth century, it is particularly noteworthy for destroying a number of early national labor unions.

Paradox of thrift. Family savings, beneficial at the individual level, are harmful at the national level because they lower aggregate demand and so must be offset by increased governmental or business spending.

Phillips curve. This is a concave trade-off between unemployment and inflation. A. W. Phillips measured this relationship for nineteenth-century Britain, but the occurrence of simultaneously high unemployment and high inflation in the United States during the 1970s was called stagflation.

Pluralism. The style of democracy found by Robert Dahl in the United States emphasizes overlapping policy pyramids, vertical mobility, and the centrality of interest groups.

Political business cycle. This is the hypothesis that the Federal Reserve system often allows the money supply to expand during the months that precede a presidential election, thereby boosting the economy and enhancing the reelection chances of the party that holds the White House. Soon after the election the money supply is contracted, thereby affecting the normal business cycle.

Political economy. This is the interaction between the worlds of politics and economics, especially the effect that political events have on economic systems, the effect of economics on politics, and a way of examining the political process through the tools of economic analysis.

***Pollock* v. *Farmers' Loan & Trust Co.* (1895).** This overruled *United States* v. *Springer.* The Supreme Court found unconstitutional the income tax provision of the Wilson-Gorman Tariff of 1894, saying it was a direct tax that must be apportioned equally among the states because of Article I, Section 9, Clause 4 in the Constitution. The Sixteenth Amendment (1913) later gave Congress the power to tax incomes "from whatever source derived, without apportionment among the several States... ."

Populism. This term referred to the People's Party of 1890–1896, but more recently it was used derisively against appeals on behalf of the masses in opposition to the interests of elites.

Positive economics. This economic analysis relies heavily on quantification, as opposed to normative argument.

Postindustrial state. This term, coined by Daniel Bell, refers to the demise of manufacturing in the United States after 1970 and the rise of less lucrative service industry occupations.

Price discrimination. When the identical product is sold in different markets and at different prices in an effort to increase monopoly profits, it is a violation of Section 2 of the Clayton Act of 1914.

Privatization. In Reaganomics, traditional governmental functions were transferred to private owners or contractors on the ground of greater productivity.

Professional Air Traffic Controllers Association (PATCO). Most of its members were federal employees who went on strike in 1981 to protest working conditions as well as wages. In showing that he would be stern in the face of labor demands, President Reagan fired those members who did not immediately return to work.

Progressivism. The Progressive movement (1900–1917) was the most successful reformist era in American history. A phenomenon of the upper-middle class, it fostered direct democracy at both the state level (the initiative, recall, and referendum) and nationally (the direct election of U.S. senators), municipal nonpartisanship, special district government for school administration, and the income tax. Although it was brought to a close by World War I, many of its principles lived on through Senator Robert LaFollette (R–WI) and in the New Deal.

Protective regulation. During the 1960s, the federal government enacted a wide range of consumer protection, environmental, and auto safety legislation that was aimed at safeguarding the public's health and safety. This is sometimes called "new-style" regulation to distinguish it from the "economic" regulation of the New Deal era.

Public aid movement. During the period from 1815 to 1860, state governments often provided financial support for private manufacturing, transportation, and other industrial ventures. Pennsylvania and Missouri were especially active in this regard.

Public goods. Goods and services are supplied by the government because it is not sufficiently profitable for the private sector to do so. This term is also applied to resources that are said not to be diminished by their consumption by any single person.

Pujo Committee. A subcommittee of the House Committee on Banking and Currency, created in 1912 under Representative Arsene Pujo (D–LA), it investigated the "money trust" and led to the Clayton Act and other Wilson administration reforms.

Pure competition. Many firms and buyers, each acting independently, offer a homogenous product in a free market.

Rational expectations economics. Only new information affects market behavior. The government exerts little independent effect because the market foresees such actions and takes them into consideration before they occur.

Reaganomics. The economic policies associated with the presidency of Ronald Reagan (1981–1989), included reduced spending for social programs, supply-side tax cuts, deregulation and marketization of decision making, devolution of social policies back to the states, and the privatization of governmental services.

Realigning election. In this election, the minority of the previous generation becomes the new majority, large numbers of a party's traditional followers desert to the historic rival, and synoptic policy change results. Such elections are believed to have occurred in 1860, 1896, and certainly in 1932; disagreement greets the claims made for 1828 or 1980.

Reciprocal Trade Agreements Act of 1934. The brainchild of Secretary of State Cordell Hull, this act removed tariff rate making from Congress by empowering the State Department to negotiate bilaterally for three years to lower (or raise) import duties by as much as 50 percent. Extended many times, the principle of authorizing the executive branch to negotiate tariffs lives on in foreign trade and is responsible for America's low import duties.

Regressive tax. In an absolute sense, this is a tax in which the rate falls as the taxable base increases, as with early Social Security. In a relative sense, it is a rise in total taxes paid as a percentage of one's income, as with most property and sales taxes.

Revolving door. People enter public service from the private sector and then return to their old corporate jobs at a higher level, only to repeat the cycle over and over again. The result is that governmental regulation is least independent of those who are supposedly being regulated. This became an important argument in favor of deregulation after 1970.

***San Mateo County* v. *Southern Pacific R.R.* (1882).** In the *San Mateo Rate* case, former Senator Roscoe Conkling argued that the congressional committee that drafted the Fourteenth Amendment had intended to include corporations along with natural persons in the phrase "due process of law." This doctrine soon made it difficult for any government to regulate corporate activity, and years later it was found that Conkling's story had been a falsehood.

Say's law. Supply creates its own demand. Jean Baptiste Say (1767–1832) believed that increasing supply would yield full employment and that economies are supply-driven. Because some producer income is eroded by savings and taxes, Keynes argued that they are demand-driven.

Second New Deal. Used to refer to Roosevelt's relationship with his second Congress (1935–1936), when the administration shifted from a focus on restructuring economic institutions to one of relying more on Keynesian notions of fiscal policy.

Sherman Antitrust Act (1890). This earliest federal antimonopoly statute attempted to prohibit both business behavior and structures intended to produce a monopoly. More than a decade passed before the law met with major success in the courtroom.

Smoot-Hawley Tariff of 1930. Enacted less than a year after Black Thursday, this was one of the highest tariff laws in American history; it was blamed for initiating a protectionist trade war that prolonged the Great Depression.

Social Darwinism. Improperly deduced by Herbert Spencer from the work of Charles Darwin, this theory became popular in the late nineteenth century. It is the notion that only the fittest will survive as society evolves and that government should not intervene to help those who are "less fit."

Socialism. According to Joseph Schumpeter, socialism is the public ownership of the means of production and distribution; but in American parlance it is often used pejoratively to describe any attempt at governmental regulation or intervention. As an economic concept, it is independent of political concepts like democracy and authoritarianism as well as of theological notions like atheism (as in "Godless Marxism") or religiosity (as in Christian or Jewish socialism).

Specific tariff rates. This import tax is levied at a fixed amount per unit rather than a percentage of the good's worth. Specific duties are used because of the difficulty of establishing a fair market value for imported goods, on which ad valorem rates could be charged.

Spencer, Herbert (1820–1903). An English social philosopher and author of *Social Statics*, his laissez-faire economic views were more popular in the United States than in his own country. It was Spencer, and not Charles Darwin, who originated the phrase "survival of the fittest."

Springer v. *U.S.* (1871). In this case the U.S. Supreme Court ruled that the Civil War–era federal income tax was not a direct tax that must be apportioned among the states and thus was a legitimate exercise of the congressional power to tax. It was overruled in *Pollock* v. *Farmers' Loan and Trust* (1895).

Stagflation. See **Phillips curve.**

St. Simon, Claude-Henri (1760–1825). This French social reformer in the Christian tradition inspired the earliest use of the term *socialism*. He saw the rise of capitalistic industries, often under the ownership of the old aristocracy, as undermining the fraternalistic goals of the French Revolution.

Subgovernments. This is the belief that public policy is made in dozens of cozy relationships involving a congressional subcommittee, an administrative agency, and a few interest-group insiders. Also known as iron triangles and policy whirlpools, subgovernments are said to be typical of pluralist politics and one of the reasons that synoptic change is rare in the United States.

Supply-side economics. This is the belief that prosperity depends on increasing the supply of goods and services rather than on stimulating demand. Reaganomics sought to do so by lowering taxes on producers like high-salaried owners and managers. Critics of supply-side economics pointed to the similarity between its ideas and the fallacy of Say's law, which states that supply creates its own demand.

Synoptic change. This is large, major change, something that is rare in American public policy. Usually caused by major electoral realignment or by some sense of emergency, it is the antithesis of incremental change.

Taft-Hartley Act of 1947. Named for Senator Robert Taft (R–OH) and Representative Fred Hartley (R–NJ) and enacted over the veto of President Truman, this act embellished the National Labor Relations Act. The law created the National Mediation and Conciliation Service, developed sixty- and eighty-day "cooling-off" periods before strikes could occur, banned the closed shop, and expanded the list of unfair labor practices that unions could commit.

Tax base. In one sense, a tax base is that which is taxed, such as annual income, personal wealth or property, or the value of goods that are being imported or sold at retail. In another sense, it is the smaller dollar amount that is subject to taxation after all exemptions, exclusions, and income not taxed have been set aside. The difference between the apparent gross income and the remaining taxable income accounts for the difference between nominal and effective rates of taxation.

Tax rate. This is the percentage of tax levied on something being taxed, such as income or property. Proportional rates are those that are the same regardless of the size of the base being taxed. Progressive rates are those that are larger as the taxable base becomes greater. Regressive rates are those that grow smaller as the base increases.

Tax theories. Taxes are based on several underlying justifications: the value of services received back from the taxing authority, the ability to pay (itself based on the equality of sacrifice or the equal utility of money), the redistribution of wealth, or the Keynesian notion of countercyclical fiscal policy.

Trade association. This organization comprises member firms and performs a number of services for them, one of which is lobbying the government. The names of many trade associations begin with National Association of ... .

Traditionalist political science. Political scientists who study politics by emphasizing historical description, that is, law and casework, and do not shy away from making value judgments of right and wrong are often called traditionalists.

Troika. This is an informal reference to the president's three closest economic advisers—the chair of the Council of Economic Advisers, the director of the Office of Management and Budget, and the Secretary of the Treasury.

Ultra vires. From the Latin, this phrase means "beyond the power." Administrative agencies and boards possess only those powers that have been delegated to them by a legislature. Thus, administrative acts that are found by a court to exceed a statutory grant of authority are null and void.

U.S. Railroad Administration. Created during World War I to prevent labor problems on the nation's railroads, this federal agency also operated railway express agencies and inland waterways during the war. Despite the hopes of many in organized labor, the railroads were returned to their 2,900 private operators at war's end.

***U.S. v. E. C. Knight Co.* (1895).** In the first important antitrust case before the U.S. Supreme Court, the sugar trust was acquitted of violating the Sherman Antitrust Act because it was found to have been engaged in manufacturing (which Congress could not regulate) rather than in commerce (which it could). This was a major setback for those opposed to the powerful trusts of that time.

Voting paradox. Also known as the cyclical majority problem, this is a problem of voting in legislatures when there are three or more groups of relatively equal size. When motions are framed dichotomously (e.g., as yes or no) there will always be a majority winner on any roll-call, barring ties. At the same time, however, there may be no true overall majority preference. Thus it is paradoxical that there both is and is not a majority at the same time.

Wagner Act. The National Labor Relations Act of 1935, colloquially named after Senator Robert Wagner (D–NY), created the National Labor Relations Board (NLRB) and empowered it to identify appropriate collective bargaining units, conduct representation elections, and define unfair labor practices.

Wagner's Law. Adolph Wagner was a nineteenth-century German economist who believed that the percentage of a nation's gross national product accounted for by the public sector will grow inexorably because of the increased costs of maintaining law and order, war, and the increasing demand for public services.

Williamson Trade-off. This graphic model developed by Oliver Williamson (b. 1932) compares the loss of consumer surplus with the cost savings that would accrue to the producer firm after a merger.

World Bank. The International Bank for Reconstruction and Development was created at the Bretton Woods conference of 1944.

INDEX

Johnson, David B., 98–99
Johnson, Hugh, 59, 60, 61
Johnson, Lyndon, 4, 66–67, 112, 134, 242
Johnson, Manuel, 177, 179
Joint Economic Committee, 64, 145
Jones, Charles O., 92
Jones, "Mother," 211
Judicial branch, 95, 119–22. *See also* U.S. Supreme
    Court
Judicial review, 119–20
Juglar, Clement, 145
Junk bonds, 84, 205

Kahn, Alfred, 69, 76, 138
Kalven, Harry, Jr., 147
Kefauver, Estes, 224
Kemp-Roth proposal for stimulating economy, 79
Kennedy, Edward, 69
Kennedy, John F., 64–66, 84, 106–7, 113, 115, 181,
    237
Kennedy, Robert, 66
Kennedy Round (1963), 237
Keretsu agreements, 237
Keynes, John Maynard, 19–22, 141, 142, 153, 163
Keynesianism, age of (1932–1980), 33, 54–71, 77, 86
    Great Society, 4, 66–67, 112
    Keynesian model, 19–22
    New Deal and, 54, 55–61
    New Frontier, 65–66
    1960s, 64–67
    stagflation and troubled 1970s, 67–69
    taxation in, 20, 153–54
    U.S. as free world leader (1945–1960), 63–64
    World War II, stimulus of, 60, 61–63
Kiewiet, D. Roderick, 98, 100–102, 103–4
King, Martin Luther, Jr., 66
Kingdon, John, 139
Kinked demand curve, 192
Kitchin, Joseph, 145
Kitchin cycles, 145, 146
Knights of Labor, 196, 216, 219, 220, 221
Kolko, Gabriel, 45
Kondratieff, Nikolai, 145, 146
Kuhn, Thomas, 29
Kuznets, Simon, 145, 146

Labor, allocation of, 18. *See also* **Organized labor**
Labor in the USA: A History (Filippelli), 49
Labor Management Reporting and Disclosure Act of
    1959 (Landrum-Griffin Act), 64, 224
Labor policy, 220–25
Labor relations:
    labor-management cooperation, 228–29
    New Deal and, 58, 62
    under Reagan, 78
    regulation of, 131
    Sherman Act used in labor disputes, 200
    during World War I, 48–49
    during World War II, 62
    See also Organized labor
Labor unions, 187–88, 197, 212
Labour party, British, 96
Laffer, Arthur B., 24, 74, 76, 154
Laffer curve, 24, 29, 154, 155, 162
Laissez-faire, 45, 50
Laissez-faire capitalism, 22
Laissez-faire school of economics, 23–24
Lamont, Thomas, 51
Lance, Bert, 114, 181
Landrum-Griffin Act of 1959, 64, 224
Large-scale enterprises, pros and cons of, 203–4. *See
    also* Monopoly(ies)
Late-phase conflict in business cycle, 179–80
Lease, Mary Elizabeth, 254
Left, economic schools on the, 22–23

Legalists, 207
Legal Tender Act of 1862, 174
Legislative branch. *See* Congress, U.S.
Legislative function of Congress, 108
LeLoup, Lance, 113, 162
Leroux, Pierre, 22
LeRoy, Gregory, 226
Levellers, 22
Lever Food and Fuel Control Act, 48
Lewis, John L., 62, 217, 218
Lewis, Meriwether, 115
Lewis-Beck, Michael, 207
Liberalism, classical, 255
Liberal party, British, 96
Liberty League, 59
Light, Paul, 147
Limited democracy, 40
Limited representative government, 40
Lincoln, Abraham, 149
Lincoln, George, 68
Liquidity trap, 19–20
Liquor monopolies, state, 127
Literature of Great Depression, 55–56
Lobbying groups, 95
Lochner v. New York, 24, 45
Locke, John, 255
Loewe v. Lawlor, 200
Logrolling, 112, 238, 245
Long, Huey, 59, 210
Long, Russell, 155
Loose combinations, 195
Lorevin, Lewis L., 60
Love, John, 68
Lowe, Thaddeus, 44
Lowi, Theodore, 92, 124
Lucas, Robert E., Jr., 24
Luxury tax, 150, 155
Lynd, Robert and Helen, 28
Lyon, Leverette S., 60

McAdoo, William G., 48
McClellan, John, 64, 224
McCrary, George, 132
McCusker, John J., 36
McGovern, George, 118
McKinley, William, 46, 199
McNary, Charles, 57
McReynolds, James, 59
Macroeconomic policy goals, regulation and, 130
Madison, James, 27
Maisel, Sherman, 179
Majoritarianism, 26–27
Majority rule, 252
Malapportionment, 109
Malbin, Richard, 111
Malcolm X, 65
Malthus, Thomas, 16
Managing the economy. *See* Fiscal policy; Monetary
    policy
Mandela, Nelson, 85
Manley, John, 28
Mann, Thomas, 74
Mann-Elkins Act of 1910, 133
Manufacturing:
    in the North, growth of, 254
    unionization of, 212
Marbury v. Madison, 95
Marginal efficiency of capital, 19
Marginality, concept of, 17–18
Marginal propensity to consume, 19
Marine Mammal Protection Act, 238
Market, national, 40
Market-based decision making, 8
Market concentration, 192–93
Market equilibrium, 18

(UNRRA), 63
United Shoe Machinery Company, 44
United States:
democracy and capitalism in, 253–56
as free world leader (1945–1960), 63–64
U.S. Department of Agriculture (USDA), 134, 178
U.S. Department of Commerce, 126, 130
Bureau of Economic Analysis (BEA) of, 145, 146
U.S. Department of Justice:
Antitrust Division of The, 193, 203, 204–5
enforcement of Sherman Act, 199–201
U.S. Department of Labor, 134
Bureau of Labor Statistics, 225
U.S. Department of State, 236
U.S. Employment Service, 62
U.S. Fuel Administration, 49
U.S. Grain Corporation, 48
U.S. House of Representatives, 26, 40, 107
Committee on Ways and Means, 110
House Democratic Caucus, 109
U.S. Maritime Commission, 134
U.S. Railroad Administration, 48
U.S. Senate, 40
Finance Committee, 110
U.S. Shipping Board, 47–48
U.S. Steel, 65
U.S. Supreme Court, 121
antitrust cases, 196, 199–201
economic power of, 119–20
New Deal and, 59, 60
on railroad regulation, 45
U.S. Treasury Department, 83, 179
Unsafe at Any Speed (Nader), 134
Upward mobility under Reagan, 83
Uruguay Round (1989–1991), 237, 238, 246, 248
USA (Dos Passos), 56
Utopia, The (More), 190

Van Buren, Martin, 93, 173
Vandenberg Resolution of 1948, 63
Van Devanter, Willis, 59
Veazie Bank v. *Fenno*, 120
Veblen, Thorstein, 23, 61
Vest, George, 198
Vietnam War, 67
Violence, organized labor and, 213, 219–20
Volcker, Paul, 73, 77, 114, 168, 178, 179, 180, 181, 183
Volsted Act of 1919, 48
Voter turnout, 98–99
Vote trading, 112
Voting behavior:
economic influences on, 98–102
electoral outcomes, effect on economy of, 102–4
turnout, 27, 98–99
type D voter, 118
Voting rights, 100, 118, 254
Voting Rights Act of 1965, 100, 118
Vreeland, Edward, 176

Wabash, St. Louis & Pacific R.R. Co. v. *Illinois*, **45, 196**
Wade, Larry L., 12
Wage and price freeze of 1971, 67
Wagner, Adolph, 63
Wagner Act of 1935, 58, 217, 223, 224, 225, 227
Waite, Morrison, 196
Wall Street Journal, 83
Ware v. *Hylton*, 120
War Industries Board, 48
War Manpower Commission (WMC), 62
War of 1812, 172, 234–35
War Production Board, 62
Waterman, Lewis, 44
Wealth:
concentration of, 203–4, 257
tax system to redistribute, 153
Wealth of Nations, The (Smith), 8, 16, 38–39, 145
Webb-Pomerene Act of 1918, 202, 204
Welfare spending, Reaganomics and, 75
Wessel, David, 179
Westinghouse, George, 43
Wheeler-Lea Act of 1938, 202
Whig party, 235, 255
Whiskey Rebellion of 1793, 150
Whiskey trust, 195
Whitney, Eli, 43, 254
Wieser, Friedrich von, 24
Wiley, Harvey, 138
Willard, Daniel, 47
Wilson, James Q., 92, 124–25, 156
Wilson, Woodrow, 46–49, 108, 133, 176
Wilson-Gorman Tariff of 1894, 151
Wobblies, 49, 217
Women in labor force, 214
organized labor and, 219, 224
strikes by, 215
Woolley, John, 178, 179, 181
Working classes, 213
Work rules, 227–28
Works Progress Administration (WPA), 58, 158
World Bank, 62, 241, 242
World War I:
American political economy and, 47–49
organized labor and, 222
World War II:
costs of, 6
international monetary policy and, 241–42
organized labor and, 223
stimulus of, 60, 61–63
Wright, Jim, 110

Yablonski, Jock, 224
Yen, 239–40
Yom Kippur war (1973), 67

Zeno, Emperor, 193
Zeno's Edict, 203